AF605852

STUDIES ON ETHNIC GROUPS IN CHINA
Stevan Harrell, Editor

PURE AND TRUE

THE EVERYDAY POLITICS OF ETHNICITY FOR CHINA'S HUI MUSLIMS

David R. Stroup

UNIVERSITY OF WASHINGTON PRESS

Seattle

Pure and True was made possible in part by a grant from the Donald R. Ellegood International Publications Endowment.

Composed in Warnock Pro typeface designed by Robert Slimbach

26 25 24 23 22 5 4 3 2 1

Printed and bound in the United States of America

Photographs are by the author. Maps are by Eve McGlynn.

UNIVERSITY OF WASHINGTON PRESS
uwapress.uw.edu

LIBRARY OF CONGRESS CATALOGING-IN-PUBLICATION DATA
Names: Stroup, David R., author.
Title: Pure and true : the everyday politics of ethnicity for China's Hui Muslims / David R. Stroup.
Description: Seattle : University of Washington Press, [2021] | Series: Studies on ethnic groups in China | Includes bibliographical references and index.
Identifiers: LCCN 2021018886 (print) | LCCN 2021018887 (ebook) | ISBN 9780295749822 (hardcover) | ISBN 9780295749839 (paperback) | ISBN 9780295749846 (ebook)
Subjects: LCSH: Hui (Chinese people)—China—History. | Hui (Chinese people)—China—Interviews. | Hui (Chinese people)—China—Ethnic identity. | Hui (Chinese people)—China—Religion. Minorities—Government policy—China—History. | Muslims—China—History. | Islam and state—China—History. | China—Ethnic relations.
Classification LCC DS731.H85 S77 2021 (print) | LCC DS731.H85 (ebook) | DDC 305.800951—dc23
LC record available at https://lccn.loc.gov/2021018886
LC ebook record available at https://lccn.loc.gov/2021018887

♾ This paper meets the requirements of ANSI/NISO Z39.48-1992 (Permanence of Paper).

To my parents, Kandy and Dan Stroup

Contents

Foreword

STEVAN HARRELL

What does it mean to be Muslim in today's China? For Uyghurs, Kazakhs, and other Turkic Muslims in Xinjiang, it means daily confrontation with state terror. Aside from the 10 percent or more of members of those ethnic nations that are incarcerated, the rest of the population faces the daily humiliation and bother of constant electronic and biometric identity checks, live-in visits by Han Chinese attempting to reform their customs of daily life, and constant reminders that their language, culture, and religion are primitive, poisonous, and detrimental to China's national unity and its place in the world.

To the ten million or so Hui Muslims portrayed in David Stroup's *Pure and True,* the Chinese Communist regime has been gentler—so far—if not exactly or always benign. Hui communities have long spoken mostly Chinese (albeit with some Arabic and Persian words inserted) and are distinguished from the majority Han primarily by their religion and the dietary and lifestyle customs that go along with it. Hui people are descendants of Muslim traders who began settling permanently in East Asia during the Ming dynasty (though they were there much earlier), who over the centuries have acculturated to Chinese ways to various degrees. Hui people now live both in concentrated rural areas, mostly in western China, and in urban enclaves in almost all of China's great cities. In recent times, many Hui have played prominent parts in China's military, literary, academic, political, and business elites; others have been farmers, shopkeepers, teachers, and long-distance traders.

Probably because they have been linguistically and politically integrated into Chinese society for so long, Hui have seemed much less "foreign" to their Han Chinese compatriots and much less threatening to successive regimes than have the Turkic Muslims of Xinjiang. Still, Hui are separate: they pray to one God every Friday; they abstain from eating pork, which is the main protein source of Han diets; and the more devout among them do not smoke or drink. For this reason, Jonathan Lipman titled his history of the Hui—the third book in the Studies on Ethnic Groups in China series—*Familiar Strangers.*

David Stroup's *Pure and True* provides a window into what being Hui was like between 2014 and 2016 in four of China's large cities: Beijing, where Hui are a small but visible minority; Jinan, Shandong's capital, where the Hui quarter is smaller and less well known; Yinchuan, the capital of the Ningxia Hui Autonomous Region, where Hui are a large minority of the urban population; and Xining in Qinghai, where Hui share the city with large numbers of Han, Tibetans, and Mongolians.

Stroup divides his account according to different ways of being Hui in these four cities. "Choosing" is about identity, kinship, and marriage; "Talking" is about both Arabic as a liturgical language and Arabic- and Persian-influenced Chinese as everyday speech; "Consuming" is about dietary habits and how they divide Hui from Han and other pork-consuming ethnic groups; and "Performing" is about religious and ritual life, both in the mosque and at home. In all these aspects of Hui life, the influence of the Chinese state interacts with attempts at community autonomy. On the one hand, state policy toward China's minority ethnopolitical groups, or *shaoshu minzu*, of which the Hui are one, mandates multiculturalism and inclusion, as Susan McCarthy laid out in an earlier volume in this series, *Communist Multiculturalism.* Even the constitution of the People's Republic guarantees religious, cultural, and linguistic rights to all the minority *minzu*. On the other hand, in recent years, especially since Xi Jinping's ascension to power, increasingly influential voices have expressed worry that multiculturalism and limited ethnic autonomy can inhibit national unity and promote "separatism" or "splittism."

Worries about splittism are primarily directed to the Turkic Muslims of Xinjiang and to the Tibetans, understandably since these are occupied nations rather than the "minority groups" with which they are classified. And indeed recent moves to curtail local languages in schools and promote acculturation to Han ways have been most severe in those two occupied territories. Other groups that have posed no threat to Chinese unity, who consider themselves to be Chinese by nationality but separate from Han culturally and linguistically, have not felt the brunt of recent policies as much as have the Tibetans, Uyghurs, and Kazakhs. But where does this leave the Hui, who are already Chinese speakers but share Islamic ritual and cultural practices with the Kazakhs, Uyghurs, and other Turkic peoples?

When Stroup was conducting his field research from 2014 to 2016, these ambivalent policies left the Hui mostly alone. They were subject to prejudice from the majority and to suspicion from the authorities, but they could still go about their daily lives of choosing, talking, consuming, and performing and, as long as they did not explicitly follow strict orthodox versions of Islamic piety recently introduced from the Middle East, they were not subject to any kind of real repression. These relatively multiculturalist policies were not only beneficial to the Hui communities themselves but allowed Stroup to gather the rich textual and visual data that document the ways in which Hui could be both ethnic and modern.

Sadly, these days seem to be coming to an end, as Stroup shows in the afterword to this book. Since Xi Jinping declared his People's War on Terror in 2017, mainly as an excuse to repress all forms of potential opposition among Uyghurs and Kazaks, the Hui have been caught, to various degrees, in the penumbra of those repressive policies. Mosques have lost their domes and their loudspeakers; Arabic calligraphy on restaurant storefronts has been painted over; even moderate forms of Islamic dress such as headscarves have been discouraged if not outright forbidden; the state has even encouraged people to drink more liquor.

It is in this period of saddening and hopefully temporary repression that Stroup's account of what things were like not so long ago acquires both its poignancy as a reminder of what might have been and its scholarly value as a record of what was. We are delighted to introduce *Pure and True* as the twenty-fifth volume of Studies on Ethnic Groups in China.

Preface

The inspiration for this book came in 2013, in the blistering heat of a July afternoon. While enrolled in a summer language program in Beijing, I had taken a long holiday weekend to visit Jinan, the city where I had lived between 2009 and 2011. I returned that summer to find a once familiar city in the midst of several dramatic changes. Like most of China's cities, Jinan was rapidly rebuilding its infrastructure and replacing shabby, old buildings with new, gleaming high-rises and shopping malls. During that summer's classes in Beijing, the subject of China's rapid urbanization and the economic, political, and social impact it had on Chinese society was the subject of many of the readings and seminar conversations that comprised our daily work. Now, on my short holiday, I couldn't help but feel I was witnessing the kinds of change discussed in our classroom firsthand. Though much of Jinan remained familiar, the many alterations that were underway felt disorienting.

The most obvious of these many changes was the ongoing construction of the city's first supertall skyscraper, near the central square. The Lüdi Center would stand over three hundred meters tall when completed, casting a literal and figurative shadow over the city and foreshadowing many more imminent transformations. Friends I spoke to in the city during that visit regarded the tower with ambivalence. Some saw it as an effort to spark economic development that was years overdue, stalled by lack of planning and localized corruption. Others saw it as a way for Jinan to catch up to Qingdao, Shandong province's other major city, which had become a more modern, prosperous, and glamorous location than the provincial capital in recent years. However, some friends saw the tower as disruptive, as it would surely bring more construction. These new projects would certainly displace the people living in their paths, causing some old friends to react with scorn.

Ambivalence to the project was felt strongest in the heart of Jinan's Hui Quarter (Huimin Xiaoqu), which sat adjacent to the site. It was no secret to anyone in the neighborhood that the city government wanted to replace the quarter's aging brutalist apartment buildings with newer structures that would raise the value of the land and the profile of the city. The people who lived in the area feared they, too, would soon be displaced. My old friend Ma Wei, who owned a barbecue (*shaokao*) restaurant in the neighborhood, did nothing to hide his contempt for the project when I stopped by to visit one afternoon.[1] Catching me admiring the construction process while we sat together outside his shop drinking beer, he wrinkled his face in annoyance. He grumbled for a few minutes that much of the area was slated for demolition. "Including this place!" he said, adding, "I'll lose this restaurant when they tear this neighborhood down."

Stunned, I tried to imagine the transformations such urban renewal might bring to the neighborhood. During my time in Jinan, the Hui Quarter was a vibrant island of ethnic minority culture surrounded by a sea of ethnic majority Han. It stood out as an area unlike the rest of Jinan, a very typical second-tier city situated on the Yellow River in eastern China's heartland. The neighborhood, overwhelmingly populated by Hui, was known throughout the city as a warren of winding alleys filled with neon signs for purveyors of grilled meats and keg beer. At night the aroma of smoke from their long trough-style grills hung in the air alongside the shouts of restaurateurs looking to attract diners from among the people wandering by. What would become of their businesses when the demolition crews came? Where would they all go? More important, what impact would their dispersal have on the city's Hui community?

In previous travels to ethnic minority tourist spots like Dali and Lijiang in Yunnan in 2008, I had witnessed firsthand how changes in configurations of urban space—and populations—impacted the way residents accessed and maintained their ethnic identities. In fact, discussions about the Chinese state's efforts to boost economic development through the commodification of ethnic identity and the creation of a large-scale ethnic tourism industry resound not only in academic fora but also in the popular press.[2] Unlike those sites, however, Jinan's Hui Quarter was not a tourist destination, and the forces of urban transformation about to be enacted upon it were not the result of an effort to create a stylized attraction for throngs of visitors on holiday. Rather, the changes occurring in Jinan's Hui Quarter stood as the kind of ordinary remaking of urban spaces taking place in cities throughout China every day.

As I pondered the impact that completely rebuilding the neighborhood might have on its residents, a number of questions began to flood into my mind: How would these changes in the Hui Quarter's physical and demographic makeup alter the daily habits that maintained residents' sense of connection to their ethnic identity? Would displacement of residents bring an end to ethnic traditions or merely cause them to adapt? Would the loss of the neighborhood as a locus of interaction and a repository of culture result in the diminishment of Hui identity in the city as a whole? Did these changes animate resentments against the state and its development initiatives? Most important, were these scenarios being enacted in other Hui communities throughout China?

Over the following years, I set out to understand how the complex interactions between changing urban landscapes and tactics of authoritarian governance influenced the daily expression of Hui identity. Through thirteen months in the field, during which I conducted 154 interviews and countless ethnographic observations in locations in six different provinces, I explored the everyday practice of Hui identity. This fieldwork allowed me to consider the ways in which new and competing conceptions of what it meant to be Hui emerged from the restructuring of urban spaces and the interactions between people that these processes of transformation facilitated. My conversations with respondents yielded a multifaceted, nuanced view of the way people lived out their ethnic identities on a daily basis and how state policies regarding ethnicity and development shaped and constrained them.

The Chinese state's crackdown on expressions of ethnic and religious identities by Muslim minorities in the years following my departure from the field in 2016 illustrate how even mundane habits of speech, diet, dress, worship, and association may convey deeply held identities. The state's increased efforts to police and standardize ethnic and religious expression in these communities reveal the importance of such seemingly commonplace practices as cultural and political acts and illustrate the vital role that maintaining control over ethnic politics plays in the state's legitimating narratives.[3]

This book is, therefore, an exploration of these dynamics from the bottom up. To understand the impacts of the forces of China's ethnic politics, economic development policies, and rapidly changing urban landscapes on the expression of identity, we must look to the everyday. Only by identifying the ways in which Ma Wei and countless other ordinary Hui people like him practice and express their identity daily may we hope to grasp the full significance of such change.

Acknowledgments

This book marks the culmination of years of conceptualization, research, fieldwork, drafting, editing, and tinkering. So many people have been integral to its production. I am grateful to all of them.

None of this research would have been possible without the funding I received from the Fulbright program and the Institute of International Education. In particular, I am thankful to Anita X. Chan and Serena Bing Han from the Beijing Fulbright office for their assistance in the field. Likewise, I am grateful for the funding awarded by the University of Oklahoma's Mergler Fellowship program, which helped support me as I wrote early drafts.

In China, I enjoyed support from sponsors and colleagues at institutions in all of my field sites. I am grateful to Minzu University in Beijing for sponsoring me while in the field. In particular, I owe thanks to Ding Hong for sponsoring me and generously introducing me to local points of contact at various field sites around the country. Additionally, many people gave me assistance at field sites. I am incredibly grateful to Rebecca Fa, Xing Fei, Alvin Gao, Ma Lai'en, Ma Lianjun, Ma Qian, Wei Wei, and Yang Yang for helping me find my feet, meet contacts, find housing, scope out interesting sites, find the best eats, and all the other small things that allowed me to not only survive but thrive while in the field.

I was fortunate to share my time in the field with a cohort of brilliant peers. Thank you to Fiona Cunningham, Liz Emrich-Rouge, Minerva Inwald, Yining Lin, James McGlone, Matt Sheehan, Samantha Vortherms, and the members of the Provincial Cuisine Club of Beijing for your friendship and companionship. My year in the field was one of the greatest adventures of my life. Thank you all for being part of it. I owe special thanks to Jesse Watson and David Porter, whose visits during my time in Jinan, Yinchuan, and Xining helped me see familiar places through fresh eyes and provided me with stimulating conversation and memories I'll cherish for a lifetime.

As this project was drafted, and redrafted, many people gave moral and emotional support in the form of food, drink, texts, phone calls, hangouts, and other expressions of solidarity and friendship. Thank you especially to Chris Anderson, Victoria Bautista, Tyler and Krystal Camarillo, Angela Chuang, Dave Conway, Chris Elford, Andrew Foglia, Steve Foglia, Keith Gaddie, Zeke and Emily Goggin, Tyler Hughes, Tammy Kreznar, Periloux Peay, Jason Pudlo, J. D. Rackey, Justin and Ruth Burr Reedy, Aaron Robinson, Rebecca Roe, Scott Saldaña, Jamie Smith, Tao Wang, and Edgar Zamora.

A number of people provided insight and clarification in the writing process. For sharing their knowledge and opinions at various stages in the process, I thank Elena Barabantseva, Ana Bracic, Daniel P. Brown, Alex Dukalskis, Timothy Grose, Guangtian Ha, Ellie Knott, Ma Chengjun, Ma Jianfu, Niu Xuan, Jesko Schmoller, and Jo Smith-Finley. Thank you to Eve McGlynn for her fantastic work on illustrating this manuscript's maps. To Isabelle Côté, I am grateful for kind and encouraging comments on an early draft. At the University of Washington Press, I am incredibly grateful to Stevan Harrell and Lorri Hagman. Steve's comments on an early draft made the work sharper and more focused, while Lorri's editing in the final stages made the work leaner and more efficient. All along the way, their positive reinforcement has driven me forward.

A few colleagues deserve extra special thanks. I am grateful to Eric Schluessel for his willingness to offer knowledge of history, linguistics, and the ins and outs of the publication process. I owe so much of my understanding of the history of the development of Hui identity to Hannah Theaker, whose meticulous attention to detail has made my work immeasurably better. Likewise, working alongside David Tobin in Manchester has made my work stronger. I thank him for our numerous conversations on contemporary Chinese politics, political theory, and weekly thrills of the top-flight leagues of European football.

Throughout my academic career I've had the privilege of working with brilliant mentors who have imparted so much wisdom to me. I thank Shelley Rigger for helping me cultivate an interest in China and learn the basics of Chinese politics. I thank Lu Yuan for teaching me invaluable lessons about China's ethnic diversity. I thank Peter Gries for helping me learn to find a writing voice and speak to a larger audience. I thank Paul Goode for helping me to conceptualize my work, making me consider its larger implications, and teaching me by his own example how to do impactful research through collaboration.

Finally, I must thank my family, who have given me immeasurable love and support throughout this process. Thank you to my sister, Caroline, my brother-in-law, Mike, and my niece, Ellie, for your love and encouragement. To my mom and dad, Kandy and Daniel: there is not enough space to thank you for everything you have done for me. From my very earliest days, you have always encouraged me to do my best, to aim as high as I possibly can, and to seize the chance for adventures that come my way. More than that, you gave me fine examples of how to love and be dedicated to your work and to others. I cannot express how grateful I am to you.

Lastly, I must thank the people of Beijing, Jinan, Yinchuan, and Xining. Without your compassion, your warmth, patience, and openness, this project would never have succeeded. It is my hope that I have held up my part of the deal and have been able to tell all of your stories.

PURE AND TRUE

MODERNIZATION AND HUI ETHNICITY IN URBAN CHINA

ON A GRAY, COLD DAY IN LATE NOVEMBER 2015, I SAT BY THE WINdow of a small shop in the Hui Quarter (Huimin Xiaoqu) of Shandong's provincial capital of Jinan, watching as snowflakes floated to the ground. Wisps of steam swirled up from the cup of strong green tea handed to me by the owner, a local Hui (a Chinese-speaking Muslim minority ethnic group) businessman in his fifties. I took a long sip from the piping hot cup and listened as he opined about the future of the neighborhood. Waving his arm out in the direction of the massive, three-hundred-meter-tall tower of the recently completed Lüdi Center that stood just across the street from the entrance to the Hui Quarter, he lamented that changes would be imminently visited upon the neighborhood. He remarked, "The government feels that this neighborhood is too chaotic [*luan*]. They're going to build new high-rise apartments [*gaolou*]."[1]

He was not the first respondent to make such claims. Others with whom I spoke in Jinan made similar pronouncements about the fate of the neighborhood. Following up, I inquired, "So, what will happen to the residents of the neighborhood?" In a resigned tone, he answered, "Some residents will be able to come back, but the prices for apartments will be higher. Some won't be able to afford it. They'll have to go somewhere else. For instance, those migrant Hui from Xibei [northwest China] will just go home.[2] Others will move farther away, and the Muslim Quarter will get smaller." We continued to sit and watch the snow fall. I posed another follow-up question: "How will this change the neighborhood?" In reply, he described in detail the centrality of the mosque to community life for many Hui. He explained that moving the community away from its place of worship would bring pervasive change:

For us Muslims, it's best to live near a mosque. But if the government wants to *chai qian* [demolish and replace (housing)]), you can't count on that. There's nothing to do about it; it's inescapable. We don't want to agree to leave, but there's nothing that can be done. If the government wants to demolish the houses, there's nothing that can be done. We'll have to move. But for us, it's different. Living near the mosque is important. You can go to pray easily. You can buy halal meat. It's easier. But if we can't afford the new apartments we'll have to leave and move farther away from the mosque. Han don't understand this.[3]

Elsewhere, in ethnic minority (*shaoshu minzu*) enclaves throughout China, such dramatic programs of urbanization frequently arouse distrust, scorn, and resistance.[4] Throughout China's history, the state used projects of urbanization that moved people and altered landscapes as part of a mission of assimilation it saw as "civilizing."[5] In many ethnic Uyghur, Tibetan, and Mongol communities, the policies that promote the demolition of enclave neighborhoods and the influx of migrants into the community provoke fears of cultural erasure and often serve as flashpoints for solidifying ethnic consciousness in resistance against the state.[6] Such grievances lie at the heart of the ethnic uprisings in Lhasa in 2008, Ürümchi in 2009, and Xilingol in 2011.[7]

The residents of Jinan's Hui Quarter, however, offered no inclinations toward active resistance. Many residents expressed a sense of inevitability about the fate of the neighborhood. They cited the government's intentions to develop the Hui Quarter, which stands at the heart of the "Old City" (Laocheng Qu), as part of a broader project of revitalization for the city center.[8] As widening began along Gongqingtuan Road on the north side of the Hui Quarter in early November 2015, one woman who served as an *ahong* (imam) at the local women's mosque remarked that further demolition would probably begin "within the next five years." When asked if she was sure, she remarked, "It's not totally certain, but it's been planned."[9] Some residents even welcomed the changes, claiming it would improve the quality of life in the neighborhood. Speaking of the new buildings to be built on the site of the neighborhood, a Hui restaurateur in his sixties remarked, "They're obviously an improvement for people's lives, aren't they? I think they're fine."[10]

The relative lack of resistance from Jinan's Hui community highlights the peculiarity of the Hui's position in Chinese society. Prior to the current era of Reform and Opening, which began in 1978, popular conceptions of the Hui in China portrayed them as restive and violent.[11] Such characterizations stemmed, in part, from a series of bloody conflicts between the Hui and the armies of the Qing empire in the eighteenth and nineteenth centuries.[12] Despite this history of Hui uprisings, resistance to the state authority does not define relations between the state and contemporary Hui communities. The occasional conflict with government actors emerging from Hui communities occurs because of local concerns rather than systemic, nationwide resistance to the state.[13] Perhaps because of this history of rebellion, the Hui present the Chinese Communist Party (CCP) with opportunities to tell stories of its success in ethnic politics. In fact, both China's domestic media and international news outlets frequently invoke the Hui as examples of China's "other," less restive, "peaceful" Muslims, painting the Hui as part of a dichotomy in contrast to their Uyghur coreligionists.[14] Such discussion of the Hui as "good Muslims" often portrays this transformation from restive rebels to model minority as one of the great successes of the Party's ethnic policies—especially in contrast to the Party's failures in managing relations with Uyghurs. However, these narratives usually focus on the actions of the Party and often overlook the economic, social, and political dynamics underway in Hui communities themselves. Such an oversight leaves unexamined questions about why widespread resistance is now less common in Hui communities. Put simply, why don't the Hui rebel anymore?

Several studies examining the construction and maintenance of Hui identity precede this one. Dru Gladney's foundational comparative ethnography of four Hui communities (Najiahu in Ningxia, the urban district of Niu Jie and suburban community of Changying in Beijing, and Quanzhou in Fujian) traces the ethnogenesis of the Hui to understand the common bonds that solidify a core Hui ethnic identity. Gladney asserts that Hui communities developed heterogeneously, and notions of Hui as a separate ethnic identity developed only after the People's Republic of China (PRC) completed its ethnic categorization project in the 1950s (historically known as *minzu shibie*).[15] Despite the recentness of articulations of a distinctly Hui ethnic identity, Gladney remarks that the common cultural resonance of *qingzhen*—which he translates as "purity" (*qing*, in the sense of ritual cleanliness and moral conduct) and "truth" (*zhen*, in the sense of authenticity and legitimacy)—hold together the Hui as an ethnic group or "nationality," as the word *minzu* is translated by the CCP.[16]

Following Gladney's early study, a number of scholars explored further branches of Hui identity. Historian Michael Dillon's broad overview of the Hui community provides a detailed account of its religious traditions and historical divisions along sectarian and regional lines.[17] With their anthropological study of Hui women's mosques, Maria Jaschok and Jingjun Shui investigate the historical role played by female *ahong* and their status—as well as that of the mosques they serve—in contemporary communities, highlighting gendered aspects of the expression of Hui identity and the distinctly localized nature of women's roles within Hui Islam.[18] Cultural anthropologist Maris Boyd Gillette's examination of economic modernization on the practices of daily life in Xi'an's Hui community illustrates how the state's development efforts allow for a reassertion of Hui identity, both through expression of Islamic modernism and through the development of a consumer culture centered around the superior quality of *qingzhen* (here understood to approximate halal) products.[19] Similarly, in her case study of religious revival among Yunnan Hui in the post-Mao era political scientist Susan McCarthy remarks that renewed interest in Hui identity provides opportunities to both rediscover lost tradition and pursue connections with the modern Islamic world.[20] Matthew Erie's study of Hui strongholds in rural, southern Gansu describes how local religious authorities reframe law in accordance with shari'a and illustrates the importance of informal relationships between clergy and state.[21]

Each of these studies stands as a landmark in the field of Chinese ethnic politics. This book builds on their foundations by assessing the ways in which internal boundaries drawn along cross-cutting identity cleavages influence the everyday contestation of Hui identity and enable the Chinese party-state's enactment of authoritarian control over ethnic politics. It explores the politics of Hui identity in "quiet times"—the moments of ordinary life outside of the rare outbursts of contentious politics, activated ethnic consciousness, mobilization, or resistance, which are frequently the subject of studies on ethnic politics.[22] Rather than focus solely on elite actors or moments of conflict, this study assesses how ethnic actors contest the significance of daily practices that sustain ethnic identity in the midst of urban change. To do so, I examine the process of ethnic boundary formation in Hui communities in the context of urbanization. I argue that the urbanization encouraged by the Chinese party-state activates cross-cutting identity cleavages like class, region, education level, and sect and sparks contestation over the proper way to express Hui identity, limiting the amount of conflict between the Hui and the state.

Identity boundaries, though they may correspond to physical units, are a socially constructed, continually negotiated set of benchmarks used to make a distinction between those who belong as members of a group and those who do not.[23] These boundaries become meaningful as they influence matters regarding group inclusion or exclusion and the treatment of those who fall into different categories.[24] Boundary setting is thus a "process of social comparison" that distinguishes the group from outsiders.[25] While *qingzhen* can mark the boundary of a common Hui identity and unify diverse expressions of Huiness (as Gladney claims), these diverse expressions also establish internal boundaries along competing cleavages of class, gender, sect, and region, among others. Interactions between these groups of Hui from different backgrounds reopen the contestation of Hui identity, offering competing understandings of which daily practices define the boundaries of Hui identity and what level of importance ought to be assigned to observing them.

In promoting transformation of urban spaces and sponsoring the internal migration in Hui communities across the country, CCP policy sparks renewed contestation of the boundaries of Hui identity. Ethnic actors offering competing views of how to properly express Hui identity generate a multitude of understandings of Huiness. Because debate unfolds around internal identity cleavages that produce intragroup boundaries, conflict concerning Hui identity rarely targets the state. By allowing such competition over what ought to stand as the markers of identity, the CCP effectively manages ethnic affairs in Hui communities without drawing organized resistance to the policies it implements. Though tenuous, such conduct of ethnic politics enables the CCP to continue to promote legitimizing narratives about the unity and stability produced by the Party's leadership.

Understanding these dynamics requires an in-depth examination of how ethnic politics unfold in the midst of the "quiet" moments of ordinary life. Pictures of ethnic politics that privilege observations of ethnic minority resistance to the state and its policies present conflict as an inevitable outcome. Those instances where states—especially those with authoritarian governments—successfully exert control over the management of ethnic politics go overlooked by the literature, leaving questions about day-to-day authoritarian governance largely unanswered. Further, cases that examine only instances of activated ethnic mobilization risk reifying or essentializing ethnic identity. If scholarship depicts both the state and ethnic minority groups as monolithic actors locked in opposition, it misses important opportunities to understand how intragroup differences exert a profound influence on the conduct of ethnic politics. To avoid reifying ethnic groups by assuming they are "real entities" rather than products of social construction, I explore how daily practices reflect the fluid, contested nature of ethnic identity.[26] Doing so enables me to develop greater understanding of why, how, and when feelings of attachment to the group—or "groupness"—are most salient.[27] This is the course taken by a growing body of scholarship in the study of nationalism and ethnic politics that focuses on the routine context of the everyday and seeks to expand observations of ethnic politics beyond these rare moments of heightened salience.[28]

QUIET POLITICS AMONG CHINA'S FAMILIAR STRANGERS: THE CASE OF THE HUI

The small Muslim Commodity Service Shop (Musilin Yongpin Fuwubu), which sells souvenirs just inside the front gate of the Niu Jie Mosque (Niujie Libasi) in Beijing, offers very few wares of interest to nonbelievers. I was told as much by the middle-aged woman who ran the sales counter. On a particularly hot Wednesday afternoon in mid-August 2015 the mosque stood mostly empty between afternoon and evening prayers. "You *can* buy these things," she gestured, surveying the shop's array of curios, including ceramic vases, prayer beads, headscarves, commentaries on the Qur'an, and incense. "But if you're not Muslim, they really won't have any significance. They won't be of any use to you." When I mentioned that I studied the Hui, she seemed to understand my curiosity and patiently began to explain how certain items (such as prayer hats and beaded prayer bracelets) fairly self-evidently aid believers in the practice of Islam.

I turned to a set of license-plate-size tin placards that displayed the words of the *Bismillah*, "In the name of God the most merciful and compassionate," in both Arabic and Chinese.[29] "What are these for?" I inquired. Just as she did for all of my questions, she replied in simple terms: "We put these signs in the doorways of our homes and businesses to say 'our family is Hui.'" This struck me as unusual. Respondents frequently blurred the line between Hui ethnicity and Islamic faith. However, Hui respondents rarely used the word Huizu to mean Muslim (Musilin). In fact, most did the reverse, not differentiating Hui from all other Muslims. "What's the difference between Hui and Muslim?" I asked tentatively. "Well, they're more or less the same," she answered. "Here in China, we call Muslims 'Hui.'" I nodded my head, although still confused by the exchange.[30]

The conflation of Hui and Muslim illustrates the peculiar status of the Hui among China's ethnic minorities and demonstrates why the Hui present an ideal case for examining noncontentious ethnic politics. Unlike the more publicized Uyghur and Tibetan cases, where contentious and occasionally violent politics reify and harden boundaries between minority groups and the majority Han and heighten the salience of ethnic difference, an examination of the Hui case reveals subtler political processes. The absence of recent violent conflict between Hui and the party-state, along with the sociocultural heterogeneity of Hui communities, provides an opportunity to break new ground in the study of ethnic politics. Thus, the Hui represent a "most likely case," as the state's attempts to harden the boundaries of identity suggests a scenario where conflict is expected. Similarly, the history of tension between Hui and Han and the cultural closeness of the groups suggest that the Hui present a most likely case for heightening the salience of ethnic boundaries that differentiate between majority and minority.[31]

One of China's largest ethnic minority groups, the Hui are often the most prominent minority group in the Han-dominated, eastern, coastal regions of the country. The 2010 census indicated a total Hui population of over 10.5 million dispersed throughout the territory of the current PRC (see table I.1).[32] The Hui differ from other groups designated by the CCP as *minzu* in several ways.[33] Unlike the nine other Islamic minority groups recognized by the Chinese government,[34] all of which possess some other unifying marker of identity, such as language, which differentiates them from the majority Han in formal ethnic categorizations, the Hui are distinguished by religion alone. By contrast, the party-state considers the Hui a "Chinese-speaking ethnicity" (*Hanyu minzu*)—a quality they share with the Han—officially setting them apart from the rest of China's minority groups.[35]

The position of the Hui relative to the majority Han, as well as to other Islamic *minzu*—such as Uyghurs, Dongxiang, or Salar—reflects both long-term distancing from the majority and historical uncertainty regarding relationships to their coreligionists. Prior to solidification of Huizu as a category by the CCP, the designation *Hui Hui* encompassed all Muslims, regardless of ethnicity. The first recorded use of *Hui Hui* in Chinese sources dates to the late eleventh or early twelfth century.[36] Later, under the ethnic class system imposed by the ruling Yuan dynasty (1271–1368), Muslims who intermarried with Chinese and their descendants fell into the category of *semu* (a broad caste whose approximate meaning translates to "assorted categories"), a designation that encompassed other non-Han subjects of the Mongol court, including Central Asian Turkic troops and others.[37] Though such distinctions separated them as something other than simply "Chinese," *Hui Hui* did not become a consistent term for Chinese-speaking Muslims until the late thirteenth century.[38]

By the Qing dynasty (1644–1912), Islam frequently appears in records of the time as *Huijiao* or "the teaching of the Hui."[39] However, records from the late Qing, most especially those from Xinjiang, suggest that despite the broad label *Hui*, clear linguistic and cultural divisions separated Sinophone Muslims and Turkic speakers of Chaghatay.[40] Elsewhere *Hui* served as an overarching category, with subgroups using a variety of terms to distinguish themselves along linguistic lines.[41] Thus, the status of Hui during the late

TABLE I.1. Hui population by province

PROVINCE	TOTAL HUI POPULATION	% OF TOTAL POPULATION
Ningxia Hui AR	2,173,820	34.5
Qinghai	834,298	14.8
Gansu	1,258,641	4.9
Xinjiang Uyghur AR	983,015	4.5
Yunnan	698,265	1.5
Tianjin	177,734	1.4
Beijing	249,223	1.3
Henan	957,964	1
Inner Mongolia AR	221,483	0.9
Hebei	570,170	0.8
Liaoning	245,798	0.6
Anhui	328,062	0.6
Shandong	535,679	0.6
Guizhou	184,788	0.5
Jilin	118,799	0.4
Tibet AR	12,630	0.4
Shaanxi	138,716	0.4
Heilongjiang	101,749	0.3
Shanghai	78,163	0.3
Zhejiang	166,276	0.3
Fujian	115,978	0.3
Shanxi	59,709	0.2
Jiangsu	130,757	0.2
Hubei	67,185	0.1
Hunan	94,705	0.1
Guangdong	45,073	0.1
Guangxi Zhuang AR	32,319	0.1
Hainan	10,670	0.1
Sichuan	104,544	0.1
Chongqing	9,056	>0.1
Jiangxi	8,902	>0.1

Note: AR = autonomous region.

Source: People's Republic of China, National Bureau of Statistics, "Sixth National Population Census of the People's Republic of China, 2010," Beijing, 2013.

Qing does not appear to be a solidified ethnic identity but rather a term whose meaning varied relative to context.[42]

During the Republican era (1911–49), the successors to the Qing held political ambitions to build a Han-centered Chinese nation-state, a more formal ethnic classification system.[43] Accordingly, the new state portrayed China as the "Republic of Five Peoples" (Wuzu Gonghe Guo), reapplying the broad designation of Hui for all Muslims.[44] As defined by Sun Yat-sen's *wuzu* model, *Hui* primarily implied Turkic-speaking Muslims.[45] Debate ensued ever the status of Sinophone Muslims, whom some Muslim intellectuals regarded merely as Han converts.[46] Others argued for their inclusion in a separate, distinct category.[47] Under the rule of the Beiyang government (1912–28), established in Beijing after the fall of the Qing under the military leadership of Yuan Shikai and his clique of generals, demands grew to treat *Hui* as two categories of identity: one that denoted ethnicity and was primarily composed of Turkic-speaking Muslims from Xinjiang, and another that denoted religious identity made up primarily of Sinophone Muslims from Inner China.[48] Later, after the Nationalists (Kuomintang) led by Chiang Kai-shek regained control of the government in 1928, state policy denoted Chinese-speaking Muslims as Han, owing largely to Chiang's Han-centric ideological nationalism, which stressed assimilation.[49]

After the establishment of the People's Republic in 1949, the category *Huizu* gained further legitimacy as the newly empowered CCP expanded the classification system and recognized differences within China's Islamic communities. Catering to minorities by offering recognition—and in some cases autonomy—became a key part of CCP strategy.[50] Thus, under the CCP, Hui sought and were granted status as a nationality distinct from both the Han and other Muslims.[51]

The CCP's ethnic propaganda frequently exalts the Hui as model patriots whose contributions to the construction of the current Chinese state evidences their devotion to the unity of all of China's *minzu*. The Chinese state frequently invokes historical examples, like that of Zheng He (1371–1433), the legendary Muslim admiral of the Ming dynasty who sailed tribute voyages on the Indian Ocean, as testament to the long-standing devotion of the Hui to the Chinese state. Even more complex Hui historical figures, such as Ma Bufang (1903–75), the Nationalist-aligned warlord who served as governor of Qinghai from 1938 to 1949, are often presented by the CCP as patriotic heroes for their efforts in fighting the Japanese during the Second Sino-Japanese War (1937–45).[52] As recently as 2016, Hui mosques throughout the country displayed state propaganda imploring the Hui to *ai guo, ai jiao* (love your country, love your faith), rhetorically placing devotion to the state on an equal footing with devotion to Islam. As a result, many Han regard the Hui as essentially assimilated. This perceived closeness of the Hui to the state, and the notion that the Hui receive favorable treatment by the state as a reward, frequently earns scorn from their Muslim coreligionists. Some Uyghurs use the word *watermelon* as a slur against the Hui, maintaining that the Hui are "green (i.e., Muslim) on the outside but red (i.e., communist) on the inside" and implying that Hui loyalties lie first and foremost with the state rather than with Islam.[53]

Such one-dimensional depictions of the Hui sweep aside a much more complicated historical picture marked by rebellion and resistance. Throughout the nineteenth century, sectarian conflicts between Hui groups led to violent unrest in both the northwest and the southwest, ultimately resulting in forceful, bloody suppression by the armies of the ruling Qing dynasty.[54] During the Beiyang period, the clique led by the family of warlord Ma Qi and other elite Hui generals enmeshed themselves in the Nationalist leadership structure and actively participated in the nation-building efforts in the northwest.[55] During the ensuing Chinese Civil War, the Ma generals' loyalty to the Nationalists and their ideological commitment to promoting the fusion of Islamic reformism and Chinese nationalism made them dogged opponents of the CCP.[56] The Communist victory in 1949 again fractured Hui communities and complicated relations between Hui and the state. Some, like Ma Liang and Ma Hongkui, staged insurgencies against the CCP in the northwest and along the Sino-Burmese border, liaising with Chiang Kai-shek and the Nationalists as late as 1954.[57]

In the early days of the PRC the CCP's ethnicization of Hui identity caused disruption and stirred up discontent by decoupling Hui identity from religion.[58] The intensity of the Party's hostility toward the Hui increased such that by 1957, the danger of severe repression made openly practicing Islam prohibitively costly.[59] While heavy-handed suppression of religious expression largely muted Hui resistance to the state, a few notable outbursts occurred during the late stages of the Mao era. Notably, the Shadian Incident of 1975 saw the state's People's Liberation Army clash with Hui villagers in the southwestern province of Yunnan in a bloody conflict that left hundreds dead.[60]

Thus, even though uprisings largely ended during the era of Reform and Opening (1978–present) and the Hui—to a large degree—have been assimilated into Chinese society, as descendants of foreign Muslims they have rarely been truly accepted as countrymen by the Han. Instead, the group's current designation as Huizu—an ethnic identity distinct from other Islamic minorities and implying Sinophone Muslims—is the final product of centuries of sustained cultural evolution that began with the Hui being conceived of as "foreign guests" (*fanke*). After generations of intermarriage with local Chinese, the Hui have come to be conceived of as "familiar strangers," an institutionalized "other" at once similar to and distinct from the majority Han.[61]

Beyond the CCP's whitewashing of a much more complicated past, such monolithic depictions of the Hui neglect the high levels of sociocultural diversity within the Hui community itself.[62] Unlike China's other ethnic minority groups, the Hui do not share a common territorial homeland. Similarly, as descendants of Muslims who blended into Chinese society through generations of intermarriage, Hui claim descent from people of a number of different linguistic backgrounds and ancestral places.[63] Because of these disparate points of historic origin, Hui communities exist in all corners of the country. However, the northwest, in particular the provinces of Qinghai and Gansu and the autonomous regions of Ningxia and Xinjiang, hold the most numerous populations.

Given such wide geographic dispersion and disparate ancestral origins, the Hui encompass a broad and diverse array of cultural and linguistic traditions. Some Hui communities bear the stamp of Sinicization as the product of generations of cohabitation with Han and the efforts of Hui intellectuals to demonstrate the compatibility of Chinese Islam with Daoist and Confucian traditions.[64] Elsewhere, however, the cultural and linguistic traditions of the Hui reflect the group's heterogeneity. Pockets of Tibetan- and Mongolian-speaking Hui scattered on China's western periphery belie the oversimplified characterization of the group as "Chinese-speaking Muslims." For example, communities of Tibetanized Hui in northwestern Yunnan and eastern Qinghai (where they are referred to as "Tibetan Hui," or Zang Hui), speak Tibetan dialects, wear Tibetan costume, and in some cases have adopted Tibetan surnames.[65] Nor is Hui religious tradition uniform. Many Hui claim they are nonpracticing and essentially secularized. Among observant Hui sectarian differences divide the community. In Linxia Hui Autonomous Prefecture in southern Gansu, Hui belong to a plethora of different Sufi lineages, while only a few hours away in Xining, the majority of Hui identify as belonging to the strictly non-Sufi, Yihewani (Ikhwan) sect.[66]

Such great differences in understanding what it means to be Hui are illustrative of the great diversity within the Hui populace. The incredible heterogeneity of the Hui demands that scholars problematize and investigate the significance of these internal differences and move beyond sweeping generalizations.[67] This study provides a thorough examination of Hui in search of a greater understanding of how this broad, multifaceted community defines the boundaries of its identity.

CASE SELECTION: EXAMINING EVERYDAY ETHNIC PRACTICES IN URBAN HUI ENCLAVES

Hui neighborhoods present ideal cases for studying the impact of daily ethnic politics in the context of urbanization because, in many Chinese cities, Hui neighborhoods function as important loci of interaction and boundary setting for the group and supply resources for the observance of a faith-based lifestyle. The neighborhood itself provides the group with social resources necessary for the reproduction of the imagined community.[68] I identify Hui enclave neighborhoods as culturally defined spaces, usually surrounding one or several community mosques and comprising residences and businesses that facilitate the daily observance of Islamic religious and cultural practices (e.g., halal grocers, restaurants, prayer goods stores). In some cases, street names—such as Xining's Qingzhen Xiang (Qinghzen Alley), Jinan's Libaisi Jie (Mosque Street), and Beijing's Jiaozi Hutong (Religious Education Alley)—may reveal the area's ethnic significance.[69] The physical boundaries that mark these areas may be imprecise or frequently shifting, but they remain clear to the residents, who often explicitly name the area the Hui Quarter, as in Jinan and Xining. As Gillette suggests of Xi'an's Huiminfang, despite a lack of officially recognized borders, locals are nonetheless able to identify the overlap of cultural and geographic boundaries and intuitively understand where the neighborhood begins and ends.[70] Close proximity to other group members imparts a sense of comfort and convenience to those who reside in such communities.[71] Thus, enclaves become crucial sites for preserving cultural traditions and sustaining connections to ethnic identity.[72]

The proliferation of Hui enclaves in cities occurs largely to accommodate the observance of Islamic lifestyle habits. In the Hui community on Niu Jie in Beijing, the concentration of co-ethnics within the same neighborhood enables Beijing's Hui community to maintain their Islamic identity by keeping a halal diet, patronizing businesses that sell ethnic goods, finding partners from within the group to marry, and sending their children to Islamic schools.[73] The streets adjacent to Niu Jie Mosque—the largest and most famous mosque in Beijing— are lined with halal grocers, bakeries, and restaurants, and department stores that cater to Muslim clientele, reinforcing the importance that ethnicity plays in residents' daily lives.[74] Enclave communities also create economic opportunities for entrepreneurs whose goods and services provide vital resources in relatively protected economic opportunity structures where they are in high demand.[75] In Xining, the city's Hui enclave spawned a number of ethnic restaurants, hostels, and transportation businesses and allowed Hui locals to continue in traditional occupations as traders and entrepreneurs.[76]

The spread of these Hui "ethnopreneurs" increases the visibility of Hui communities nationwide.[77] A mark of successful ethnic branding and widespread cultural diffusion into mainstream Chinese society, Hui restaurants serving halal dishes, in particular the famous *niurou lamian* (handmade beef noodles), sprout up in nearly every city in the country.[78] Prior to a nationwide campaign of de-Islamification in 2018, the typical green signs adorned with Chinese Islamic calligraphy used by Hui restaurants made them instantly recognizable.[79] Even in heavily Han Chinese eastern cities, like Shandong's capital, Jinan, Hui ethnic businesses and places of association clearly distinguish enclave communities. Jinan's Hui Quarter encircles the Great Southern Mosque (Jinan Qingzhen Nandasi), one of the oldest and most important in eastern China. Despite the mosque's prominence, the local populace knows the neighborhood mostly as a place where they can get barbecued mutton. Indeed, Jinan's taxi drivers, when asked to transport passengers to the neighborhood, frequently confirm that those passengers want to go to "the place where you can eat barbecue" (*chi shaokao de difang*).[80]

To assess how changes to the geographic and demographic makeup of these enclave spaces affected the daily practice of Hui identity for those living within them, I undertook extended fieldwork in urban Hui neighborhoods. I took careful steps to ensure my fieldwork sampled a broadly representative and theoretically relevant collection of Hui communities. I conducted in-depth case studies in four cities—Beijing, Jinan in Shandong, Xining in Qinghai, and Yinchuan in Ningxia Hui Autonomous Region—between July 2015 and July 2016. I chose these sites (shown in Map I.1) with care following preliminary field research conducted between July and August 2014. In addition, I made ethnographic observations in Nanjing in Jiangsu, Weizhou township in Tongxin County in Ningxia Hui Autonomous Region, Linxia Hui Autonomous Prefecture in Gansu, and Xunhua Salar Autonmous County and Hualong Hui Autonomous County in Qinghai. In total, I conducted 154 semistructured interviews. (See appendix A for details.) These sites were selected because they each meet a set of common criteria. Each city is a provincial capital or province-level municipality and thus may be considered urban centers. In each community the Hui have a strong historical presence and are the second most populous ethnic group behind the majority Han.[81] Additionally, each city is home to a notable and important mosque around which the Hui community has traditionally been centered.[82]

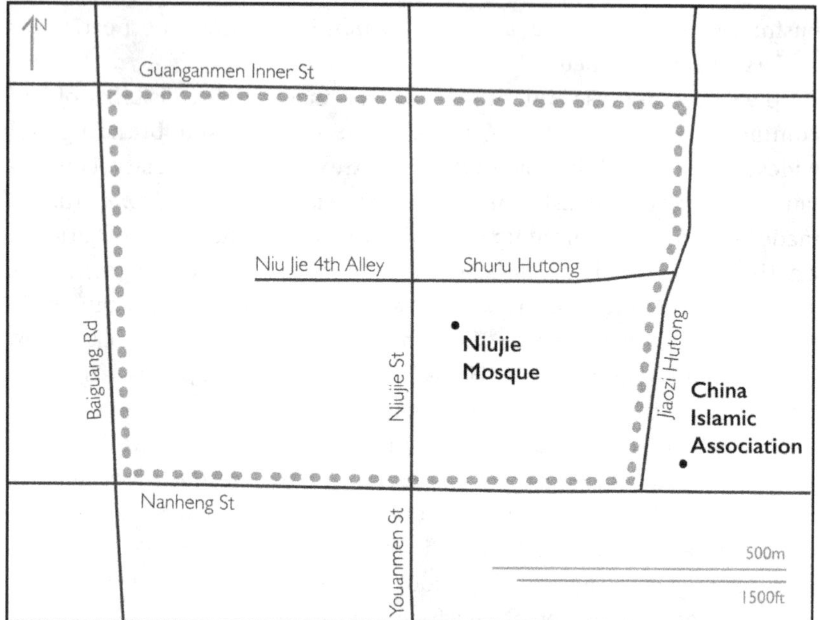

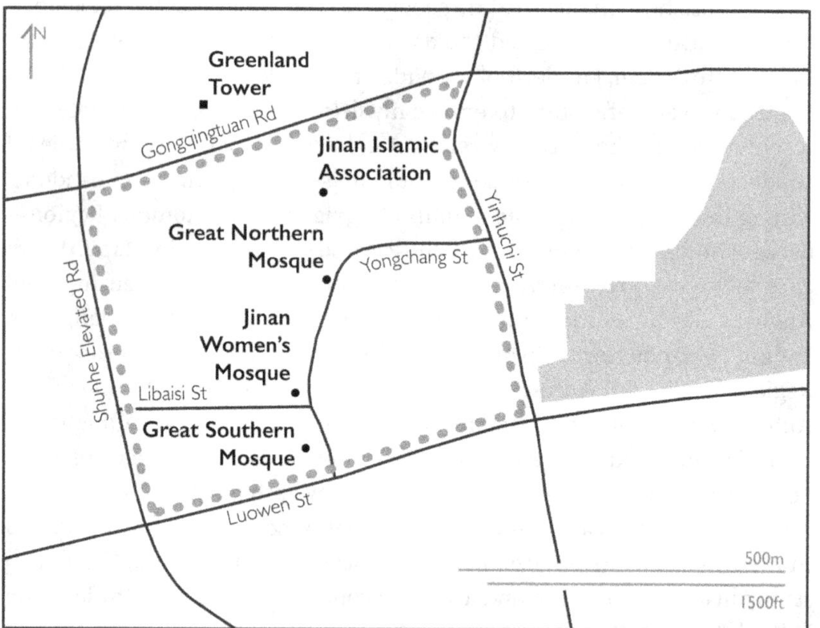

MAP I.1. Maps of case study sites. (a) Beijing case study site; (b) Jinan case study site; (c) Yinchuan case study site; (d) Xining case study site.

Nanliang
Village
(25 km)
Shanghai Rd
Ningxia
Museum
Beijing Rd
Tongxin Lu
Market
(10 km)
Minzu St
G109
Xiguan
Mosque
Grand
Central
Mosque
Zhengyuan St
Zhongshan St
Qinghe St
G102
Jiefang St
Dongguan
Mosque
Xinhua Rd
Changcheng Rd
Fenghuang St
Yuhuangge St
Nanguan
Mosque
G102
Najihu
Mosque
(20 km)
2km
1mi
C

N
Huangshui R
Shuichengmen Mosque
(Northeast Gate)
Ma Bufang
Residence
Beiguan
Mosque
Huayuan St
Qingzhen Alley
Nanguan
Mosque
Dongguan
Mosque
Qiyi St
Dongguan St
Ledu St
Jianguo St
Xiadu St
Yangjiazhuang
Mosque
Shulinxiang
Mosque
500m
1500ft
D

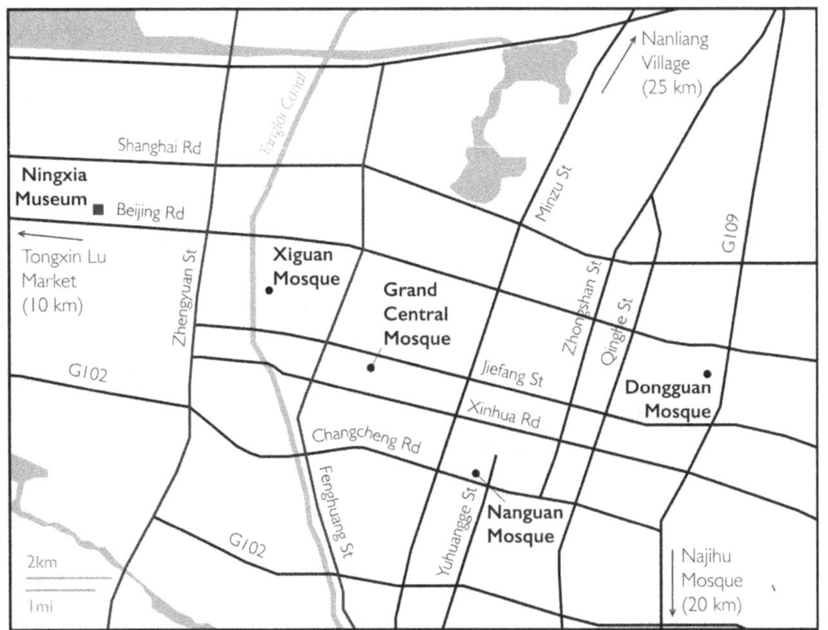

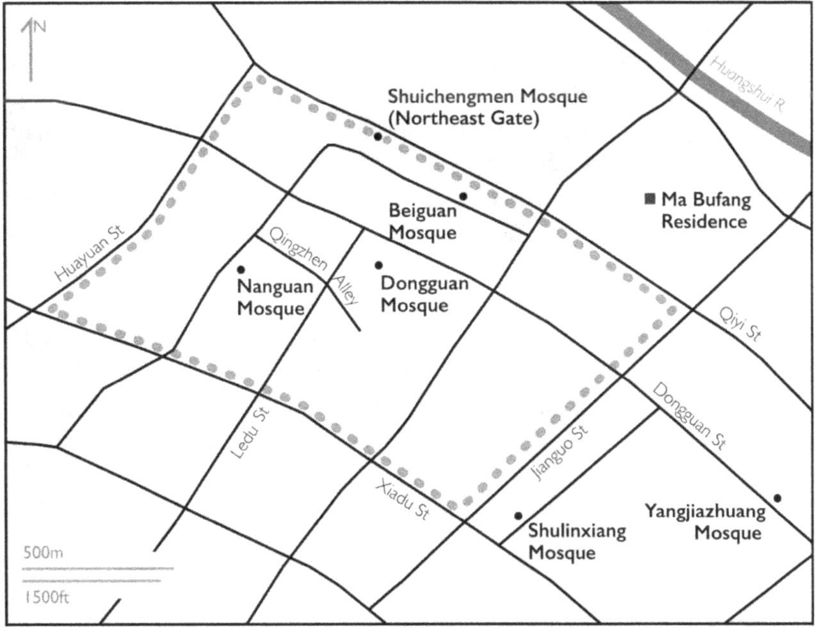

These cases present variation in several key aspects. First, the selected cases vary in terms of demographic configuration, falling into one of three categories: (1) isolated Hui communities, (2) titular autonomous Hui communities, and (3) multiethnic communities. Isolated communities are those in which the Hui represent the only substantial minority ethnic group and comprise less than 5 percent of the total population. In these communities, Hui culture is implicitly held up as "other," in contrast to the majority Han culture, and Hui cultural visibility remains low. In titular autonomous communities, however, the state permits Hui limited ability to make preferential policies on the basis of ethnicity. In these communities, the state affords prominence of place for public (if superficial) displays of Hui culture, privileging Hui identity vis-à-vis other groups, especially the Han. In multiethnic communities where the Hui are one of two or more ethnic minority groups that comprise greater than 5 percent of the total population, contrasts are drawn not just between Hui and Han but between Hui and those other ethnic groups. In these communities, the Hui may be grouped with others as part of a highly visible, broadly construed, generalized "minority" in comparison to the majority Han. Of these three types, isolated Hui communities occur most frequently throughout China. While Gansu, Hebei, Henan, Ningxia, Qinghai, Xinjiang, and Yunnan all contain Hui autonomous communities at the subprefectural level (i.e., government-designated autonomous counties or districts), much of China's Hui population does not live in an autonomous community. Likewise, while Hui communities in Gansu, Qinghai, Xinjiang, and Yunnan coexist alongside various other ethnic groups, Hui in most other parts of China are surrounded by the majority Han.

In addition to demographic diversity, the selected case sites also provide substantial geographic variation between eastern and western China. Historically, Chinese ruling dynasties regarded the west as not just peripheral in physical distance from the coastal provinces, but also as culturally distant.[83] Thus, east and west are still often read, even in contemporary China, as markers for closeness to Chinese civilization. The sites selected for this study exhibit this geographic range: Jinan and Beijing are eastern Chinese cities; Yinchuan is situated between the central plains and the northwest; Xining lies out on the northwestern periphery.

OVERVIEW OF CASE SITES

In Beijing, the heart of the Hui community lies on Niu Jie, located to the southwest of the city's center at the edge of Xicheng District.[84] Built around the Niu Jie Mosque—Beijing's earliest, built in approximately 916—the neighborhood shows evidence of concentrated Muslim inhabitation since at least the twelfth century.[85] Then, as now, the neighborhood stood on the periphery of central Beijing. By the early seventeenth century, the city had developed other prominent Muslim enclaves, such as the community at Madian, located just to the north of the former imperial center in today's Haidian District.[86]

The twentieth and twenty-first centuries saw large-scale alterations that dramatically transformed much of the city.[87] Since the early 2000s, reconstruction plans have altered the makeup of both the Niu Jie and Madian communities. On Niu Jie the construction of new apartment buildings was undertaken to replace single-floor *pingfang*-style homes. The project was undertaken with the intent of allowing locals to stay in the area, and well over half of the original residents have moved to new housing in the neighborhood. Buildings constructed since 2002 feature Islamic motifs and intend to solidify the neighborhood as a Muslim area. On Madian, by contrast, road-widening projects dispersed the Hui community, and now the mosque is the only space in the area that reflects Hui heritage.[88] Respondents in the neighborhoods note that, with the decline of Madian's cultural vitality, the axis of Beijing's Hui community now tilts strongly in the direction of Niu Jie.[89] Though many of the Hui living in the Niu Jie enclave consider themselves local Beijingers, in recent years in-migration of Hui from rural areas changed the demographics of residents.[90] The neighborhood attracts Hui from throughout China who have come to the capital to conduct business, to do temporary work (*dagong*), or to work in the government. While former Hui spaces like Madian, Douban Hutong, and Dong Si decline, Niu Jie is an isolated island of Hui identity in the midst of Beijing's cityscape—one in many ways defined by traditional Han culture.

Likewise, in Jinan the Hui Quarter represents the city's only substantial, concentrated, ethnic minority population center. Historically, additional pockets of Hui residences appeared in Dikou Zhuang in the northwest of the city, but development undertaken in the past thirty years dispersed them.[91] Though small enclaves of ethnic minorities exist throughout the city, Han comprise the overwhelming majority of the city's population.[92] As Jinan is a far less cosmopolitan city than Beijing, the city's Hui Quarter provides the only space in which Han residents routinely encounter non-Han culture.

Shandong has grown rapidly over the past thirty years, becoming one of the country's most economically developed, wealthy, and cosmopolitan provinces.[93] Though the city's population is overwhelmingly Han, Jinan is also home to a long-standing Hui community that, according to some sources, dates back to the Song dynasty (960–1279).[94] At the turn of the twentieth century, Jinan's Islamic Association served as a locus for the production of important Islamic scholarship.[95]

In Yinchuan, by contrast, the Hui comprise roughly one third (36.8 percent) of the total population.[96] The city lies just inside the far western reaches of the Ming dynasty Great Wall, close to the edge of the Mongolian steppe. As such, cultural interchange between China and Inner Asia has defined the city's culture.[97] In the contemporary context Nigxia serves as a nexus for Chinese and Muslim cultures, with exchanges flowing in both directions.[98]

Yinchuan's political status as the capital city of Ningxia Hui Autonomous Region reflects this position of in-betweeness. Within the Autonomous Region, the Hui ostensibly retain some rights to self-governance, and as the region's capital Yinchuan acts as a showcase for Hui culture. In principle, ethnic minority cadres cooperate in the creation of policies that would accommodate local ethnic or religious traditions. In practice, however, avenues for genuine autonomy are limited. Visible markers of Hui identity, like monuments or street signs in Arabic, are dispersed throughout the city, but often in superficial, patriotic ways. Moreover, critics assert that opportunities for genuine representation for the Hui in local government amount to little more than symbolism. Minority cadres are expected to toe the Party line.[99]

Farther west, in Xining, the dynamics of interethnic relations become more complicated, as a multiplicity of ethnic groups stand in contrast to the Han majority. Located in Qinghai on the edge of the Tibetan Plateau, the city falls within the geographic northwest. The region traditionally marked the edges of the Chinese civilizational and administrative sphere. Well into the Qing dynasty, the Chinese understood the Ganqing (a colloquial portmanteau of Gansu-Qinghai) region in which Xining sat as a culturally alien border region. Throughout much of its history the region served as a node of interaction between empires.[100] The multicultural diversity and economic vitality of trade-route cities in the northwest, like Xining, ensured connection to vital trade networks and allowed these outposts to remain influential despite their peripheral locations.[101] To the Han, however, Xining represented a remote point on the edge of empire. Incorporation of the northwest occurred largely through conquest and annexation.[102] Han viewed these boundaries as cultural as well as geographic. Small differences in lifestyle between different groups of Han arriving from the east paled in comparison to those differences that separated them from the nomadic pastoralist communities of the Plateau. Such contrasts leveled the cultural distances between Han and increased them between Han and others.[103]

In the early twenty-first century, Xining's ethnically diverse demographics reflect the city's historic status as a place of exchange. In addition to its

MAP I.2. Location of case study sites within China.

sizable Hui community, the city is home to communities of the Tibetan, Salar, and Tu (Mongour) ethnicities, as well as the majority Han. The eastern Chengdong District not only contains a prominent Hui Quarter centered around the Dongguan Mosque but is also home to a small Tibetan enclave and Qinghai Nationalities University. Thus, while the interethnic relations in Jinan and Yinchuan primarily unfold in interactions between Han and Hui, Xining presents an ethnic mosaic with many different components, creating a more complex picture.

The geographic range of these cases provides variation in physical landscape and level of economic development but also cultural proximity to "civilization" as historically defined by Han scholars and administrators. Map I.2 shows locations of these cities within China.

Providing variation on a number of dimensions such as these allows for a theoretically significant and broadly representative account of the everyday ethnic politics of Hui enclaves in the context of rapid urbanization, while

TABLE I.2. Characteristics of case studies

CASE	GEOGRAPHIC	DEMOGRAPHIC	% HUI (OF TOTAL POPULATION)	URBAN PROCESSES
Beijing	East	Isolated	1.74	*Chai qian*
Jinan	East	Isolated	< 1	*Chai qian* Migration
Yinchuan	Central plains/ Northwest	Titular autonomous	36.8	Migration City expansion
Xining	Northwest	Multiethnic	16.26	*Chai qian* Migration City expansion

still allowing for nuance and contextual richness. Table I.2 illustrates these characteristics.

BETTER CITY, BETTER LIFE? STUDYING EVERYDAY ETHNIC POLITICS IN THE CONTEXT OF URBANIZATION

Urban spaces provide two distinct advantages for conducting ethnographic observations of everyday ethnicity.[104] First, cities provide an especially illuminating context for observing daily ethnic practices. In concentrating people in large numbers, cities serve as "repositories of cultural identity." In these spaces, identity and physical boundaries often overlap, as identities become mapped onto specific parts of cities. Where associations between space and ethnicity develop, differentiation—both physical and cultural—between self and other may become more starkly pronounced.[105] Enclaves with high concentrations of ethnic minority group members act as a forum for contestation of the content and boundaries of groups, creating spaces for consumption of, performance of, and participation in identity. Urban development, as it changes and alters the physical landscape, becomes a field for the assertion, negotiation, commodification, and redefinition of ethnic boundaries, making them more visible. Second, because states frequently use programs of urban development to centralize state power and increase the state's ability to exercise control, choosing case sites where urbanization is ongoing allows researchers to study interactions between ethnic actors and the state. The deeply political nature of urbanization makes urban renewal and city planning powerful tools in the hands of the state. Throughout history, centralizing states have frequently implemented such measures as tools for increasing the power of the state to exercise control.[106] Rendering a city more "legible" is thus a primary objective of states.[107]

In addition to centralizing authority by reshaping urban space, states may attempt to exert control by reconfiguring urban populations. Migration therefore makes up a second, powerfully transformative facet of urbanization. The state often incentivizes migration through economic means. It may provide migrants—especially those moving to regions where ethnic minorities comprise a majority of the population—with incentives in the form of jobs, housing subsidies, and preferential language policy.[108] In this sense, migration occurs neither as a purely strategic, individual choice nor as the inevitable result of macrosociological phenomena, but instead because of a combination of both.[109]

In China, programs of urban transformation take two primary forms: *chai qian* (demolition and relocation style urban renewal) and the migration of the *liudong renkou* (transient population). Both of these types of urbanization form a backdrop against which everyday ethnic politics unfold. (See table I.2 regarding how these conditions unfold across various case sites.) This context informs the conduct of ethnic boundary formation and the practice of daily ethnic politics in China.

"CHAI QIAN" AND "CHAI NA'ER?": PROCESSES OF URBAN RENEWAL IN CHINA

As I strolled down the gravel path that cut through the construction site, wind blew clouds of dust through what remained of the Beida Huaishu neighborhood, located just west of Jinan's central train station. A few years prior to that afternoon in November 2015, clusters of small, aging *pingfang* houses dotted the neighborhood. Now a forest of high-rise apartments stood in their place, many still without tenants. In the center of the scene, green scaffolding covered the just recognizable frame of a mosque, its minaret and domes not quite finished. As I approached the site, the foreman of the construction crew approached me. When I asked what had happened to the old mosque that stood on the site, a building dating back to the Ming dynasty (1368–1644), he remarked that it, like all the other houses in the neighborhood, had fallen victim to the widening of the adjacent thoroughfare, Jing Shi'er Lu, a few years prior. The site's previous mosque would be replaced with the larger, "Arabic-style" building currently under construction.[110] I asked him if the residents of the neighborhood, a small Hui enclave on the city's western edge, would be able to return after the buildings were complete. "Yes," he responded, seeming somewhat unconvinced by his own answer.

The scene at the site of the former Beida Huaishu Mosque recurs throughout urban China. Over the past few decades, the country's transformation into a primarily urbanized society captured the attention of policymakers, journalists, and academics alike. As China builds modern infrastructure in its cities, observers scrutinize the means and methods of construction to an increasingly high degree. As in the Beida Huaishu community, urban renewal frequently comes in the form of demolition and relocation, in which old or dilapidated structures are dismantled in order to clear space for new residences or commercial property. This kind of destruction and rebirth of neighborhoods occurs in nearly every urban center in China.

Unsurprisingly, when asked to describe the changes in their neighborhoods over the past ten years, Chinese residents often mention demolition and relocation among the first differences from the past. In the postreform era, demolition (*chai*) was so pervasive that Beijing was likened to "a city of *chai*."[111] Similarly, Peter Hessler notes in his memoirs of his time in Beijing that demolition was so prominent during the early 2000s that residents began to quip that their country was called Chai Na'er?, or "Demolish Where?"[112]

At first, the local government relocated displaced residents from these neighborhoods to new apartments in a different location. However, as the process of urban renewal became more responsive to market demands, the government abandoned the practice of relocation and replaced it with a policy that paid displaced residents a stipend for the purpose of purchasing new homes.[113] Such tactics suggest a form of "repressive assistance" in which the regime uses the targeted distribution of compensation as a warning against resistance meant to preemptively stifle dissent that might cause instability.[114] This shift from relocation to compensation illustrates a larger dialectic between notions of community and property and mirrors the tensions between state planning and market economics present throughout the Chinese economic system.[115]

Often, official propaganda heralds demolition and relocation projects as intrinsically linked to the realization of a better, more beautiful, more livable cityscape. Such slogans frame the process as one of beautification that requires mutual cooperation in order to yield mutual benefit. For example, a large billboard near a construction site in the northern suburbs of Shandong's capital of Jinan proclaimed, "The purpose of demolition and relocation is to allow the construction of a better place."[116] The residents of redeveloped neighborhoods often lack the financial resources to share in or benefit from the "better places" built in place of their former homes. The compensation that most of the lower-income residents living in redeveloped neighborhoods receive fails to cover the cost of the upscale or luxury residences that replace their old homes. Consequentially, the process of demolition and relocation effectively brings about the gentrification and increased economic stratification of the neighborhoods in which it occurs.[117] Furthermore, the relocation of poorer residents to outlying suburbs and wealthier residents to redeveloped areas in the urban core results in increased class differentiation between neighborhoods throughout China's cities.[118]

Increasingly, urban renewal is a flashpoint for social protest among residents unwilling to leave their homes.[119] The emergence of "nail houses" (*dingzi hu*)—those belonging to citizens who refuse to vacate, even while foundations for new construction are dug out around them—has captured international attention. Faced with no clear legal recourse, citizens are often forced to take extralegal action to defend their property rights.[120]

In ethnic minority communities, urban renewal programs often seek to standardize non-Han culture, crystallizing it in a politically correct form that compliments the state's narratives. For example, a pervasive modernization campaign begun in the early 2000s transformed the Uyghur-majority Old Town neighborhood of Kashgar, enabling further state supervision of ethnic politics and regulation of Uyghur identity. By demolishing traditional buildings, widening and straightening streets, and repurposing buildings (e.g., turning community mosques into cafés) the project formally established state control over the expression of Uyghur identity and sought to prevent the proliferation of nonapproved forms of local culture. Unsurprisingly, locals met the campaign with antipathy.[121]

BUILDING NEW CITIES FOR CHINA'S "TRANSIENT POPULATION": MIGRATION AND URBANIZATION

In addition to the physical reshaping of cities through *chai qian*, the state changes China's urban landscape through the movement of people. Over the past forty years, internal migration in China has precipitated a massive shift in the country's demographics. By 2011, the percentage of the population living within cities surpassed those living in the countryside for the first time ever.[122] The flow of migrants arriving at the field sites fluctuated in the decade prior to my fieldwork. (See appendix C for specific figures.) Across sites, the inflow of migrants hit high marks in the middle years of the 2000s, slowing somewhat by the time I entered the field in 2015. In Jinan, migration peaked in 2006 with over 150,000 migrants arriving in the city and declined to just under 50,000 by 2016. In Xining, rates of arriving migrants moved up and down: over 120,000 migrants arrived in 2006, marking a high point for the city, which saw rates decline below 50,000 within the next two years. A spike in migration occurred in Xining in 2013, with almost 70,000 arrivals, but the number fell to about 36,000 by 2016. In Beijing, rates of migration remained between 150,000 and 200,000 arrivals per year between 2006 and 2016, with a high of over 210,000 in 2011. Though the rates of migration began to slow by the middle of the 2010s, across field sites people I spoke to described the net effect of such large numbers of migrants moving to their cities. In total, over 2 million migrants arrived in Beijing between 2006 and 2016, while over 830,000 arrived in Jinan and 569,000 arrived in Xining. Such a massive shift of people from small, primarily agricultural villages to cities brought with it dramatic socioeconomic changes. Many studies conducted over the past few decades document the challenges posed by the so-called transient population engaged in migration from China's villages to its cities and from its periphery to its coast.[123] These studies detail the struggles migrants face finding places of residence, receiving social service provisions, providing for the care of their children, finding steady sources of income, and surviving on the margins of urban society. However, the impact of migration on ethnic identity in minority communities, from which many migrants originate, remains comparatively unexamined.

Indeed, even though ethnic minorities constitute a lower percentage of the population than Han, they migrate at higher rates in similar demographic categories, especially at the lower end of income and education spectrums.[124] Migration among ethnic minorities occurs mostly when rural migrants move to urban settings, usually leaving the peripheral west to arrive in cities on the comparatively developed eastern coast. Mandatory or state-compelled relocation does not drive minorities to migrate as much as the dictates of the market and the availability of economic opportunities. Moving from rural, primarily agricultural communities to urban spaces where more opportunities to engage in wage labor or entrepreneurship exist affords minority migrants the promise of upward socioeconomic mobility. Once they reach new, urban environments, minority migrants depend upon ethnic networks to secure jobs and housing and to establish themselves in unfamiliar settings.[125]

After arrival, migrants face difficulties in dealing with prejudice and discrimination from locals. Much of this conflict arises from the wealth gap between migrants and locals and often overlaps with differences in ethnic identification. "Sons of the soil" conflicts occur more frequently in locations where economic discrepancies exist between locals and migrants of different ethnic groups. In China, where locals are usually majority Han Chinese and migrants often belong to ethnic minority groups, migration may lead to conflict over job opportunities, land rights, cultural status, and government policies.[126] Beyond discrimination, minority migrants also frequently express fear of cultural degradation as they leave their homes to live in Han-dominated communities. After moving to the city many migrants lose touch with cultural institutions or their mother language.[127]

These difficulties affect both those who move outside of their home province to far-flung destinations like Beijing or Shanghai and also those who move from small villages to provincial capitals. For example, a respondent in Yinchuan observed that Hui migrants who came to the city from rural villages within the province often struggled to adapt to life in the region's capital. He explained that for rural migrants whose lives in the village revolved around the habits and routines of single-story courtyards, living in high-rise apartments was disorienting. Being disconnected from the ground, he reasoned, caused many of them to feel as if they had lost the roots that held them in place.[128] Even when migrants move within the province, they still may feel alienation in the place of their arrival.

Both urban renewal and migration exert profound and transformative effects on ethnic identity. Given the importance of the cultural institutions at the core of most Hui neighborhoods (e.g., halal butchers, mosques), the urban landscape provides an illuminating backdrop against which everyday ethnic politics may unfold. Hui neighborhoods provide an excellent case for examining the conduct of ethnic politics in the context of urbanization.

METHODOLOGY: STUDYING CHINA'S ETHNIC POLITICS ETHNOGRAPHICALLY

Unlike studies of contentious politics, where relevant evidence occurs in easily discernable bursts of intense action, documentation and analysis of everyday politics requires special considerations. Taking the framework of everyday ethnicity seriously entails reconceptualizing what scholars should consider a basic unit of observation. Rather than focusing on individual actors or institutions, everyday ethnicity allows researchers to examine ethnicity via observations of practices.[129] Sociologists Jon E. Fox and Cynthia Miller-Idriss envision the nation as a "cultural construct of collective belonging realized and legitimated through institutional and discursive practices," such as "talking," "choosing," "performing," and "consuming" the nation.[130] Thus, observations of everyday ethnicity are practices that maintain ethnic

TABLE I.3. Examples of everyday ethnic practices in Hui communities

KIND OF PRACTICE	TYPE OF OBSERVATION
Talking the nation	Using Qur'anic, Arabic, or Persian phrases in daily conversation
	Attending Arabic/Qur'anic study group
	Becoming literate in written Arabic
	Using Arabic pidgin
Choosing the nation	Referring to oneself as Hui (*Huizu*, 回族)
	Marrying a Hui partner
	Insisting on non-Hui partner's conversion to Islam in interethnic marriages
	Living in a predominantly Hui neighborhood
	Educating children about Islamic/Hui culture (家庭教育)
Performing the nation	Attending Friday prayers
	Observing Islamic holidays (e.g., Ei'd al-Fitr) and rituals (e.g., fasting)
	Wearing traditional Hui or Islamic costume (white prayer hats, hijab, etc.)
	Nonobservance of traditional Chinese festivals (Lunar New Year, Mid-Autumn Festival, etc.)
Consuming the nation	Shopping at halal groceries, butchers, etc.
	Eating at halal restaurants
	Abstaining from consumption of alcohol and pork

boundaries. Table I.3 lists practices associated with each of Fox and Miller-Idriss's categories.

Following Fox and Miller-Idriss's example, my observations of Hui ethnicity focus "on the ways in which ethno-national idioms—once in circulation—are enacted and invoked by ordinary people in the routine contexts of their everyday lives."[131] To this end, my fieldwork sought to find the "micro-interactional moments" and "institutionally embedded and repetitive routines" that maintain ethnicity in quiet times.[132]

However, when attempting to observe these types of practices, researchers must use caution. Studies that seek to measure the influence of ethnicity on a set of social phenomena (or vice versa) often suffer from a paradoxical condition: ethnicity is nowhere, and it is also everywhere. The ethnic significance of a particular event may be buried in hidden transcripts that prove difficult to unearth. In these cases, even the most sensitive and careful questioning may fail to yield an understanding of an event's ethnic significance. Conversely, as Rogers Brubaker et al. caution, "Ethnicity is all too easy to find if one goes looking for it."[133] Careless observations may imbue almost any action with ethnic significance.

I conducted observations in a variety of official and unofficial spaces where quotidian replications of ethnicity occur. While my status as a foreign non-Muslim perhaps most closely matches anthropologist H. Russell Bernard's model of the participating observer—a category of ethnographers he characterizes as "outsiders who participate in some aspects of life around them and record what they can"—my identity limited my ability to embed in the community.[134] In particular, taboos on non-Muslims entering religious spaces in devout communities prohibited me from full participation in the manner usually described under the banner of participant observation. While I did eat, converse, walk, and live in the same communities as my respondents, my religious identity meant that I did not worship alongside them but rather observed from respectful distance. Though studies that gain participant access provide keen insight on the interaction of religious doctrine and ethnic identity, my observations yield insight related to more mundane, daily practices.[135] I also observed local institutions that provide official venues for the maintenance of ethnicity: mosques, schools, and museums. Additionally, I observed informal spaces where practices of consumerism and leisure reproduce and maintain identity: Hui restaurants, department stores, marketplaces, shops, and other businesses.

Verification of the insights I gained from field observations required targeted conversations with local residents.[136] Assessing the impact of urban renewal in Hui neighborhoods depended upon my ability to speak directly with local elites and important figures in the community. Local government officials and prominent community figures like imams, heads of local Hui or Islamic associations, and teachers provided vital perspectives that helped to confirm my account. Likewise, ordinary residents of the neighborhood, local entrepreneurs and small business owners, and members of the neighborhood's working and professional community offered outlooks on daily ethnic practices that differed from those of elites. To provide a satisfactory account I strove to interview a diverse sampling of people and represent the wide diversity of opinion and difference in perspective that occurred even within the space of a small neighborhood.

Interviewers must be cautious about asking questions that might prompt interviewees to respond in ethnic terms. Thus, when formulating queries, I avoided making presuppositions about how respondents might view or understand subjects, particularly regarding abstractions like ethnicity.

Purposefully invoking ethnicity threatened to skew respondents' answers or lead me to interpret remarks in a way that a respondent would deem inappropriate.[137] Instead, I attempted to treat interviews as learning experiences in which I might encounter new or surprising information. This posture of "deliberate naiveté" prevents priming respondents to answer in a particular way.[138] Rather than imposing my own presuppositions on respondent's remarks, I sought to listen for the significance offered by the interviewees, themselves.[139] Through careful probing and follow-up questions, I allowed the ethnic significance of responses to emerge naturally. Rather than directly questioning residents about their conceptions of their own ethnicity or how it is impacted by urban renewal, I tried to elicit such information indirectly. Posing questions that asked respondents to describe their daily habits, consumer purchases, relationships with neighbors, changes in the neighborhood over time, and other ostensibly nonethnic matters allowed for ethnicity to emerge organically, without prompting.[140] Analyzing the way in which ethnic frames were imposed or not imposed on these discussions yielded insights about the role played by ethnicity in the community. This approach produced a more nuanced account than the kind of rote or overly practiced answers that I might have gained through direct questioning.

In total, I conducted 154 semistructured interviews across all case sites. Through the use of snowball sampling, in which an initial respondent recommended and put me in contact with further respondents, I was able to speak with a diverse array of respondents from different regions, professions, genders, and age cohorts.[141] Interviews were informal and conversational; in addition to set, planned questions I asked probing follow-up questions as interviews progressed. The conversations were conducted in standard Chinese (Putonghua; Mandarin) and ranged in length, some as brief as ten minutes, while one lasted over two hours. Where respondents consented, I recorded these interviews on my smartphone, and in all other cases interviews were reproduced from notes taken during the conversation or immediately afterward. These respondents represent a broad sampling of the Hui community and provide a thorough picture of the diversity of expressions of Hui identity.

The following chapters describe the everyday practices that maintain the boundaries of ethnic identity in urban Hui communities, as well as assess how China's rapid urbanization impacts the way residents identify and contest these practices. These everyday practices represent the spectrum of ways in which ordinary urban Hui residents choose, talk about, consume, and perform identity in the course of their daily lives.

CHAPTER ONE

"GOD IS A DRUG"

Ethnic Politics in the Xi Jinping Era

Han people rarely come to this part of the city.

—A TWENTY-EIGHT-YEAR-OLD HUI GRADUATE STUDENT, XINING

ACROSS THE STREET FROM BEIJING'S VENERABLE NIU JIE MOSQUE, A long banner sits atop a high wall and stretches the length of a block. At the far end, in vertical text, white characters that read "The Great United Family of Minzu" (*minzu tuanjie da jia ting*) stand out against the plain blue background. As the banner unfolds down the street, it depicts a man and woman from each of China's fifty-six *minzu* dressed in traditional costumes. Some dance and play instruments; others hold the tools needed for the time-honored livelihoods of hunting, herding, or harvesting. All smile brightly in joyous celebration of a united homeland.[1] The Han are pictured at the center of the wall, surrounded by all of China's minority *minzu*. Like the others, they don bright costumes and celebrate the diversity and vibrancy of the nation.[2]

Portraying the Han and ethnic minorities as joyfully living together in peaceful harmony under the leadership of the CCP casts them as contented, willing members of China's large multiethnic family and legitimates the Party's rule.[3] These images of jubilant harmony among all ethnic groups highlight China's status as a vibrant, diverse, multiethnic society. Depicting minorities engaged in song and dance renders them exotic, colorful, and flourishing under the Party's benevolent and tolerant governance.[4] Such rosy depictions of interethnic relations closely mirror the State Council's official rhetoric: "Although the origins and histories of ethnic groups in China are different, the overall trend of their development was to form a unified, stable country with multiple ethnic groups. The boundaries and territory of today's China were developed by all ethnic groups in the big family of the Chinese nation during the long course of historical development."[5]

Nearly three hundred miles away, outside of Shandong's capital city of Jinan, a message on another wall displayed a very different picture of inter-ethnic relations. In Laozhaicun, a small, mostly Hui suburban village, located on the edge of the city's Tianqiao District, the words "God is a drug" (*renzhu duyi*) appear as crudely scrawled black spray-painted characters on the side of a home. During my visit to Laozhai in mid-December 2015, the respondent leading me through the village drew my attention to the graffiti, making sure to explain its significance as a bit of anti-Hui ethnic chauvinism. The phrase, he explained, was meant as a homophone for the *shahada* (*qingzhen yan*), the Islamic declaration of faith: "There is but one God" (*renzhu duyi*).[6] By switching the homophone *du* 毒 for *du* 独, the graffiti belittled the Muslim Hui. Such an act, my contact reasoned, could have been made only by Han from the neighboring village.

The virulent language of the vandalism echoes a hostility toward religion similar to that which is expressed by the CCP. Harkening back to the beginning of the PRC in 1949, the official statements made by the Party regarding religion suggest that, while free practice of faith is to be tolerated, religion itself is fundamentally false and dangerous to society.[7] The foundational "Document 19," a treatise on religion published by the Party in 1982, proclaims that bourgeois capitalists "use religion as an opiate and as an important and vital means in its control of the masses."[8] The same enmity toward religion voiced by official memos also informs the slur defacing the wall in Laozhai. Instances of bigotry like this were common, my guide remarked. Frequent competition between the predominantly Hui residents of Laozhai and the Han from neighboring villages, usually over contracting or land-use rights, sparked antipathy between the groups, sometimes resulting in ethnically motivated vandalism.[9]

While the smiling, jubilant minorities shown in propaganda suggest harmonious relations among all groups, the slurs scribbled out in coarse graffiti reveal the enduring prejudices directed toward China's ethnic minorities. Rhetorical claims about the unity and indivisibility of the Chinese state, like those depicted on the Niu Jie mural and made on official records by the State Council, form a critical piece of the legitimating strategy employed by the CCP. Proclaiming stable and familial relations for all of China's ethnic groups allows the Party to position itself as the guardian of China's growth and prosperity. In so doing, the CCP aims to exert control in ethnic politics by minimizing grounds for conflict between itself and minorities and redirecting contentious politics that would challenge the Party's narratives of unity and harmony.

However, the persistence of inequality between the Han and minority groups, of casual Han chauvinism, and of the kind of bigotry that gives rise to the anti-Hui graffiti found in Laozhai belies the hollowness of these claims. While the CCP touts its role in fostering economic progress and social harmony shared by all of China's *minzu*, sharing in these public goods requires acculturation on the part of minorities. Instead of showcasing tolerance and ethnic unity, the daily instances of prejudice experienced by ethnic minorities reveal a continued stigmatization and othering of non-Han Chinese. Ordinary Han-Hui interactions are marked by physical and cultural separation that results in stereotyping, discrimination, and resentments that highlight the hollowness of the CCP's *minzu* policies and legitimating claims and the precariousness of the Party's control.

The everyday negotiation of Hui ethnic identity occurs against a background of policy, politics, and interethnic relations. Examining the CCP's policies and rhetoric illustrates how official discourse attempts to constrain ethnic expression by filtering it through a state-approved lens. Creating this framework in which the negotiation of ethnic boundaries unfolds provides the CCP with the ability to oversee and manage ethnic politics in a way that reinforces its legitimating narratives of the Party as a guarantor of societal stability. Daily experiences of prejudice, however, disrupt and discredit this narrative. Exploring daily interactions between Hui and Han—and by proxy the Han-centric state—allows for a clearer picture of when interethnic relations matter and when they do not. Though tensions between Hui and Han rarely rise above the level of stereotyping and micro-aggressions, persistent gaps between state narratives about the equity of all *minzu* and the daily lived experiences of prejudice between Han and Hui may raise the salience of ethnic identity. In both cases, an overview of the general state of interethnic relations helps to illustrate the ways in which the CCP attempts to implement control over ethnic expression and how the everyday negotiation of Hui ethnic identity fits into the larger picture of ethnic politics under authoritarian regimes.

ETHNICITY AND AUTHORITARIAN LEGITIMATION IN THE XI JINPING ERA

Understanding the importance of interethnic relations for the CCP's strategy requires an examination of the way authoritarian regimes construct and invoke legitimating narratives. By imposing categories of ethnicity and placing hard boundaries around official definitions of ethnic identity, the CCP makes ethnic registration and categorization an essential part of its strategy for governance and control. The state's official categories provide a background against which the everyday negotiation of identity unfolds. Thus, understanding the social and political significance of quotidian expressions of Hui identity necessitates an examination of the Party's "politics of categories." Studying how categories are formulated, cataloged, imposed, and maintained by the state allows us to better understand whether and why actors accept or reject the state's categories, where state policy meets resistance, and how debates over identity change in response to state-imposed measures.[10]

The CCP's conduct of ethnic politics is intimately connected to concerns for preserving the societal stability (*wending*) that bolsters the regime's legitimating claims. As the effectiveness of other legitimating narratives declines, the Party increasingly emphasizes its role as a guarantor of a stable, harmonious domestic atmosphere. The CCP's overriding concern for stability causes "seepage," wherein a fixation on a single concern effectively reorients the regime's resources, messaging, and interpretation of social phenomena such that all matters become focused on addressing the issue.[11]

The current seepage surrounding the politics of stability is the culmination of a trend begun under the leadership of Deng Xiaoping as the CCP sought new legitimating narratives in the aftermath of the Mao era (1949–76). Deng staked the CCP's right to rule on its ability to improve China's economic state. Thereafter, the Party's leadership proclaimed a performance-based model of legitimacy as the pursuit of a *xiaokang shehui* (variously translated as "comfortable society" or "moderately prosperous society"), which became a central pillar of the legitimating narrative during the subsequent Jiang Zemin and Hu Jintao administrations.[12]

While economic performance remains a cornerstone of the regime's legitimating claims under the Xi Jinping administration (2012–present), the CCP also increasingly invokes its role as guardian of social stability and national unity to bolster its arguments for rightful control, insisting that it alone can provide the order that allows for China's prosperity.[13] By linking stability and prosperity together, the Party poses each as the necessary precondition for the other. Such logic is best expressed through the slogan that positions "development as an unyielding principle and stability as non-negotiable responsibility."[14] The Party's legitimating claims rely upon its self-presentation as the only actor capable of presiding over both the governance of the state and the guidance of the economy without losing control or allowing the country to lapse into disorder.[15] Moreover, the regime links stability and economic growth to the restoration of China's position as a world power.[16] Consequently, the Party's concern for order becomes an overriding prerogative that drives policy formation and implementation across countless aspects of regime governance.[17]

While the regime construes stability broadly, any understanding of the term necessarily encompasses proper maintenance of ethnic relations. The CCP implements a web of interconnected policy measures in order to manage and oversee the politics of ethnic identity. Interethnic relations in China occur in the context of a system of ethnic categorization that regulates the expression of ethnic identity, referred to as the *minzu* system.[18] Under this system fifty-six groups are officially recognized as *minzu* by the state.[19] *Minzu* status is defined with the use of criteria derived primarily from a similar system implemented by Stalin in the former Soviet Union but also influenced by systems put in place by the British in colonial India.[20] The *minzu* system demands that an ethnic group possess the "four commons": a common language, a common territory, a common economic life, and a common "psychological make-up," which has been reinterpreted by the state to mean a common culture.[21] Despite that fact that, even in the earliest stages of ethnic classification, state-sponsored taxonomists only loosely adhered to these "four commons," they nonetheless remain as the Party's official criteria for recognizing a *minzu* identity.[22]

By officially investing the state with the power to classify ethnicity, the CCP attempts to assert control over the expression of ethnicity and reinforce narratives that downplay ethnic resentments or cause for conflict with the state. In offering minorities a state-sanctioned version of ethnic identity, the state allows for the expression of "permissible forms of difference" while also precluding competing versions that might conflict with state interests.[23] Gaining control over official expression of the content of a group's identity also allows the state to control the territory these groups inhabit, a matter of crucial importance to state security and survival.[24] Placing the power to supervise and manage this categorization system in the hands of the state allows the regime to harness the positive capabilities of minority collective action. Thus, since the beginning of the era of Reform and Opening, China has made great efforts to encourage people to identify as minorities and revive the perpetuation of minority ethnic culture.[25]

China's political leaders take great care to link successful ethnic policy with the country's overall security. The Party leadership views the insecurity stemming from occasional ethnic unrest, especially in Xinjiang and Tibet, as a threat to derail the CCP's ability to trumpet the accomplishments of Xi's "China Dream," campaign.[26] These worries about the potential of ethnic conflict to contribute to the PRC's unraveling are shared by Xi himself; writings from his early career urgently connect proper management of ethnic policy to China's survival.[27] In 2014, on a visit to Xinjiang Uyghur Autonomous Region following attacks in Kunming and Ürümchi, Xi stressed that proper management of ethnic politics formed an integral part of the security of the nation as a whole, and he urged the importance of interethnic exchange and integration.[28]

Accordingly, preventing the outbreak of unrest in ethnic minority regions and maintaining the stability viewed as necessary for continued economic and military security are primary objectives of the Xi administration. Party leaders believe that China's ascent into a "rich and strong country" (*fumin qianguo*) relies on establishing stable ethnic relations and the extension of development to impoverished, peripheral, minority-populated regions.[29] Rhetorically including minorities as a part of *Zhonghua minzu* (variously translated as "Chinese nationalities" or "the Chinese race") attempts to make them citizens of the Chinese state rather than subordinates of the majority Han nation.[30] In so doing the Party enacts a kind of forcible inclusion of minorities into the framework of the state and stakes a claim to being the sole guardian of their well-being.[31]

To curb the threat of tensions in ethnic communities leading to more widespread destabilization, Xi's administration has expressed the necessity of aligning ethnic minority culture with the goals of the state. Though an increasingly prominent group of scholars and officials, most notably Ma Rong, Hu Lianhe, and Hu Angang, argue that the best way to achieve this integration is to dismantle the system of ethnic differentiation and affirmative action policies that encourage multiculturalism in order to form an integrated and homogeneous race-state (*guozu*), the Party had, until the early stages of the Xi administration, sought to exert control over the expression of minority identity through a system of ethnic classification.[32] The *minzu* system of ethnic classification allows the state to oversee the expression of ethnicity by controlling census categories, determining which ethnic practices are official markers of ethnic identity, and reducing minority culture to "certain permissible forms of difference," which fit in a state-approved framework.[33]

"ALLOW THE FLOWERS OF ETHNIC UNITY TO BLOOM EVERYWHERE": ETHNICITY, CONTROL, PROPAGANDA, AND LEGITIMATION UNDER XI JINPING

The *minzu* system is the culmination of a long-standing effort to incorporate minorities into the Chinese state.[34] Indeed, promises of official recognition and governmental autonomy made by the CCP to minorities on China's periphery during the Long March period of the Chinese Civil War (approximately 1932–33) aided the Communists in winning minority support against the Nationalists. Extending these offers to groups unrecognized by the Nationalists, whose official minority categorization system recognized only five groups, made up a critical part of the CCP's early "united front" strategy for ethnic governance.[35] The Party's goal of reestablishing control over former imperial territory is apparent in these overtures.

Maintaining the vast and diverse—both territorially and ethnically—geobody of the former Qing Empire requires the current regime to invoke a larger notion of Chineseness that implies multiculturalism, harmony, and equality under the Party's leadership. The ultimate result is a "mestizo-like" notion of Chinese civilization.[36]

These metaphors of a "family" of *Zhonghua minzu* are reinforced by extensive government "*minzu* publicity" (*minzu xuanchuan*) campaigns, which emphasize the indivisibility of the ethnic peoples of China and downplay notions of ethnic conflict.[37] In this way, the CCP uses "cultural management" in an attempt to mitigate the cultural tensions that adversely affect China's sociopolitical stability.[38] Posters prominently placed in public spaces within minority neighborhoods urge cooperation and harmony in relations among China's many ethnic groups. In Qinghai's Tibetan and Hui community of Lusha'er (known in Tibetan as Rushar) outside of Xining, such signs boldly proclaimed, "Ethnic minorities cannot be separated from the Han, and the Han cannot be separated from ethnic minorities. All minorities are mutually inseparable."[39] Similarly, a billboard behind Lanzhou's Great Western Mosque proclaimed, "A unified homeland revitalizes China."[40]

By tying China's geographic and social unity to its economic prosperity, the CCP positions itself as the guardian of the state's borders and its people, as well as their economic well-being. A billboard near the Dongguan Mosque in Xining emphasized the necessity of ethnic unity for sustaining prosperity: "All nationalities strive together in unity, and develop together prosperously."[41] The message being conveyed is clear: without the CCP to maintain a unified China, prosperity and economic growth cannot occur. China's wealth and safety rely on the continued participation of minorities in the state under the leadership of the Party. To hold together this diverse "family" of Chinese peoples, official propaganda implores citizens to build "ethnic unity" (*minzu tuanjie*). Various signs throughout the ethnically diverse city of Xining announce, "Ethnic unity builds a better home," "Let everyone follow the model of ethnic unity and allow the flowers of ethnic unity to blossom everywhere," and "Let the blossoms of ethnic unity eagerly bloom."[42]

Slogans promoting equality and harmony attempt to reduce grounds for conflict with the state and reinforce a narrative about the Party's provision of stability. However, persistent prejudice and unequal treatment in daily interactions hollow out these claims and potentially undermine the Party's strategy for management and control. While interethnic contact that occurs through regular, associational channels may provide a means for mitigating instances of conflict, limited or negative contact may cause relations between groups to steadily worsen.[43] Repeated negative contacts may lead to hardening of boundaries between groups and contribute to a cycle wherein further exclusion breeds further mistrust.[44] These experiences of prejudice raise the salience of external boundaries between Hui and Han and highlight the CCP's failures to deliver on its promises of unity.

The CCP's rhetoric and policies surrounding ethnicity do not foster such positive associational contact, instead fostering feelings of prejudice and instances of discrimination. Though the PRC Constitution establishes the equality of all Chinese citizens, critics assert that such guarantees are inflected with condescending Han chauvinism.[45] By laying bare the regime's inability to deliver on its promises of equality and shared stakes in the state's prosperity, such instances of discrimination discredit the state-sponsored rhetoric that proclaims the Party's role as a purveyor of prosperity and stability. In assessing the efficacy of the regime's stability management (*weiwen*) tactics, the CCP's paranoia about losing legitimacy spurs the Party to use a heavy hand in employing stabilizing measures, often violating the law in the process. The more the regime enforces stability maintenance, the more unstable society becomes.[46] Likewise, the more effort the CCP expends in trumpeting a message of *minzu tuanjie*, harmony, and family-like relations, the more the daily experiences of prejudice and discrimination undercut the regime's legitimating claims.

Discrepancies between regime narratives and lived reality undercut the CCP's efforts to manage interethnic politics by drawing points of conflict away from the state—which is largely viewed as Han-centric. Prejudices encountered in daily life increase the salience of boundaries between majority and minority, thus increasing the likelihood of tensions along ethnic lines. In the most extreme cases, this increase in salience gives rise to contentious politics and occasionally violence. Further, CCP attempts to intervene and restrict ethnic expression to squelch tensions may provoke further conflict. The well-publicized resistance to the CCP—and the Party's heavy-handed and frequently violent suppression in response—in the minority autonomous regions of Tibet and Xinjiang illustrates this potential quite clearly.[47]

However, even in far less contentious cases, disjuncture between the regime's rhetoric and daily realities exposes the precariousness of the Party's management style. The Hui enjoy a reputation as a thoroughly integrated, "model religious minority," often described in news articles as "state-approved" Muslims.[48] However, a closer examination of Han-Hui relations indicates a continued, pervasive cultural and physical separateness between Han and Hui. Though some assert that Hui have achieved near total integration with Han, evidence suggests continued misunderstanding and resentment between the groups.[49] The persistence of prejudice between Han and Hui underlines the regime's lack of success in delivering on its promises of promoting *minzu tuanjie*.

Mutual ignorance between Han and Hui stemming from lack of substantive intergroup contact creates mutual prejudice and suspicion. By raising the salience of boundaries between majority and minority, such mistrust erodes the Party's ability to minimize contentious politics and maintain control.

Indeed, prior to sweeping nationwide crackdowns on Islam and Muslim minorities begun in 2017, the CCP presented the Hui as a highly assimilated *minzu*. Such thorough incorporation of the Hui into Chinese society provided the CCP with a major narrative victory, given the Hui's history of resistance to central authority prior to the establishment of the PRC.[50] After the founding of the People's Republic, the CCP made great efforts to co-opt Hui leadership into collaboration with the state.[51]

Though these attempts mostly succeeded, one incident of violence, the 1975 Shadian Incident (*Shadian shijian*), merits mention. Violence erupted in the overwhelmingly Hui stronghold of Shadian in Yunnan in July 1975 after years of simmering tensions, stemming initially from resentments over Red Guard attempts to suppress Islam in the village. As early as 1968, Red Guard units tried to rid the village of "feudal" Islamic practices by force, including, by some accounts, closing or vandalizing mosques, subjecting residents to struggle sessions, forcing them to eat pork, and requiring them to wear pigs' heads around their necks.[52] As strife between villagers and the Party intensified over the ensuing years, the community came under scrutiny. In 1974, nearly eight hundred villagers demonstrated in the provincial capital of Kunming to appeal to the state to honor its constitutional guarantees of religious freedom and were labeled a "disturbance." In the wake of these protests, small-scale clashes broke out between a self-appointed local Islamic militia and the county government's military administration. These conflicts led to an abortive attempt at negotiation between the parties orchestrated by Beijing in early 1975. Under orders from the central government, the People's Liberation Army (PLA) arrived in summer 1975 to restore state authority and end a tax protest undertaken by local villagers. By late July, after negotiations had deteriorated further, the PLA surrounded and besieged the village.[53] On July 29, the PLA entered the village, beginning a lengthy pitched battle that claimed 1,600 lives and destroyed as many as 4,400 houses.[54] Eyewitnesses recount the use of heavy artillery to subdue the villagers. Some attest to the PLA's use of fighter jets on the village.[55] Eventually, in 1979, after the end of the Cultural Revolution, blame for the incident fell on the deposed Gang of Four.[56] As restitution, the government sponsored massive projects of rehabilitation and reconstruction in Shadian and memorialized the victims with a marker to the martyrs (*shexide* for the Arabic *shahid*).[57] In the ensuing years, Shadian grew into a prosperous, devoutly Islamic community that marketed itself to the outside world as the center of China's Islamic revival. The Grand Mosque, reputedly one of the largest in China, is the centerpiece of the community.[58]

Shadian's revival in the 1990s and 2000s illustrates the CCP's approach toward the Hui in the era of Reform and Opening, wherein the Party began to tout the Hui as a model Islamic minority.[59] In recent years, the relationship between Hui communities and the state has garnered increased attention in international media, particularly as a contrast to the more restive and conflictual relations between the PRC and Uyghur communities.[60]

Especially in the period after the announcement of China's ambitious Belt and Road Initiative (*yidai, yilu*) in 2013, the regime's frequent citing of the Hui as an example of an Islamic minority living contentedly and cooperatively under the leadership of the CCP illustrates the importance of the Hui to the CCP's legitimating strategy, both domestically and abroad. The Hui occupy a median position on the civilizational spectrum between the two poles of Islamic and Chinese spheres.[61] As an imam in Xining explained, "Hui culture is like the child of two major cultures: Chinese culture and Islamic culture. Chinese culture is our mother culture, and Islamic culture is like our father culture. Even if we are currently closer to mother culture, the father culture is most important. We can't forget this father culture."[62] This position of in-betweeness made the Hui symbolically important as cultural envoys in the CCP's attempts to court the larger Islamic world. Likewise, Hui communities have been the beneficiaries of extensive outreach and funding from Muslim-majority states—particularly Saudi Arabia—hoping to promote the growth of faith and Islamic identity.[63]

While a number of *minzu*, such as the Miao, Bai, Yao, and Naxi, also represent relatively successful conduct of interethnic politics on the part of the CCP, the shared linguistic and cultural heritage of the Hui and Han and the Hui's ties to the international Islamic community make the Hui a

FIGURE 1.1. Mural at the Great Mosque in Najiahu in both Chinese and Arabic: "Love your country, love your faith. Know the law, abide by the law."

revealing case. Further, the centrality of the Hui to the Party's claims of providing unity and equality provides an ideal case for illustrating the tenuousness of the regime's ability to maintain control over ethnic politics.

"LOVE YOUR COUNTRY, LOVE YOUR FAITH": HAN-HUI RELATIONS THROUGH AN OFFICIAL LENS

State propaganda paints a picture of the Hui as eager participants in the Chinese nation. Signs at mosques throughout northwest China encourage patriotic behavior. In 2016, a mural at the Great Mosque of Najiahu in Yongning County, Ningxia, implored its congregants, "Love your country, love your faith. Know the law, abide by the law" (see figure 1.1).[64] Since 2017, when a nationwide crackdown on religious expression in Muslim communities began, the CCP changed many such signs to display an even more patriotic slogan: "Love Your Country, Love the Party" (*aiguo aidang*).[65] In Xining, a banner at a small mosque to the north of the city's Hui Quarter urges residents to be a bulwark against terrorism by beseeching, "Don't let terrorism destroy ethnic unity and society stability!"[66] Messages like these that emphasize the Chinese citizenship of the Hui as coequal to their membership in the Islamic community of faith (umma) suggest that in the officially sanctioned understanding of Hui identity, the group's religious and civic identities overlap and do not conflict. In this sense, the government presents the Hui as a compliant, exemplary group, not prone to religious extremism or separatist tendencies.

Likewise, official sites of Hui culture strive to portray the Hui as key contributors to the development of modern China and the establishment of the PRC. At the Ningxia Provincial Museum, an explanatory sign states, in English, that the Hui "are just as patriotic as they once were with their beliefs remain unchanged [*sic*]!" In the same exhibit another sign proclaims, "We welcome and embrace this group with firm belief and with striking characteristics, which, in the time-honored process of development has well blended with the age-old Chinese civilizations," suggesting that widespread assimilation is a natural outcome of development.[67]

The Hui Culture Park in Najiahu, a predominantly Hui suburb to the south of Yinchuan, devotes two of its five exhibit halls to "contributions of the Hui ethnic group to Chinese civilization." The English-language introductory signs to these exhibits proclaim, "The Hui ethnic group's progress and development is consistently associated with the fate of the Chinese nation" and assert that the Hui "defended their national dignity courageously" and were "devoted to rejuvenating the Chinese nation." Displays that feature biographies of prominent Hui revolutionaries who fought alongside the CCP in its campaign against the Japanese and Nationalist armies, and Hui thinkers who contributed to the consolidation of the current PRC, stand next to these signs. Sweeping aside Hui such as the notorious warlord Ma Bufang (1903–1975), who fought alongside the Nationalists, such exhibits uncritically emphasize the commitment of the Hui as Chinese patriots.[68] Any historical troubles are pushed aside, while the Hui are presented as willing and eager participants in the founding of the new Chinese state.[69]

Such characterizations of the Hui buttress claims that they are integrated into Chinese society, politically and culturally. In the minds of many Han, the assimilation and Sinicization of the Hui are all but complete. One young woman, a Han university student studying Chinese Islamic architecture in Yinchuan, remarked that no tensions existed between Han and Hui. Asked why she believed this, she offered only the simple explanation "The Hui have already been Han-ified."[70]

HAN IGNORANCE AND HUI STEREOTYPES: THE HUI AS CARICATURED IN DAILY INTERACTIONS

Ignorance of Islam and its influence on the daily life of practicing Muslims often clouds Han perceptions of Hui culture. For example, Han tourists visiting the Hui Culture Park in Najiahu expressed confusion about the manner of observance and purpose of the Ramadan fast in the rudimentary questions they posed to the young Hui woman serving as their tour guide. "But don't you get hungry?" many inquired, prompting a patient, if slightly annoyed, retort from the guide that faith allowed her to endure such difficulty. Later, at the park's replica prayer hall, the Han guests removed their shoes, donned head coverings, and knelt on the floor in simulation of prayer while a young Hui man gave an introductory talk. "Han visitors often ask me why we Hui do not eat pork," he remarked, adding that they often want to know if it is because "pigs are the Hui's ancestors."[71] The guide's speech, which explained other rudimentary elements of a Muslim lifestyle, such as dressing modestly and not partaking in alcohol, illustrated just how little knowledge the Han tourists possessed about Islam.

Prior to the onset of the de-Islamification campaign, museum displays reinforced such caricatures. Before its closure for renovation in mid-2015, the Hui Culture Park's museum greeted visitors with a twenty-minute film explaining the Hui and Hui culture, portraying them as a rural, agrarian, or pastoral people. The film's depictions of Hui traditions, food, ceremonies, and music all centered on Hui living in the countryside and paid little attention to urban Hui communities.[72] Likewise, in early 2016, at the Hui exhibit at the Ningxia Provincial Museum, a series of miniature dioramas of rural Hui villages presented illustrations of Hui lifestyle practices, including prayer, weddings, and harvest.

At the exit of the exhibit, visitors confronted a display featuring life-size mannequins of a Hui family wearing ethnic costumes. A mother and father sat together while their two children played traditional instruments on the floor. The father read the Qur'an while the mother sewed.[73] By showing only scenes of rural life, these tableaux failed to capture the experiences of urban Hui or showcase a strong tradition of Hui scholasticism and theology. Each of these portrayals neglected significant in-group geographic, socioeconomic, and cultural diversity and instead reduced Hui culture to a single, easily stereotyped dimension.

Han interaction with Hui culture beyond these official museum displays reveals a similar lack of substance. Due to increased rates of internal migration from less prosperous western China to the wealthier eastern coastal regions, nearly every city in China—even those with historically small Hui populations—boasts restaurants serving *qingzhen* cuisine, usually bowls of *lamian*.[74] For many Han, eateries like these provide the most common point of contact with Hui culture, often depicted in caricature. At a noodle shop in the Hui Quarter of Jinan, for instance, a series of posters depicts cartoon Hui cooks, wearing traditional white Islamic prayer caps (*baimaozi*), as they happily stretch the dough for noodles, slice beef, and pour water for the soup's broth. Some of the cartoons depict elderly men with long, wispy white beards.[75] A *qingzhen* restaurant inside the WanDa Plaza Mall in Yinchuan lures customers with two life-size mannequins of a man and woman wearing the "official" traditional ethnic costumes of the Hui depicted in state propaganda, sitting cross-legged on a carpet at a low table. The sign behind them reads, "Chat and eat noodles; rest and drink tea."[76]

Hui entrepreneurs doubtless find such caricatures useful in their pursuit of marketization and profit and thus employ them to suggest authenticity or novelty to Han consumers.[77] However, these depictions perpetuate a cartoonish and one-dimensional view of the Hui as pork-abstaining, bearded noodle makers in white hats. Such reductive stereotypes about Hui culture and the tenets of Islam seem due to the absence of associational or quotidian interaction between the Han and the Hui. Because *lamian* restaurants are the most common venue for most Han people's interaction with Hui people and Hui culture, popular understandings of the community may never develop beyond such kitschy and skewed representations. Ignorance of the cultural traditions behind Hui diet and dress raises the possibility of micro-aggressions or more overt forms of discrimination in Han-Hui interactions.

While many Han understand that the Hui adhere to a dietary code that prohibits eating pork, they may misunderstand the foundations of these restrictions. A twenty-six-year-old Han woman in Jinan remarked, "We [Han] eat pork and they [Hui] don't eat pork, and so this leads to a lot of difficulties."[78] Though she never elaborated what such "difficulties" might entail, her irritation implied that menu choices were a source of arguments; she also betrayed her contempt for Hui who might refuse Han food. A thirty-two-year-old Han graduate student studying education in Yinchuan explained that, prior to visiting a Hui suburb for a class field trip, she had not understood why Hui practiced different lifestyles from Han. Only after speaking with Hui residents did she realize that they observed such different practices because they were following the dictates of Islamic law.[79] The Han owner of a dive bar in Yinchuan that advertised itself as a "*qingzhen* bar" displayed a similar lack of awareness of the religious foundations of the Hui dietary code. When asked how an establishment that served alcohol (which is expressly prohibited by

Islam) could be considered *qingzhen*, he offered his own bizarre rationalization that the bar could be considered *qingzhen* because it was a place that was quiet and tranquil (*qing*) and served only "real" (*zhen*) imported beer from Europe and Singapore. Further questions revealed that he saw no problem with appropriating *qingzhen* to advertise his establishment.[80] Ignorance of even these most basic aspects of Hui lifestyle can lead to disrespect and conflict. A Jinan Hui respondent in his fifties explained, "They [Han] only understand a little bit and aren't really clear [about the Hui]. And if they're not really clear, it's really easy to offend Hui, or show disrespect to Hui. For example, if you're all eating together, you shouldn't eat pork, but they share it with everyone. Stuff like that really easily starts fights."[81]

SEPARATION AND PREJUDICE IN HAN-HUI RELATIONS

Physical separation contributes to this cultural distance between Han and Hui. Hui neighborhoods often stand apart from the rest of a city. A twenty-eight-year-old Hui teacher from Jinan described her experience growing up in a small village on the edge of the city. A road ran through the village, dividing the east from the west. The western half of the village was inhabited exclusively by Hui; the eastern half exclusively by Han.[82] In the town of Weizhou in Tongxin County, south of Yinchuan, residents estimated that Hui comprised 95 percent of the population and claimed that Han residents stayed for only short durations before moving elsewhere.[83] As such, Han frequently perceive these spaces to be overwhelmingly Hui, and thus avoid them.

In urban centers, such physical separation stands out even more clearly, as historically Hui neighborhoods stood apart from the core of cities.[84] Such separation often occurred as a result of the Hui's tendency to cluster homes and businesses around a central mosque.[85] The insularity of these Hui enclaves makes them impenetrable to non-Muslim outsiders. Han residents of Jinan's Dikou Lu, a large avenue near the city's central train station, were almost completely oblivious to the existence of a small neighboring Hui enclave surrounding a historic mosque. Those Han living on nearby Wansheng Alley claimed to be unaware of the existence of the mosque and uncertain whether any Hui people lived nearby.[86]

In Xining, the city's primary Muslim enclave was historically separated from the core by city walls, segregating the community physically as well as by habit and custom.[87] Though the walls have since been razed, the boundaries they once demarcated remain salient as Xining's contemporary street grid follows the path where they once stood. Most residents still recognize the city's Chengdong District, which sits on top of the former Muslim city, as the Hui Quarter. A Hui graduate student in anthropology remarked that these neighborhood configurations still influence the course of daily life in Xining. While walking down Dongguan Da Jie, the large boulevard that lies at the core of the neighborhood, he said that, despite the close proximity of Xining's many minority groups, interactions among them continue to be rare: "Han people rarely come to this part of the city."[88] Those Han who do live in the area, he explained, often look for somewhere else to live. The Han tenants who previously rented the apartment in which his parents lived felt out of place in the neighborhood and were eager to leave the predominantly Hui enclave. The visibly Hui character of areas like the Chengdong District leads Han to feel alienated by their surroundings and may contribute to negative feelings about the neighborhood and those who live there. To the west of Dongguan Da Jie, the Hui population becomes scarce. "You rarely see people wearing white prayer hats or hijabs outside of this neighborhood," the student observed.[89] Another Xining resident, a forty-three-year-old Hui professor of sociology, remarked that non-Hui regarded the Hui Quarter as backward, poor, and dirty:

> The Chengdong District is a very old one, because it's the Hui Quarter, the Muslim Quarter. It gives people, especially us Hui, a feeling of closeness. But to other *minzu*? They feel that the place is dirty and disorderly, that the people are uncouth and of low *suzhi*, that it's chaotic and such.[90] And because they feel that it's such low *suzhi*, taxi drivers don't agree to go there. If they [potential passengers] are Hui, especially if they're Hui women, like the middle-aged women who wear headscarves, they [the drivers] won't agree to stop the car for them, because they're afraid that they're so uncouth that they'll argue about the fare.[91]

The claims that Han looked negatively on Hui *suzhi*, or lack thereof, illustrates the standing of the Hui within larger social hierarchies that place urban, educated, middle-class Han in a central position. The association of Hanness with possession of *suzhi* mark those who are working class, migrants, or non-Han as socially backward and uncivilized "others." Hui arriving in cities as migrants, like many of those who live in Xining's Chengdong District, may feel doubly excluded, as both their rurality and their ethnicity carry markers of backwardness that lead to othering.[92]

Respondents elsewhere echoed these claims that the Hui were stigmatized as poor and backward. One Beijing Hui respondent in his seventies grumbled that Han in the community looked down upon the Hui: "The Hui are an ethnic minority, and ethnic minorities are all poor, including the Hui. You can see that the jobs Hui have are all really bad. They all have small carts that sell *nian gao* [a kind of sweet snack] for one to two *kuai* a slice. This isn't good work. You can't earn money."[93] Such economic disadvantage, the respondent implied, placed Hui in a position of perpetual weakness and marginalization and led Han to look down on them. Likewise, in Jinan, Han residents described the Hui Quarter as a "dirty, disorderly, and dilapidated" (*zang, luan, cha*) place. One Han respondent, a thirty-year-old English teacher from Jinan, admitted that her discomfort going into the city's Hui Quarter came close to physical disgust: "The Hui don't eat pork, and instead they eat lots of mutton. The smell of mutton really disgusts me, and so I feel that the Hui Quarter is just dirty and disorderly."[94] The association of Hui with low-wage jobs and ethnic products caused Han respondents, like the English teacher, to associate the Hui Quarter—and its residents—with squalor and unpleasant, if not unsanitary, sights and smells.

Due to a substantial lack of knowledge and interaction, differences in culture, such as Hui avoidance of foods or lifestyle habits they deem "impure" (*feiqingzhen*), are frequently interpreted by the Han as condescension or disdain. Perhaps giving credence to this perception, Hui often profess that, by consuming only that which is *qingzhen*, they are purer than Han.[95] To some Han, this showy observance of *qingzhen* becomes grating. For example, the twenty-six-year-old Han woman believed that the Hui treated the Han with high-handed contempt. Though she admitted to not truly understanding the reasons for the Hui's lifestyle differences, she cited them as a sign of self-importance: "I just feel that the Hui are naturally a little arrogant. Which is to say, 'I'm Hui. I'm a minority.' They have that kind of attitude."[96] The Han teacher echoed this: "In my view, Hui aren't very friendly, especially toward Han. Hui are very friendly to other Hui, but in my view, Hui act a little superior."[97] According to this respondent, the Hui took their status as a recognized minority as a sign of special status that they flaunted, particularly in their interactions with the Han.

Other Han complained that Hui used their special status to flout rules and regulations that Han would not be allowed to break. In so doing, some complained, Hui took advantage of the state's tolerance. Han in Jinan expressed frustration that the Hui Quarter got away with ignoring many environmental and sanitary regulations because the government feared provoking a response along ethnic lines. Several respondents claimed that the local government hesitated in enforcing regulations or conducting urban renewal to remedy the neighborhood's dilapidated state because of a fear that these actions would provoke Hui resistance. One Hui woman in her late twenties who ran a small English school in Jinan recalled that attempts by developers to buy land in the Hui Quarter failed because of fear that Hui might resist if they weren't compensated at a higher price than market value.[98] One resident in the Jinan Hui Quarter lamented that the neighborhood's problems with air pollution from barbecue smoke continued because the government would not dare enforce a ban on open-air grills in the neighborhood in order to avoid a riot by the Hui.[99] In both cases, respondents complained that the Hui used intimidating displays of solidarity to gain preferential treatment from local authorities seeking to assuage ethnic tensions. These instances provoked anger among Han, who felt that Hui acted as if they were exempt from following the rules due to their minority status.

Often these Han cited government policies favoring the Hui and other minorities for creating and promoting such feelings of superiority and entitlement. A middle-aged Han man who had grown up in Yantai, about three hours to the east of Jinan, described Han-Hui relations as marked by an elevated form of dislike stemming from governmental policies:

> Outside of Ningxia Hui Autonomous Region, Gansu, Xining, and a few Hui areas of Henan, most Han really exclude the Hui. This kind of exclusion isn't like the way Tibetans are excluded. It's completely different from that kind of exclusion. This kind of exclusion in my opinion is done with a lot of enmity. As opposed to Tibetans, who are excluded because of cultural misunderstanding. I feel like Han reserve that kind of feeling toward the Hui. The exclusion carries a little hostility. I've never experienced that, so I don't know how that hostility comes to be. But I feel like it's possible that some of the reasons come from the government.[100]

This respondent's oblique reference to the government as the source of resentments points to the regime's preferential policies (*youhui zhengce*) for minorities. A growing crowd of critics regards this broad array of policies—which include nominal autonomy in designated autonomous communities, limited subsidies for housing and farming, exemption from state family-planning policies, and benefits in college entrance examinations—as perpetuating and exacerbating tensions between groups.[101] A former head of the State Ethnic and Religious Affairs Committee of the Chinese People's Political Consultative Committee, Zhu Weiqun, expressed such sentiments in 2014, claiming that preferential treatment policies "make citizens aware of the differences between ethnic minorities," thus promoting discord and antipathy rather than unity.[102]

These resentments, which imagine the Hui as an advantaged, contemptuous, superior "other," also give rise to notions that the Hui are clannish and unwelcoming. One woman, a Hui factory worker in her mid-forties who lived in the Hui Quarter, boasted, "We who live in this neighborhood are more unified than others because we're all ethnic minorities."[103] However, such displays of solidarity may be a coping mechanism. As one Hui respondent in Jinan explained, "There's really nothing we can do [about prejudice]. We can only unify and deal with this ethnic bullying together."[104] Because associational ties between Han and Hui are weak, actions that Hui regard as positive and indicative of the strength of their community, Han interpret as secretive, suspicious, and exclusionary.

While such expressions of solidarity and unity may strengthen the Hui community internally, outsiders often view such togetherness negatively. Han commenting on Hui unity expressed fear that such tribalism led Hui to gang up on and bully or intimidate the Han. The Hui sense of solidarity, many complained, resulted in every conflict between Han and Hui residents falling along ethnic lines, no matter what initially caused the quarrel. The Han English teacher remarked that whenever conflicts arise between Han and Hui in Jinan's Hui Quarter, "Hui think of it as an ethnic problem. That neighborhood has a lot of Hui who will come help out other Hui." For these Han, being outnumbered by Hui while visiting Hui communities led to discomfort, and for some, like the English teacher, a fear of danger. Fears that Hui ethnic solidarity would lead to their being outnumbered caused these Han to feel intimidated by Hui while in the neighborhood and contributed to their desire to avoid going there.

Resentments based on the Hui's perceived clannishness and arrogance and the perception that they receive favorable treatment from the state because of their minority status, create the potential for conflict. In Laozhai village, a respondent claimed that tensions between the villagers often resulted in anti-Islamic vandalism. The previous year, he recounted, a dispute over contracting rights for the construction of a set of apartment towers between competing Han and Hui construction firms escalated into full-blown conflict when the Han nailed a pig's head to the door of the residence of the foreman of the Hui team in the dead of night. In the end, the respondent noted, local Party officials intervened to prevent further escalation, siding with the Hui team, much to the chagrin of the rival Han team.[105] In Xining, a Hui respondent explained how Han provoked fights by using the Islamic taboo on pork as an epithet against the Hui: "[Pigs] are incredibly taboo. For example, some Han will swear at you by calling you Zhu HuiHui [literally, 'Piggy Hui' or 'Hui Pig'] or something like that, and maybe you want to strike back, maybe even to the point of fighting. This is maybe a kind of subconscious effect."[106]

Instances of bigotry like these firmly challenge the assertion that while the Hui are certainly "familiar," they are no longer "strangers." Instead, they indicate that relations between urban Han and Hui residents remain marked by ignorance, separation, and prejudice. While many Han regard the Hui as assimilated, or essentially "Hanified," gaps in understanding continue to perpetuate small resentments and suspicions between the groups. The lack of genuine knowledge about the Hui and resentment toward what they view as Hui privilege suggests that, to most Han, the Hui remain a distant "other." Despite being held up as an integrated, model minority, the Hui remain "familiar strangers" in the eyes of many Han.

THE LIMITATIONS OF ETHNIC UNITY AS A LEGITIMATING NARRATIVE

As the self-proclaimed guardian of China's national interest, the CCP hangs its legitimating claims on its ability to serve as a guarantor of prosperity and domestic stability. Providing stable interethnic relations is a crucial part of this climate of stability. While the rhetoric of the state may proclaim ethnic unity and mutual benefit for all peoples, the daily interactions between Han and Hui suggest a very different reality. The failure to deliver on the promise of stable, equal, prosperous interethnic relations poses a thorny problem for the regime. Such failure threatens not just the regime's policies on ethnicity but its legitimation strategy more broadly. Routine experiences of discrimination and prejudice thwart the state's attempts to use rhetoric and targeted programs of autonomy and preferential policies for minorities to reduce tensions with the state and create a climate of stability. These difficulties suggest that the CCP's own interventions, which intend to reduce the salience of boundaries between ethnic groups and channel contentious politics away from the state, instead succeed in highlighting ethnic identity. Everyday prejudice throws the CCP's policy failures into sharper relief, potentially redirecting grievances back toward the state and creating instability. Therefore, the CCP's legitimation strategy falls short in two major respects.

First, many Han resent state policies they perceive as creating minority privilege and special treatment at the Han's expense. These resentments revolve particularly around the slate of benefits awarded to Hui on the basis of minority status. Such antipathy is clearly exemplified by Han respondents who argued that Hui acted arrogantly or flaunted minority privilege. Han respondents expressed frustration over their perception that Hui acted as if minority status made them special or superior. Moreover, the complaints of Jinan residents about the local Party's unwillingness to interfere in Hui neighborhoods reveal a belief on the part of many Han that the state treats minorities differently. Such frustration leads some Han to believe these policies contribute to a loss of Han culture.[107] These perceptions produce the very prejudice and ethnic resentment the Party seeks to avoid.

Second, the regime's failure to deliver on the promises of unity and prosperity lays bare the discrepancies between Han and minorities. Despite preferential policies intended to tie minorities to the state and extensive campaigns emphasizing the indivisibility of *Zhonghua minzu*, the state's actions risk raising the salience of boundaries, threatening destabilizing tension. Despite the regime's insistence that all *minzu* "develop together prosperously," persistent inequalities and prejudices undermine these claims. A lack of substantive contact between Han and Hui leads to the development of negative associations rooted in stereotypes. The stigmatization of the Hui Quarters in Jinan and Xining as poor and backward illustrates the unevenness of the benefits of China's economic development and the failures of preferential policy or largely hollow rhetoric to overcome these gaps. As Hui continue to experience discrimination in their daily lives, the potential for conflict with the Han, and by proxy the state, increases. Further interventions by the state to suppress such conflict may inflame such tensions.

More damaging still are the occasional instances, like those in Laozhai, where micro-aggressions or petty instances of discrimination in interethnic relations lapse into more malicious incidents of vandalism or violence. The outbreak of such conflicts renders hollow the CCP's claim that its leadership delivers harmony and stability to all *minzu*. If even the Hui, whom many in the Party and the public more generally consider to be a model minority, consistently experience this kind of discrimination, the CCP's efforts to use propaganda or state-administered benefits to lessen the salience of boundaries between majority and minorities have been unsuccessful. Such incidences mar the CCP's rosy picture of the various ethnicities of China coming together as the larger family of *Zhonghua minzu* and underline the precariousness of the CCP's efforts to maintain control over ethnic affairs by downplaying contentious politics.

CHAPTER TWO

CHOOSING

Citizenship, Faith, and Marriage

Conversion must come from your heart.

—A THIRTY-TWO-YEAR-OLD HAN WOMAN PREPARING TO MARRY A HUI MAN, YINCHUAN

SITTING IN A CHAIR BY THE WINDOW ON THE FIFTEENTH FLOOR OF a sleek, modern office tower in Yinchuan's Jinfeng District, my respondent, a thirty-two-year-old Han woman who worked as an executive for the creative design company housed on the floor, beamed as she described the television production she was set to oversee. As one of the leading cultural production companies in the capital city of the Ningxia Hui Autonomous Region, the company had decided to showcase colorful aspects of Hui culture by filming a series of documentary programs to air on local TV. The next of these, she explained, would be a traditional Hui wedding. Her excitement stemmed from the fact that the wedding set to be filmed was her own.

As a Han woman marrying into a Hui household in a city where such marriages rarely occurred, my respondent occupied an uncommon position. When asked whether her marriage required her to make lifestyle changes, she remarked that her fiancé's family expected her to convert to Islam. Doing so entailed a preparatory course. "I've got to go to an *ahong* [imam] at the mosque," she explained, "and the *ahong* will teach me a course about how to observe matters of the faith after I've converted." She described the path toward conversion to be completed before the wedding: "[The *ahong*] will also ask me why I want to convert to Islam, because before I join the faith, everyone needs to know if my conversion is voluntary and free. If I was forced to join, he wouldn't really approve of the conversion. Their requirement is that conversion must come from your heart. You must think this faith is good."[1]

The conversion journey my respondent described illustrates the powerful connection between ordinary lifestyle choices like marriage and cohabitation, and deeply held identity. In choosing to marry a Hui man, she also took on a different religious faith and the lifestyle practices involved in observing it. Her choice reflects the complicated role that cultural and religious norms about partnership play in ethnic identification. While she noted that the imam required her conversion to be free, her remarks also suggest that her in-laws' insistence on her becoming a Muslim in order to marry their son steered her choice. Her story highlights the asymmetries in autonomy and ability to choose freely surrounding matters of ethnic and religious identification.

Choices made in the course of everyday life maintain the boundary of ethnic identity.[2] Among the many choices that reproduce the boundaries of ethnonational identity, decisions about marriage and family often have special ethnic or national significance. Choices concerning whom to marry and under what conditions become imbued with ethnonational weight, especially in cases where institutions of the state attempt to limit or restrict the form ethnic identity may take, and the ability of citizens to choose it.

In more conservative communities, a literalist reading of Islamic law may take choice entirely out of the equation where matters of partnership are concerned. These Hui sometimes cite Islamic *fiqh* (religious jurisprudence) based on conservative interpretations of the Qur'an (2:221) in their insistence that non-Muslim women must convert before marrying Hui men and that Hui women are forbidden to marry non-Muslim men altogether.[3] However, in less strict communities Hui may cite more pragmatic justifications—such as eligibility for state-issued benefits for minorities—for relaxing norms about conversion or allowing intermarriage with non-Muslims. Such a wide range of attitudes about choices related to marriage not only illustrates the ways in which ordinary choices about partnership may resonate with ethnic significance but also highlights the ways in which gender may limit autonomy—especially for Hui women—and limit the ability to exercise choice at all.

REPRODUCING THE NATION: MARRIAGE, CHILDBIRTH, AND MAKING ETHNIC CHOICES

Even choices that ostensibly have little to do with ethnic or national identity can be structured by institutional framing that reveals ethnic significance. If the ethnic significance of the choice lies hidden, actors may still directly acknowledge it in the decision-making process.[4] Matters such as choosing where to live, whom to keep as friends, or whom to marry are not explicitly ethnonational in nature, but the logics of institutions or long-standing cultural norms may imbue these choices with ethnonational significance. Institutions that require actors to make choices reveal the "edges" of an identity—those situations in which identity is "lurking just beneath the surface"—by rendering implicit meanings explicit. In demanding that participants take declarative actions that make the otherwise obscured peripheries of identity manifest, institutions breach and reveal the edges of identity.[5]

As an example of how institutions can permeate relatively mundane lifestyle choices with enhanced ethnic meaning, consider the processes associated with citizenship. Choices related to citizenship most strongly demonstrate the ways in which citizens makes decisions in an ethnically motivated manner. Citizenship offers those who seek it the "symbolic reward" of being a member of a community.[6] Though in some cases claimants may hold membership in multiple communities, citizenship often acts as a form of enclosure, asking would-be citizens to select a single membership at the exclusion of others. As such, citizenship choices make attachments to community overt.[7]

Citizenship also provides the state with a means of establishing social control over what options for identification those under its jurisdiction may choose. The national census provides a tool for measuring citizenship that directly prompts selections, often within a limited menu of options defined by the state.[8] In granting the state the power to identify the categories into which its citizens fall, the census empowers the state to limit or control the forms of ethnic or national identities its citizens may claim.[9] As a result, the state gains the ability to favor or disempower certain groups.[10]

Given the state's ability to limit or control choices surrounding self-identification, the way citizens respond on a census frequently becomes a strategic choice that is constrained by the influence of politics. Census respondents must consider the social, cultural, and (occasionally) material advantages and disadvantages of the choices they make.[11] In some cases, the incentives that come attached to self-identification as a member of a particular group may prove strong enough to revive moribund or waning cultures.[12] For example, benefits associated with choosing to be officially counted as Manchu by the Chinese census led to a revival of interest in Manchu culture and history and a rise in the total population of Manchus in China, beginning in the early 1980s.[13]

In forcing citizens to select a single, official identity, states may turn matters of citizenship into a strategic choice to secure the benefits of preferential policies.[14] In treating ethnic identity as singular, indivisible, and permanent, the policies of the state present ethnicity as immutable and rooted in descent. Such a picture of ethnicity may mirror the descent-based, popular understandings about ethnic identity held by ordinary citizens.[15] Such a belief in the primordial nature of ethnicity among ethnic actors may lead ostensibly quotidian matters such as selecting a neighborhood to live in or engaging in socializing, marriage, or childbearing, to become freighted with ethnic connotations. Pairing these social norms with state preferential policies that incentivize identifying as one identity over another only intensifies the ethnifications of these decisions.

Citizenship status influences a host of other, less formal practices as well, particularly those related to partnership and childbirth. In these circumstances ethnicity and gender inextricably inform and construct one another.[16] Societal pressures may make the choice of whether or not to have children one influenced by community norms rather than individual preferences.[17] Notions of "appropriate" or "proper" maintenance of boundaries govern women's choices concerning marriage.[18] Groups frequently emphasize the role of women to reproduce the community both as literal mothers and as "cultural reproducers" who symbolically embody the group.[19]

Choices about marriage and childbirth are therefore often linked to the survival of the group and to the transmission of culture. States frequently invoke such symbolic discourses surrounding motherhood as part of political campaigns to increase population.[20] Such rhetorical and social pressures ethnicize matters related to marriage and registration. In these instances, choices related to partnership or child rearing may become explicitly tied to acceptance or exclusion.[21] Individuals must weigh these social and cultural constraints when making these decisions.[22] Notably, such restrictions are not distributed evenly across gender boundaries. In some instances, the imposition about taboos concerning childbearing or norms about purity may effectively negate women's autonomy in these matters. In some cases, women's primary method for gaining citizenship comes through marriage and birth.[23]

CHOOSING TO BE "OFFICIALLY ETHNIC": THE *MINZU* SYSTEM AND ETHNONATIONAL IDENTITY IN CHINA

By filtering the identities of its minority populations through the process of strict categorization and census, China has reified the boundaries of minority identities through codification and established a fixed set of criteria that establishes recognition. A number of policy measures that provide benefits to those registered as ethnic minorities encourage participation in this system. Indeed, these benefits make being officially designated as minority *minzu* desirable to some.

Presently, the *minzu* system allows the state to play a supervisory role over the contestation of identity within its borders. In controlling which groups receive recognition and which do not, the CCP dramatically impacts contestation of identity. As of the 2010 census, 640,101 people lack any categorization at all and are what the PRC refers to as unrecognized (*wei shibie*) *minzu*.[24] Effectively, the system makes the CCP the final arbiter of the content of ethnic boundaries for the purposes of recognition. Though expressions of group identity remain negotiable, particularly when dealing with lower-level local officials, the Party's power to recognize or promote certain practices and characteristics as essential features of a particular *minzu* identity and empower some actors over others enables the CCP to exert authority and guidance over ethnic expression.[25] Control over the content of a group's identity gives the state a position of relative advantage when attempting to minimize resistance and incorporate ethnic borderlands into the state.[26]

The *minzu* system presents China's citizens with a choice. Because the system does not allow for multiethnic identification, nor are citizens easily reclassified once given a designated *minzu* status, the system forces citizens to make decisions concerning their ethnic registration. While for many citizens one is simply born into a *minzu*, those from multiethnic backgrounds must select official membership in only one group. For those whose ethnic identity does not conform to the tidy categories outlined by the state, the *minzu* system may contribute to loss of identity, as claimants either adapt to a minority identity that does not align with their self-identification or, in cases where acculturation is more complete, simply choose to identify as Han.[27]

Because of such rigidity, the *minzu* system makes all Chinese citizens countable and sortable.[28] One of the major consequences of China's institutionalizing of ethnicity is the attempt to promote homogenization within groups by consolidating various subgroups into a single uniform category for expedient classification. Paradoxically, the state's attempts to create "discrete categories" of identity actually result in greater variation within identity.[29]

The case of the Tibetan-speaking Muslims (Zang-Hui) of Kaligang (referred to in Tibetan as Khargang) in Hualong Hui Autonomous County of Qinghai provides an example. The PRC officially classifies these Muslims as Hui.[30] However, the group's identity blends Muslim and Tibetan cultural traits. They often wear Tibetan clothing, speak in local Amdo Tibetan dialects, and resist the label Zang-Hui. Due to the rigidity of the Chinese ethnic classification system, the group's self-identification diverges from official state classification.[31] Similar ambiguities exist among the Naxi, Zhuang, Yao, Yi, Miao, and various other *minzu* that cobble together several disparate groups under the heading of a single nationality.[32]

Such heterogeneity illustrates a fundamental dilemma that China's ethnic minorities face under the *minzu* system. The inability of the rigid system of categories to accommodate intragroup differences or allow for multiethnic identities places citizens into one of fifty-six tidy boxes of ethnic self-identification. These categories do not reflect the diversity within groups but instead reify differences and harden otherwise blurred ethnic boundary lines. In imposing state-mandated categories of identity on top of existing, informal markers between groups—often in a way that does not perfectly align—the *minzu* system complicates practices of ethnic identification.[33] By forcing citizens to select one and only one *minzu* identity, the system turns the process of self-identification into an ethnically motivated choice for reasons of self-preservation and adds heavy ethnic significance to choices concerning marriage and childbirth.

MARRIAGE AND ETHNIC IDENTITY IN CHINA

Official categories of ethnicity have encouraged China's ethnic minority communities to engage in endogamy and having additional children as attempts at ethnic preservation. For example, increased Han migration to Xinjiang Uyghur Autonomous Region has prompted a self-enforced taboo among Uyghurs on interethnic marriage. Uyghurs—especially those living in rural, southern Xinjiang who consider children "a blessing from Allah"—chafe at family-planning policies imposed by the Chinese state.[34] Both issues heighten the salience of the boundaries between Han and Uyghur. Goldstein et al.'s 2002 examination of family-planning practices in Tibetan communities identifies competition with Han and Hui migrants as one of the primary drivers of Tibetans' preferences for having large families.[35] Because the *minzu* system does not allow for citizens to select multiple ethnicities, they must often weigh matters of ethnic preservation when considering whether or not to marry outside the group.

Previous scholarship on Hui identity notes the importance of intra-Hui marriage for maintaining Hui identity.[36] Even in non-majority-Hui urban settings, the Hui are more likely to prefer endogamy to intermarriage. Likewise, Hui are more likely to express the idea that religion and ethnic differences put up barriers that make exogamy difficult, if not undesirable.[37] Those rare partnerships between Han and Hui that do occur almost always result in the adoption of Islam by the Han partner. Interethnic marriages like these provide one of the "most important channels for conversion," genuine or otherwise. To many Hui clergy, Hui identity is "constitutively gendered" and rooted firmly in patriarchal lineage, necessitating religious conversion in exogamous marriages, especially of Han women to Hui men.[38] Likewise many Hui frown on intermarriage, especially of Hui women to Han men, as they fear that women who marry outside the community might abandon Islam.[39]

In many rural Hui communities, the primary ethnic entrepreneurs are the unmarried young men and women. Endogamy enables Hui to increase the size of their community without fear of losing traditions or of cultural dilution. Because isolated, rural communities seek Hui marriage partners in neighboring towns and villages, endogamy not only serves the role of preserving Hui lineages; it also plays the important dual role of facilitating increased contact with co-ethnics and strengthening the communities' experience in dealing with other Muslims.[40] Individuals attempting to navigate these social pressures may feel the weight of the implications of their partnership choices most acutely.

"MY FAMILY WOULD NOT HAVE ACCEPTED A NON-MUSLIM": SOCIAL PRESSURE AND MARRIAGE CHOICE

A long history of exclusion, differentiation, and partial assimilation complicates the uniformity of the contemporary category of Huizu.[41] In cautioning scholars against simply replicating the logic of these PRC-established categories, Jonathan Lipman writes that, "upon even cursory examination, the supposedly exclusive *minzu* categories break down, become muddled, invite deconstruction."[42] Some, like historian Raphael Israeli, have cast doubt on the applicability of terms like "ethnicity" or "nationality" in reference to the Hui, noting that Hui have not used such terms to describe themselves in either a historical or contemporary context.[43] On one rare occasion, a twenty-eight-year-old man from Yinchuan echoed these sentiments. He insisted that the category of Hui did not make sense and that he was merely a Han who believed in Islam.[44]

Contrary to Israeli's assertions, however, most respondents saw Huizu as a distinct and separate category. Many reasons explain why, despite such heterogeneity and complicated history, this is the case. Most notably, interactions with the state reinforce the legitimacy of the category. Hui actors and the Chinese state have administered ethnic politics to Muslim communities not just as a religious group but as a *minzu*.[45] As my own observations suggest, the importance attached to choices related to *minzu* registration reflect that *Hui* stands not only as a meaningful category but as one that inspires contestation.

Notions of ethnic identity in Hui communities are often framed in relation to the *minzu* system. While some respondents cited the incompatibility of the system's rigid categorization with the ambiguity that pervaded lived reality, several claimed that the process of registering an ethnic identity provided the primary means of association with being Hui.[46] A fifty-five-year-old Hui retiree from Xining recounted, "The first concept I had [of being Hui], when I was young, with a child's understanding, I just knew I was Hui. Because at that time, when I went to sign up for school, I had a *hukou* [household registration], and that *hukou* said my *minzu* was Hui."[47] In this respondent's case, without the state-imposed definition, being Hui lacked specific meaning or significance. For him and others I interviewed, access to Hui identity came primarily through the state's formal designations rather than daily lived practice.

Some respondents' discussions of their ethnic identification echoed the logic of the *minzu* system, asserting the singularity and indivisibility of ethnonational identity. These respondents connected ethnic registration status to transmission by descent. One, a nineteen-year-old college student from Jinan, posited that ethnicity was always passed on in patrilineal fashion: "In China, it seems like this kind of thing goes according to the father. So, because my father is Hui, my *hukou* is also Hui, just like my father's."[48] Others insisted that so long as one partner was Hui, the system would automatically treat their children as Hui. "My little brother and I, our *hukou* are both written down as Hui," recalled a forty-four-year-old woman who worked as a bank teller in Jinan. "My children are also written down as Hui. My little brother's children are also written down as Hui. But my spouse is Han. My brother's wife is also Han. It's that kind of situation [*qing kuang*]." As to whether she might register her children as Han, she remarked that this would be impossible: "Regarding this kind of situation, there's absolutely no dispute whatsoever. Moreover, when going to write down your *hukou*, so long as one party is known to be Hui, the public security will take the initiative to ask you whether or not you wrote down Hui."[49] Her experiences with public registration illustrate bureaucrats' rather rigid understandings of ethnic identification as promoted by the *minzu* system. So long as one parent registers as a minority, the children automatically receive that designation, whether or not such descent comes through the mother's or the father's family.

Regardless of patrilineality, both these respondents' conceptions of ethnicity hinged on biologically determined membership in the group. If one parent was Hui, a child would be considered Hui. Interestingly, the bank teller's comments suggest that children of interethnic marriages retain only the ethnicity of the minority parent. The dismissal of the notion that a child with one Han parent and one Hui parent might also be considered Han reveals that the *minzu* system deals with even such ambiguous cases of multiethnic citizens by employing a one-size-fits-all solution: if a citizen holds any minority descent, they may be registered as a minority. Such inflexibility places added ethnic significance on the selection of a partner.

Several respondents, both married and unmarried, reported feeling that their families expected them to marry within the group. One man, a Jinan fitness instructor in his late twenties, recalled, "Choosing a Hui partner was my decision. I wanted to marry a woman who was devout and knowledgeable about Islam. But regardless, my family would not have accepted a non-Muslim. They would tell me that it's imperative that I find a Muslim girl to marry."[50] A nineteen-year-old college student in Jinan remarked that even without pressure from family and friends, young Hui may consider marriage in ethnic terms: "Sometimes even though parents don't have any preference, their children do. For instance, my little sister, she's like this. My parents did not say, 'You have to marry a Hui,' but she really wants to marry a Hui."[51] Even absent explicit admonishment to marry within the community, unmarried Hui—like the respondent's sister—may infer pressure from parents or others in the community. The unspoken expectations of the community place limits on the ability to exercise autonomy in partnership choice, lest the chooser suffer disapproval.

The kind of social pressure that surrounds marriage often leads to public scrutiny from members of the community. Especially in rural communities, such pressure may dramatically influence marriage choices. Several respondents explained that marriage outside of the group might draw unflattering attention. One woman, a student in Jinan, remarked that in her rural Shanxi hometown, "Han and Hui intermarriage is really rare. Marrying outside of the group is especially rare. In any case, every Hui in the village knows about almost every family's daughter that marries a Han."[52] In other cases, tradition may prohibit choice in matters connected to marriage, especially for women, upon whom prohibitions derived from religious law may be more stringently enforced. A respondent in Xining contrasted the environment in the city with nearby Xunhua: "Here [in Xining] people choose who they marry, but in Xunhua people usually don't."[53] In Xining, where the larger population and the presence of other ethnic and religious groups lessened the compulsions to marry within the community, partnership was a matter of choice. The same could not be said for the more traditional confines of the countryside, where norms were enforced with greater vigor.

Those who choose to marry outside the group may suffer the scorn of others in the community. The Hui fitness instructor in Jinan expressed his disapproval of friends who had married non-Hui partners, stating his belief that they had compromised their identity. "I know some people who got married to a Han person and kept an Islamic lifestyle," he remarked, adding disdainfully, "I don't really get along too well with these people."[54] Another respondent in Xining explained that marriage to a Han might be met with disapproval, reasoning, "More traditional Muslims might say it's important to marry a Muslim and wouldn't accept otherwise."[55] In more conservative communities the choice a person makes when selecting a partner boils down to marrying within the community or being disavowed.

"IF MY DAUGHTER MARRIES A HAN, MAYBE SHE'LL START TO FOLLOW HIS LIFESTYLE": CULTURAL SURVIVAL AND MARRIAGE TABOOS

Concerns about cultural preservation help to explain the rarity of Han-Hui intermarriage. Hui respondents frequently cite cultural distance between Han and Hui as the major obstacle to intermarriage between the two. A Xining shopkeeper in her forties contended that Hui rarely married Han because "most Han are Daoist or Confucian or Buddhist. It's not a good arrangement because of the religious differences."[56] However, a factory worker in his thirties in Jinan insisted that fear of a loss of tradition and ethnic identity, not religious concerns, compelled the taboo on intermarriage with Han: "It's definitely not because of religious reasons. It's because of ethnic reasons. I've heard a funny explanation: people say, 'My daughter isn't allowed to marry a Han, because if my daughter marries a Han, maybe she'll start to follow his lifestyle.'"[57]

The man's citation of the adoption of Han cultural practices, like celebrating secular holidays, engaging in ancestor veneration, or consenting to being cremated after death as opposed to being buried reflect a fear that living with Han would lead to Hanification (Hanhua) was behind respondents' declaration that differences in lifestyle, particularly regarding cleanliness and diet, made marriage between Han and Hui "inconvenient" (*bu fangbian*).[58] In explaining why her parents wouldn't accept her marrying a Han, a fifty-two-year-old receptionist in Jinan said, "In China, the theory is like this: normally you hope your son or daughter can find a partner of the same *minzu*. Firstly, it's because it makes diet and matters of food and drink easier. There are also a few customs that aren't alike, just like between you and me there are Chinese and Western customs that aren't alike. So, that's the reason."[59] These lifestyle differences put a strain on families, especially when dealing with in-laws or extended family members who may not place similar emphasis on tolerance and understanding. Some respondents said these fault lines broke families apart. For example, one Jinan respondent, the child of a marriage between a Hui father and a Han mother, recalled the divisions that happened between in-laws because of her parents' marriage: "Even after they got married, [the two families] would still break out into quarrels, and it was just really hard to deal with."[60]

These cultural and religious differences, some respondents attested, became especially problematic when dealing with rituals related to death and burial. Respondents expressed concern that a non-Hui spouse might fail to observe the Islamic prohibition on cremation.[61] A twenty-nine-year-old Hui woman in Xining illustrated this dilemma with an anecdote: "A friend of mine married a Han woman who converted to Islam. But her parents are still Han. She died suddenly, before she turned thirty. Her parents wanted to cremate her, and her husband didn't want to because we Muslims can't be cremated. We have to bury our dead. But her parents didn't care. They said 'We're not Muslims. We have our own traditions and you have yours, but she's *our* daughter.' And so they cremated her. It was a problem, but there was nothing her husband could do about it."[62] Such gulfs in understanding and fear of a loss of Islamic tradition drive many Hui to deem marriage to Han undesirable. A woman in her twenties in Xining explained, "Very few people intermarry, and after they get married, they're also more likely to get divorced. This is because lifestyles are just too different, and you're not used to it if you haven't lived that way since you were young."[63] Having to endure the strain put on interethnic relationships by the perception of incompatible lifestyles, pressure from less sympathetic members of a couple's extended family, and looming fear of eventual divorce make these partnerships appear less desirable and lead Hui to avoid them altogether.

"THEY HAVE TO BECOME MUSLIMS FIRST": RELIGIOUS CONVERSION AND BRIDGING CULTURAL DIFFERENCES IN INTERETHNIC MARRIAGE

To bridge the cultural gaps that complicate intermarriage between Han and Hui, many respondents argued, Han partners should convert to Islam. In traditionalist Hui communities, restrictions go even further by stipulating that these standards be applied only to Han women, while Hui women are not allowed to marry Han men at all. This mandate originated from Islamic jurisprudence that utilized a conservative reading of the Qu'ran (specifically,

2:221), yet few respondents explained the practice in these terms. Instead, they claimed conversion was necessary for convenience of lifestyle habits and maintenance of tradition. Though few seem to believe that Han women take their conversions seriously, the act provides a symbolically important function by adhering to norms that encourage a woman's submission to Hui male hegemony.[64] Cultural motivations bolster citations of religious law. The idea among religiously conservative Hui that only those interethnic marriages between Hui men and non-Hui women may be deemed acceptable—and even then, only upon the condition of religious conversion—rests upon long-standing myths of ethnogenesis telling of Arab or Persian traders taking local Chinese women as brides. Stories like these place Hui communities on the "receiving" end of a marriage exchange. Even though scant historical evidence exists to uphold the veracity of these tales, they are accepted as truth in devoutly religious Hui communities.[65]

Some respondents noted a recent change in attitudes regarding such strictures. In previous eras, some recalled, the community considered conversion in cases of intermarriage to be mandatory. Noting that intermarriage between Han and Hui occurred more commonly than in previous eras, a Beijing author in his seventies explained the kinds of stipulations typically put on interethnic relationships in the days of his youth. Conversion to Islam, he remarked, was the minimum requirement for a couple to get married. Further, different standards applied to Hui men and women. He described the traditional attitudes regarding intermarriage, recalling that in his youth women were not permitted to marry outside the Hui community.[66] His memories, and the contrast they draw with more accommodating attitudes of Beijing Hui in the present, illustrate the greater flexibility and autonomy Hui men have traditionally possessed in marriage practices, especially in religiously devout communities.

Though such absolute prohibitions softened in the years since the start of the era of Reform and Opening in 1978, many respondents cited conversion of the non-Hui partner to Islam as a necessity for interethnic couples. One respondent in Xining laid out these terms bluntly, asserting, "Hui can marry Han, and Tibetans and Tu, but they have to become Muslims first. Otherwise, it can't happen."[67]

Some respondents saw the imposition of this requirement as a way for accommodating parents to support their children while still upholding cultural norms. A respondent in Xining, a teacher in his late forties who was himself the son of a Hui mother and a Salar father, suggested conversion might smooth over any objections parents might raise to the union: "It's just that maybe if two people love each other, then maybe the families won't oppose [the marriage]. Maybe it's normally just that the man must convert to Islam, that kind of thing. He'll go to the mosque, and the *ahong* can give him an Islamic name [*jingming*]."[68] A nineteen-year-old Hui man from Heze in Shandong studying in Jinan explained his parents' position on the matter: "About this problem . . . If, say, I go home and my girlfriend is Han, if I bring her home to meet my parents, and say we want to get married, my mom and dad certainly won't say that they object, but they also won't say that they consent. If she agrees, then before we get married, we've got to give her some education. It's like that. Education and a *xili*."[69]

Even marriage within the faith presents obstacles for many Hui, if the partner belongs to another of China's Islamic minorities. While many Hui respondents considered marriage outside the faith—to Han or other non-Muslims—as impermissible, attitudes concerning intermarriage between Hui and one of China's other Islamic minorities varied. A forty-year-old Hui professor from Xining observed that the relatively unified religious atmosphere of his city allowed for a more accommodating attitude toward marriages between Muslim groups: "People here have a mentality of *zujiao yiti* [ethnoreligious integration]. This means Hui are Muslims and Muslims are Hui. We don't really separate into minorities." He added, "The Salar speak a different language. But otherwise, the cultural differences aren't so large." However, despite such a positive outlook, he concluded that such marriages "only sometimes happen."[70]

Many respondents commented on the infrequency of interethnic marriages, even between Muslim groups. While most agreed that nothing prohibited partnering with a non-Hui Muslim, many cited cultural and linguistic concerns that made such marriages rare. A Hui government service worker from Xining his fifties remarked that nothing prohibited marriage to other Islamic minorities, but that such relationships often struggled because of cultural incompatibility: "Hui and Salar or Dongxiang *can* marry, but there may be different traditions."[71] Likewise, a Salar prayer goods salesman in Xining mentioned that marriage between Muslim ethnic groups was not forbidden but pointed to language differences as the primary reason for the rarity of such occurrence. In his hometown of Xunhua, for example, "everyone there speaks Salar." Most Hui, he reasoned, would struggle to communicate in such an environment.[72] A twenty-nine-year-old from Xining with a Hui mother and a Salar father mentioned language as a reason she identified as Hui. Despite her Salar heritage, she bemoaned the linguistic limitations that distanced her from the Salar community: "Mostly at home I speak Qinghai Hui dialect [Qinghai Huihua]. I can't really speak much Salar."[73]

"OUR *MINZU* PROBLEM IS ALSO A MARRIAGE PROBLEM": URBAN SPACES AND ATTITUDES TOWARD INTERETHNIC MARRIAGE

Urban spaces present particular challenges in regard to making marriage choices. Unlike small and often homogeneous rural enclaves, urban settings provide greater opportunities for interethnic interactions and thus increase the likelihood of interethnic relationships. Cities also provide greater stratification of income, education, profession, and other factors. As such, in these contexts other dimensions of identity that in rural settings seem less salient gain importance. For instance, in urban contexts where community norms around ethnic or religious practices are weaker and cultural institutions that normally enforce them have a less powerful presence, norms surrounding class, profession, level of education, or other competing identities may take on greater salience.

Longtime Beijing residents note increasing tolerance in local Hui's attitudes toward marrying non-Hui. Some attribute such changes to loss of tradition following the upheavals of the 1960s and 1970s. One resident, an author in his seventies, remarked that prior to the Cultural Revolution (approx. 1966–76), when the Party prohibited open practice of religion, Beijing Hui observed far more restrictive limitations on marriage: "Before, Hui didn't ever marry Han. Or if they did it was a Hui man marrying a Han woman, and she had to accept Islam and learn how to be Muslim. Generally speaking, we didn't allow Hui women to marry Han men. But after the Cultural Revolution this changed a lot."[74] As religious traditionalism waned, so too did concern over ethnic identity in matters related to partnership. In particular, women's ability to exercise choice in selecting a partner increased as insistence on observing Qur'anic dictates on marriage subsided. Respondents explained that these types of restrictions softened during the era of Reform and Opening. A twenty-nine-year-old artist described how her parents' experiences during that period made them more tolerant to the idea of her marrying her Han partner: "My parents, because they were sent down to the countryside in Inner Mongolia to work for so many years, they're more convinced that two people need to be in love, and hope that I can find a partner that I like. So they actually haven't really restricted me."[75] For her, choosing a partner rested primarily on romantic attraction, and ethnic identity played little part in her choice to marry a Han man.

A fifty-seven-year-old woman working as a cab driver in Shijiazhuang in nearby Hebei described the choice facing her daughter who lived in Beijing, where she was married to a non-Hui man. Recently she had given birth to her first child, a boy. In response to questions about her grandson's *minzu* status, the cab driver expressed her hope that the child would embrace his Hui identity. Ultimately, she admitted, *minzu* status remained a choice that he alone could make later in life. She reasoned, "When he's older he can choose to be Hui like his mother or choose to be not Hui like his father."[76]

However, relationships outside the Hui community did not come without complications. The twenty-nine-year-old artist bemoaned the difficulties that her own marriage had caused for those in her extended family. Of the restrictions they had sought to impose, she remarked, "For us, the question of marriage was especially messy [*jiujie*]. Because for our family this situation has been messy for a long time. They [extended family members], of course, want us to find a Hui partner to marry. It's not permissible to marry another *minzu*, and marrying someone from another country is even less permissible. We must find Hui partners." She continued, commenting that many young Hui experienced these difficulties, even amid changing social attitudes. "If you have conservative parents, they will completely disagree about these things." Volunteering an example, she said, "My uncle—my dad's older brother—his two daughters both must marry a Muslim." She explained her uncle firmly believed that "if both sides are Muslim, then the family atmosphere will be stronger—it will be very strong." She reasoned that fear of cultural loss drove many to these positions. "Our *minzu* problem is also a marriage problem. In order to protect their own *minzu*'s purity [*chunzheng*], everyone must be with their own *minzu*."[77] Her concern illustrates her understanding of an intrinsic tie between identity and descent. The notion that an ethnic identity might become diluted through marriage outside the group highlights the idea that the group must be literally reproduced through childbirth and continuing lineages.

In Beijing, historic Hui communities like those at Madian, Douban Hutong, and Dong Si were dispersed by urban renewal that made marrying within the community less common. With Hui populations scattered throughout Beijing, partnering outside of the community occurred with greater frequency. As migrants from rural Hui communities in China's interior—especially the northwest—arrived in the capital, attitudes changed yet again. These arrivals coincided with a consolidation of Hui cultural and religious institutions around Niu Jie, with the neighborhood becoming Beijing's de facto Muslim stronghold. A thirty-three-year-old Hui software engineer who moved from his hometown in Harbin to attend university described the changes in Beijing's community following his arrival: "Most of the residents on Niu Jie are not long-term residents. They're only temporarily living here.

Most are *waidi* [outsiders]."[78] As these Hui from other places arrived in Beijing, respondents told me, they changed the social landscape of the Hui community. Such change was twofold. First, migrants coming to Beijing, especially younger singles, might adjust expectations about partnership after living in an urban environment where the norms about marrying within the group weighed less heavily. Second, the arrival of rural, more religiously observant Hui to Niu Jie underscored differences in understandings of religious and cultural norms held by local, usually more secular Beijing Hui. As the artist reasoned, "The situation in Beijing is a totally different environment from Xinjiang and the northwest."[79]

In Jinan—where the Hui represent the only non-Han population of any size—many respondents reported an ongoing loosening in attitudes regarding intermarriage.[80] Respondents frequently asserted that while older generations insisted that Hui marry other Hui, younger Hui felt less strongly bound by these norms.[81] One woman, the owner of a small pan-fried dumpling (*guotie)* shop in Jinan, lamented her adult son's romantic choices : "It would be best to marry a Hui girl. Hui should be with Hui and Han should be with Han, but young people don't really listen."[82] Young Hui in Jinan, who often grow up in largely secular homes, aspire to choosing a partner based on romantic attraction rather than prerogatives related to ethnicity or religion. While many recognize that a relationship with a Hui partner would smooth over some difficulties, this did not override the more important factor of being in love. One woman, a twenty-two-year-old working in the airline industry, explained her family's shifting attitude toward Han-Hui intermarriage:

> My grandparents hope I can find a Hui spouse. Although our family already has two Han members, they still hope this. After all, the need to continue tradition is important. But in my parents' opinion . . . My dad was also previously insistent and would say, "You must find a Hui spouse." It was a rigid rule he gave me, saying, "It's mandatory for you to marry a Hui." But my mom talked with him about it afterward, I think, and so he said, "It would be best for you to marry a Hui, but if you can't find a Hui spouse, just find one who will respect you and who will understand our *minzu*, and that will do."[83]

Some Jinan respondents cited the small size of the Hui population as a reason for the lower resistance to marrying outside the group, claiming it was hard to find Hui partners who were suitable.[84] An engineer in his fifties likened the tendency of Hui to marry only other Hui to inbreeding and declared that, in his opinion, finding partners of another *minzu* would be "good for the children of the next generation."[85] Middle-class, secular Hui like this engineer dismissed the idea of mandating marriage within the Hui community as backward and unsuitable. Instead, they insisted that their children find partners whom they liked and who were of capable of looking after and providing for a family. The fifty-two-year-old receptionist explained why she did not follow her parents' example in forcing her daughter to seek a Hui husband: "The Hui social circle is too small. If you want to find someone you like, and fulfill these requirements [to marry another Hui], it's not easy. So, for the sake of my child's happiness, I broadened this category. If I absolutely wanted to require [my daughter] to find a Hui man, I maybe could find one, but I imagine this wouldn't be that great. I want her to find someone who's outstanding in all respects."[86]

Another woman noted that living in Jinan allowed for more flexibility when compared to rural Hui communities. In her rural hometown, she observed, marriage to a Han might require him to become Muslim: "In order to marry a Han there would be some formalities to go through. Here, where we're pretty far away, we wouldn't go through those formalities."[87] Though the village's conditions of allowing women to marry outside the group if their partner agreed to convert provided slightly more autonomy than those communities in which such marriages were prohibited to women, these requirements still proved limiting. In Jinan's looser environment, however, such cultural norms held less power, and as such granted Hui women more autonomy in marriage choices. Compared to the village setting, where Hui ethnic and religious norms predominated, in Jinan's urban atmosphere a partner's identity as Hui proved less salient.

In stark contrast to Jinan, in Xining, where Hui are one of many different ethnic groups living in a truly multiethnic environment, Hui largely remain firmly opposed to marriage with Han. Many respondents argued that Hui could marry Muslims of different minorities (e.g., Salar, Baonan, Dongxiang) without any controversy but not Han.[88] An entrepreneur in her late thirties claimed that such marriages couldn't work because Han converts rarely took Islam seriously: "If Han and Hui get married, the Han person certainly has to convert. If not, it's impermissible [*bu yunxu de*]. But we try as much as we can to not promote marrying Han, because converting to Islam for marriage isn't meaningful belief. Instead, it's because 'I like this person, so I'll follow them. At best, I won't eat pork.' But it's not serious belief, so going about your life can be really troublesome."[89] When asked if Han-Hui marriages ever occurred, one young man in his late twenties insisted, "That's something that happens more often in places back east."[90] He held up local Hui as an example of more pious Muslims who did not marry outside the community. Another respondent observed that intermarriage "was more common in those situations where children strived their hardest" and made great effort at making the marriage work despite cultural differences or their parents' objections. She admitted, however, that these were exceptional cases.[91]

Preservation of Islamic customs motivated several respondents' opposition to marriage across ethnic lines. When explaining why she would not accept her son's marriage to a Han, one woman said that fear of cultural degradation motivated her stance: "I'm afraid they'll become Hanified. Because I think a *minzu* can be maintained, passed down. I'm not saying this because of bloodlines, it's just *minzu* traditions. It's best if you can keep them completely intact and maintain them as best as you possibly can. If Hui, especially women, marry Han, then they'll lose a lot of our culture, and it's very sad. Of course, because I'm a minority, I'm really concerned about this."[92]

While residents in Xining emphasized the importance of cultural preservation, many in Yinchuan complained about the fact that these traditions had, in large part, already eroded. Over the course of the past twenty years, Yinchuan's population had swollen due to waves of internal migration from all parts of China. The effects this migration exerted on the city, and its culture, led numerous respondents to remark that Yinchuan had become a "city of migrants" (*yimin chengshi*).[93] As wave after wave arrived, many locals groused about the disappearance of Yinchuan's distinctive Muslim culture and griped that leniency and permissiveness in regard to Islamic traditions contributed to a decline in the quality of the city's religious atmosphere. Interethnic marriages, they argued, were partly to blame. One man in his early thirties moaned that standards in Yinchuan had grown too lax and families weren't serious enough about religious observance: "There are some people who, because the religious atmosphere in this city is very lax, might have one eye open and one eye closed. Of course, on the surface, they they won't accept it. If a boy and girl have a good relationship, there's nothing the family can do, and they'll get married. The non-Muslim bride or groom will convert to Islam. But this conversion is only in appearance. You tell me, those converts, are they really Muslim? I don't think so."[94]

A restaurant owner in the suburban community of Najiahu echoed these sentiments and longed for a return to the era where members of the community took a more active role in making sure their children married other Hui. He recounted that, in the past, people felt obligated to persuade other families not to allow their children to marry Han, lest they be complicit.

"Now," he admitted, "in this society, there's nothing you can do about it. Everyone minds their own business. Just looking after your own children is enough."[95] A woman in her early twenties who worked as a secretary in the offices of a neighborhood association recalled parental disapproval led to a breakup with a former boyfriend: "I dated a Han guy before, but my family didn't approve, and I think it was because we had different religious faiths."[96] The social pressure exerted by the family's unwillingness to accept the relationship illustrates just how the judgment of the community acts as a constraint on individual autonomy.

Despite these concerns about Hanification, several respondents described a change in the community. The Han woman working in marketing and preparing to marry a Hui man told me that her decision provoked strong reactions from her parents, who feared that her conversion would prohibit her from observing the practices of ancestor veneration and wearing mourning clothes. Her husband's family, however, showed great tolerance in allowing her to observe such traditions, even after she became Muslim: "This is where two families must be comparatively open-minded. My husband's family is very open-minded, and they can accept Han-Hui intermarriage, and they must tolerate these traditions. For instance, with respect to the rules about dying, they surely approve of my doing these things."[97] Others mentioned that young couples were beginning to disregard such concerns altogether. One Han woman in her early thirties who worked as an elementary school teacher related the story of a Hui friend: "Intermarriage between Han and Hui is becoming more common. My coworker's new boyfriend is Han. Her parents weren't very accepting, but she told them she doesn't want to marry a Hui man."[98] Thus, while community censure still influences the decisions made regarding marriage and partnership, the social landscape of Yinchuan also reflects changing attitudes among young people. This shift in attitudes toward a more tolerant stance on intermarriage occurs simultaneously with transformations in the demographics of Yinchuan wrought by migration to the city—both from inside and outside Ningxia.

CHOOSING HUINESS IN THE CITY: MARRIAGE AND ETHNICITY IN A CHANGING SOCIAL LANDSCAPE

The wide array of difference in attitudes found across these communities illustrates how and when marriage choices take on ethnic significance. Importantly, cross-cutting gender and religious cleavages significantly impact the amount of autonomy individuals possess in making choices about partnership. Predominantly secular Hui may view marriage outside of the group as workable, even though it requires compromise and mutual accommodation. Elsewhere decisions about who one marries may not allow considerations about marrying outside the group, particularly for women. Especially in more religiously devout Hui communities, marriage within the community may be compulsory for women and may be enforced by family members or community authorities. Thus, for more pious Hui women, ethnicity is highly salient in matters concerning marriage and childbirth, and as such these practices may not be matters of choice at all. Men in such communities, by contrast, may feel less pressure to marry within the group but may still be bound by norms derived from conservative interpretations of Islamic law that mandate a non-Muslim partner must convert to Islam.

Because the state set hard parameters on official ethnic registration, choosing to marry within or outside of the community varies with the importance attached to ethnic identity relative to other identities. The concentration or dispersion of a population may heighten the degree to which ethnic identity takes precedence over others. When the concentration of the group is small, other identities may take precedence. Where multiple ethnic identities interact, the urge to prevent cultural degradation may give ethnicity precedence where marriage is concerned or perhaps lead to resignation that ethnic degradation is inevitable.

In isolated communities like Jinan, Hui are less likely to consider marriage strictly as an ethnonational choice and less likely to consider ethnic intermarriage as taboo. In these communities, where the Hui population is smaller and the community is surrounded by Han, ethnic salience wanes when making marriage choices in favor of class difference, level of education, or even romantic attraction between partners. Respondents' willingness to accept marriage between Han and Hui without requiring religious conversion exemplifies flexibility and adaption in the face of demographic isolation. In these cases, a Han partner's promise to show tolerance and respect for Hui culture and lifestyle habits provides a form of compromise.

By contrast, in multiethnic communities like Xining, where religious observance is more stringent and linguistic divisions between ethnic groups may complicate relationships, marriage is framed as an explicitly ethnonational choice. The insistence on the part of many Hui parents that their children marry Hui for the sake of cultural preservation illustrates a fear for cultural survival in the face of increased interaction with other groups. That many Xining residents consider conversion of Han partners to Islam as a minimal requirement before allowing interethnic marriage clearly illustrates these urges. Residents may prioritize religious and ethnic choices over others, electing to return to enclave neighborhoods and marry within the faith. In these cases, ethnicity gains increased salience over other forms of identity.

In Yinchuan attitudes are shaped, in part, by the city's formal institutional status. In this capital city of a titular autonomous region, Hui culture and identity take a prominent, if superficial, place. However, the recent influx of rural migrants raises specific challenges concerning marriage and partnership. Migrants arriving from more conservative rural locations observe different standards about partnership from those urbanites who view themselves as open-minded and cosmopolitan. Likewise, children of rural migrant parents who grow up in urban settings may form different attitudes than those of older generations. In this sense, in cities like Yinchuan, questions about the appropriateness of interethnic marriage may be subject to debate even within generations of the same family.

As a "city of migrants," Yinchuan illustrates a broader trend occurring throughout the country. China's push toward urbanization (*chengzhenhua*) moves Hui migrants from various locations into close proximity with each other, as well as with other ethnicities and religions. In Yinchuan, the interactions of Hui with Han, as well as with Hui from different parts of China, reopen contestation over the appropriateness of interethnic marriage. As these arguments unfold, they renegotiate the boundary markers that define Hui identity. Debating whether or not non-Hui spouses should convert, or whether children of Han-Hui intermarriage should be claimed as Hui, may lead to drawing internal distinctions within the Hui community that divide it along regional, sectarian, class, age, or gender lines. The reignition of these debates prevents the *minzu* system from achieving the political goal of solidifying a singular, standardized Hui identity that aligns with the state's definitions. Instead, the divisions that emerge from within the community expand notions of what it means to claim Hui identity.

CHAPTER THREE

TALKING

Arabic Language and Literacy

Our Qur'ans all have Chinese characters.

—AN EIGHTEEN-YEAR-OLD HUI UNIVERSITY STUDENT, JINAN

AS I ENTERED THE LARGE COURTYARD IN FRONT OF THE MAUSOLEUM at Fenghuang Shan Gongbei in Xining, I greeted the complex's caretaker, a short, middle-aged man who wore a white knit skullcap (*baimaozi*), with a friendly wave.[1] I walked up to the ornately chiseled dividing wall of stone and gray brick that separated the larger, outer courtyard from the inner courtyard containing the tomb and shrine. Peering inside, I prepared to step through the rounded archway and stand in front of the tomb. As I began to move forward, a voice from behind startled me. "Hey!" it rang out. I turned around to see the caretaker waving his arms emphatically and signaling for me to stop. "You can't go in there!" he told me. "You're not Muslim!" Curious, as I was unaware of restrictions against non-Muslims standing in front of the tomb, I asked how he had made such a determination. After all, I asked him, what does a Muslim look like? "I knew you weren't Muslim, because when you walked in, you didn't say *salamu* [the Chinese transliteration of the Arabic *salaam*]," the man replied emphatically. "That's how we Hui greet each other."[2]

Over the course of conducting my field research, the subject of one's proficiency in speaking and reading Qur'anic Arabic became a recurring theme in my interviews. When I asked about language use in Hui communities, respondents cited a variety of ways in which Arabic impacted Hui identity. Some, like the *gongbei* caretaker, placed emphasis on the importance of the language for signaling shared Hui identity. Others went as far as to liken it to a de facto minority language for the Sinophone Hui. Some remarked that, as a language of faith, the ability to speak Arabic properly served as a barometer for religious piety. Others noted the language's impact on Hui dialects—often marked by the use of loanwords from Arabic, Persian, or Turkic languages—across the country.

In each of these cases, Arabic language influenced the day-to-day conduct of life in Hui communities. For instance, while conducting interviews in Yinchuan, a local Hui university professor encouraged me to offer the Islamic greeting *As-salaam-alaikum* (Peace be upon you) to my Hui interviewees before shaking their hand. Doing so, he insisted, was standard among Hui in Yinchuan.[3] In Xining, I was told by many respondents that greeting friends and neighbors by saying *salamu* was an important expression of community. They elaborated that greeting each other in Arabic at the end of services on E'id al-fitr (in Chinese, Kaizhai jie) was an important part of the festivities that marked the end of Ramadan.[4] Throughout the country, respondents frequently suggested that the use of Arabic language acted as a kind of shibboleth or marker of belonging among Hui.

Language plays an especially important role in establishing the boundaries of Hui identity. Official state classifications regard the Hui as a Chinese-speaking minority who lack their own minority language. However, despite this status, Hui give special significance to *jingwen* ("scriptural language"; in this case, Qur'anic Arabic) as a language of faith. Throughout the course of my fieldwork, respondents described how, in the absence of an officially recognized, vernacular minority language, *jingwen* became the language most frequently associated with Hui identity. The prominent status of *jingwen* in Hui communities has consequences for promotion and preservation of the language in official institutions. Though the state frequently uses Arabic script on public signs and documents in Hui autonomous areas, largely as a performative gesture to showcase tolerance and diversity, Hui lack linguistic resources afforded other *minzu*. Unlike many *minzu* who are offered minority-language education programs in public schools, coursework in Arabic is not offered in public schools, even in Hui autonomous areas. As a result, most Hui living in these spaces are unable to read these signs and posters. Those Hui who do pursue the study of Arabic often do so at the expense of learning other subjects that might advance their economic interests.

Given the rarity of Qur'anic literacy or spoken proficiency among my respondents, the ability to read and, perhaps more important, pronounce *jingwen* became a litmus test for one's Hui identity in the eyes of many.

Additionally, multiple respondents described how the languages of the Turks, Persians, and Arabs from whom they claimed descent influenced the development of locally specific Huihua (Hui dialects of Chinese), which distinguished Hui from the majority Han. The variability of these linguistic markers from one community to another illustrates the absence of unified and coherent Huihua. Not only do these ordinary habits of speech serve as markers of Hui identity; they also serve as grounds for drawing intragroup distinctions that cut across Hui.

In particular, questions about the use of Chinese language to transcribe *jingwen* and recite from the Qu'ran showcase sectarian and regional divisions. Followers of the Yihewani (a Chinese transliteration of Ikhwan, or Muslim Brotherhood) school, a reform-oriented Hanafi sect, frequently disparage other traditions, in particular the Gedimu (a Chinese transliteration of the Arabic Qadim, also sometimes referred to as *laojiao*) school, for their use of Chinese to read and recite Islamic texts. Such a practice, they maintain, provides evidence of the Gedimu's inferiority and Hanification.[5] Such divergence between sects over the importance of language frequently also aligns with regional divides. In eastern China, where Muslim literati began the practice of relating Islam to native Chinese philosophical and religious traditions like Daoism and Confucianism as early as the fourteenth century, translating the Qur'an into Chinese or reciting Qur'anic Arabic with the use of Chinese characters is common practice.[6] However, in the northwest respondents insisted that such practices degraded the authenticity of scripture and could not be considered the proper practice of Islam. Likewise, Islamic terms derived from highly localized Hui vocabularies contribute to the salience of regional identities within the Hui community.

That linguistic habits starkly define the boundaries of Hui identity comes as no surprise. Language is fundamental for building shared identity. Even casual conversations carried out between people in the course of their daily lives can establish a sense of common belonging among members of a community.[7] Classrooms, office breakrooms, storefronts, restaurants, playing fields, and a host of other ordinary locations become venues for everyday discourse about identity.[8] Accordingly, habits of speech such as dialect choice, word choice, accent, and intonation are often strong markers of identity.[9] These markers may provide the basis for inclusion, exclusion, or stigmatization.[10] They may also give way to concerns about language preservation and survival in the face of assimilation. Further, written language, like that used on road signs and official buildings, may inspire and mobilize ethnonational sentiments.[11]

FORGETTING THE MOTHER TONGUE? MINORITY LANGUAGES, ETHNIC IDENTITY, AND THE STATE IN CHINA

Linguistic rights form a crucial component of China's ethnic minority autonomy policy. Consistent with the Marxist-Leninist principle that the state must promote the values of socialism through minority autonomy and using minority languages, the CCP enshrined linguistic rights for ethnic minorities in its founding creed.[12] These statuary and constitutional commitments to ethnic autonomy and linguistic preservation notwithstanding, the state's policies often facilitate the Hanification of China's minority groups. Critics argue that because the state offers only minimal or token opportunities to study their ethnic languages, minorities must choose between obtaining minority-language proficiency and pursuing other studies that would enhance their economic interests. Thus, though the minority autonomy system ostensibly intends to promote cultural and linguistic preservation, in practice ethnic minorities often perceive the policies it generates as eroding minority culture.[13]

One area in which these tensions between cultural preservation and integration arise is in minority-language education.[14] China's public schools within minority autonomous regions act both as institutions for the conservation of culture and as a means for fostering loyalty to the state and reinforcing Han-centrism.[15] In enshrining minority language and culture in the curriculum, public schools exert a powerful influence on the maintenance of ethnic identity. State-sponsored language instruction in schools dictates how students learn to reproduce ethnic minority culture and allows the state to supervise and shape cultural expression.[16] Regarding the Hui, the CCP emphasizes the group's Sinophone identity. For example, the overwhelming use of the Chinese language in the curriculum of the state-affiliated Chinese Islamic Association illustrates ethnic bias in the instruction of clergy in exigesis, or scriptural interpretation (*jiejing*). The use of Chinese language favors the Hui over Uyghurs and other Muslim ethnic groups that speak Turkic or non-Sinitc languages and attempts to use language and textual interpretation to shape and control ethnic and religious expression.[17]

Beyond the classroom, ethnic minorities must weigh matters of language preservation against economic viability. As ethnic minorities from undeveloped regions of China move to urban centers to pursue their economic interests, incentives to learn and speak standard Chinese (Putonghua) increase. One ethnic Salar interviewee in Xining explained, "I really worry that if a large number of kids live outside of their hometowns and study Chinese and slowly forget their mother tongue [*muyu*], how can we pass on our ethnic culture?"[18] Such remarks illustrate how language acts as a transmission belt for culture. Without fluency in a minority language, members of the group fail to grasp the significance of other elements of culture. Minority-language instruction becomes the fundamental basis for cultural survival. However, the perception is strong among many minorities that the path to economic advancement demands that students learn the dominant national language and leave such traditions behind. Some may see learning a minority language as akin to choosing poverty over prosperity.

Other groups besides the Hui share these concerns. Among China's Mongol community, loss of ability to speak the Mongol language ranks as one of the primary concerns related to the group's cultural survival.[19] Observers argue that, because Mongolian-language monolingualism has been functionally abolished in Inner Mongolia and almost all Mongols speak at least some Mandarin, the complete linguistic assimilation of Mongols in Inner Mongolia may occur in the near future, barring dramatic changes in language education and cultural preservation policies.[20] However, a curriculum in only the Mongol language puts Mongols at a distinct social and economic disadvantage in a Han-dominated linguistic environment. In autonomous areas some minority citizens worry that these programs harm their ability to gain high-wage jobs or move up the social ladder since Chinese is the language of business.[21] Uradyn Bulag asserts that learning only Mongol makes Mongolians "economically, politically, and even socially incompetent citizens in a Chinese-dominated society that, from the 1980s onward, was increasingly market oriented."[22] These simultaneous pressures trap Mongol communities between the fear of language extinction and of economic marginalization. The CCP's campaigns begun in the summer of 2020 to curtail Mongol-language instruction in schools in Inner Mongolia exacerbated these fears.[23] In response, Mongol activists accused the CCP of violating the principle of minority autonomous governance and running counter to the spirit of ethnic unity as envisioned by the ideology of Xi Jinping Thought. In July 2020, protests against the policy broke out across the Inner Mongolia Autonomous Region and the government received over 4,300 petitions from activists asking the state to protect Mongol-language education.[24]

Prior to a crackdown on Uyghur culture in the mid-2010s, Uyghurs expressed similar resentments concerning language loss and economic viability. Many complained that the local schools did not teach courses in Uyghur beyond the elementary level and that opportunities for economic advancement required them to gain fluency in spoken Mandarin Chinese.[25] Many of sociologist Blaine Kaltman's respondents remarked that Uyghur-language-only education placed Uyghurs at a comparative disadvantage on the job market. Thus, Uyghurs are faced with a dilemma: preserving their native language in lower levels of education limits their ability to gain access to the top-level higher education needed for economic advancement, which is conducted in Chinese.[26] Those Uyghurs who elect to conduct their studies in Mandarin (the so-called Minkaohan) to better their economic chances must make complicated and nuanced choices about how to remain attached to their culture and cope with their position within their own community.[27] Some of Kaltman's respondents even claimed that language education was a means by which the government attempted to deliberately marginalize Uyghurs.[28]

"WE HUI DON'T HAVE OUR OWN LANGUAGE": LANGUAGES OF FAITH AND DAILY LIFE IN HUI COMMUNITIES

Language tethers the Hui to Chinese culture, and Han culture in particular, due to their official status as a "Chinese-speaking ethnicity" (*hanyu minzu*). Though the Hui are a linguistically diverse group whose members speak a number of different languages—including a variety of regional Chinese dialects and dialects of Mongolian, Tibetan, Chamic, and Austronesian languages—the Arabic language exerts a heavy influence on Hui culture as a language of faith.[29] For religiously devout Hui, Qur'anic Arabic is the language of worship. Even among relatively secular Hui, Arabic—alongside Persian and Turkic languages—influences daily speech patterns by contributing loanwords to local Hui vocabularies.[30] Though Arabic is not an official minority language as recognized by the PRC, Hui often cite proficiency (or lack thereof) in speaking and reading Arabic as a boundary marker for group identity.

Historical accounts differ about how the Hui have balanced the use Arabic and Chinese. Raphael Israeli claims that early Chinese Muslim communities attempted to ground their faith and their origins in a Chinese context and situate Islamic terms within a Chinese linguistic environment. From the introduction of Islam during the Tang dynasty in the early seventh century up through the Yuan (1271–1368), foreign Muslims in China kept Arabic alive in daily use. However, Israeli contends that, due to their gradual assimilation into Chinese society, by the start of the Ming dynasty Chinese Muslims had adopted Chinese names and spoke the Chinese language in public spaces but maintained Islamic names and spoke Arabic among themselves, resulting in a split between public and private identity. Though virtually no contemporary Hui speak Arabic as a native language, Israeli suggests that the division between public use of local Chinese dialects and private use of Arabic-derived terms persists within the community even today.[31]

Li Juan, Ma Shaobiao, and Ma Shaohu's account of the development of language in China's Muslim communities largely accords with Israeli's; they found that, despite the emergence of an elite cohort of Chinese-born, Chinese-speaking Muslim literati by the late Yuan dynasty, the majority of Muslims continued to use Arabic or Persian in their daily lives until the early Qing. The authors note that the elite among these Muslims established a number of Arabic-language institutions, such as the HuiHui Imperial College (Huihui Guozijian), and the discipline of Huihui national studies (Huihui *guozixue*) to promote Arabic use and study religious texts.[32] Likewise, Zvi Ben-Dor Benite proposes that eighteenth-century commentaries on Islam written in Chinese by Hui literati, such as the *Han Kitab* (*Han Ketabu*), served as a means by which Hui scholars could explain Islamic theology in Confucian terms to demonstrate the compatibility of Islam with Chinese tradition.[33] Jin Zhongjie and other historians suggest these institutions also existed outside of the imperial court, in Ningxia, for instance. Jin's account of the establishment of mosque education in Ningxia suggests that by the mid-sixteenth century Muslim scholars such as Hu Dengzhou had implemented local institutions to promote Arabic-language learning and Islamic knowledge.[34]

Others offer an account of Hui identity that emphasizes fusion and innovation rather than bifurcation. For example, historian Ma Tong's account of language transmission starkly differs from Israeli's, suggesting that the diversity of cultural and linguistic backgrounds among Muslims necessitated the use of Chinese as a lingua franca, even within the Islamic community. As these Muslims intermarried and lived in China they adopted Chinese dialects as a means of providing common communication. Ma suggests that the Chinese language served an important role in communicating not just outside of the community of faith but also within it.[35] As these communities forged a new, distinctly Hui identity, forces of historical development rendered this kind of cultural fusion inevitable.[36]

Jonathan Lipman contends that as Muslims integrated into Chinese society, a number of linguistic innovations allowed them to bridge the language gap between Chinese and Arabic, Turkic, and Persian. Lipman documents the use of mosque education (*jingtang jiaoyu*) beginning as early as the later Ming dynasty to provide instruction in Arabic for Chinese Muslim communities. In these mosque schools, imams developed systems that Chinese students could use to learn to recite religious texts written in Arabic or Persian by using Chinese characters to approximate the sounds of the original language. Likewise, the creation of *xiaojing* (also known as *xiao'erjing*), an Arabic alphabetic system to write local dialects of Chinese, allowed those

Chinese Muslims who could speak but not read Chinese characters to produce texts in their native language.[37]

These innovations allowed the transmission of Islamic religious knowledge and Muslim identity in a context where Chinese, not Arabic, was the dominant language. This system produced a community of Hui intellectuals fully literate in both languages.[38] However, despite the development of this localized Islamic literary tradition, the Hui community did not universally embrace such tools, and Hui identity did not solidify around these texts. Rather, the appropriateness of such innovations divides contemporary Hui. While *xiaojing* and phonetic translation of the Qur'an allowed for the adaptation of Islamic texts to suit a Chinese context, religious traditionalists in the Hui community decried such texts. As a result, a wide range of attitudes toward language education developed among Hui families, including those in rural areas who elected to teach their children to read only Persian and Arabic.[39]

Even today Hui disagree about what level of Arabic proficiency should be considered sufficient for being properly Hui. As an example, two Hui men interviewed in Lanzhou boasted that ability to read the Qur'an in the original Arabic and use standard pronunciation in reciting it distinguished northwestern Hui as the least Hanified, most authentic Hui. One of the men mocked the Hui in *neidi* (interior China) for having to rely on Chinese characters to pronounce Arabic. "They can't even say the words correctly!" he exclaimed incredulously.[40]

A Hui scholar in his seventies from Jinan confirmed that this inability to read—and thus correctly pronounce—the Qur'an was indeed a source of shame for locals. "Because older people have learned a Sinicized Arabic, they view it as incorrect," he said, and some felt that this illiteracy represented a failure to embody their Hui heritage.[41] Others in the community expressed this sentiment as well. One man, a baker in his forties, expressed sadness at the loss of Arabic literacy in the community, confessing, "Here, we haven't spoken [Arabic] in a long time. Only the people from Xibei can speak it. Long ago, we spoke Persian and Arabic, but now we're all relatively Hanified [Hanhua]."[42] A factory worker in his mid-thirties expressed admiration for migrants from the northwest whose proficiency in Arabic inspired his own rediscovery of his Hui identity. He claimed he did not feel especially strong ties to his Hui identity until he decided to start a Qur'anic study class at the Great Southern Mosque. Learning the language of faith, he explained, made him want to further explore his culture. In part, he recalled, the examples of other Hui drove his interest. The arrival of migrants from Gansu and Qinghai in Jinan provided a model for how to study and pray. Noting their devotion to the language, he remarked that unlike Jinanese Hui, Xibei Hui kept their children from learning to write Chinese characters (Hanzi) to prevent them from being Hanified.[43] For him, the practice seemed to be an admirable commitment to teaching children about their ethnic heritage. By virtue of their ability to read and pronounce the Arabic of the Qur'an without relying on aid from Chinese-language devices, Xibei Hui guarded against the loss of identity that he believed afflicted Jinan's Hui.

AN UNOFFICIAL MINZU LANGUAGE? STATE PROMOTION OF ARABIC IN HUI COMMUNITIES

Though the state does not recognize Arabic as a minority language of the Hui, it does acknowledge its importance to the Hui community. An introductory sign in a museum inside the complex surrounding Yinchuan's Nanguan Mosque described the relationship between the Hui and Arabic: "The Hui are a Chinese Islamic *minzu*. They don't have their own language. Their language is Chinese [Hanwenhua]. Therefore, lots of people use the Qur'an and Arabic as Huiwen [Hui language]."[44]

In recent years, the state has both promoted and restricted the use of Arabic in public spaces within Hui communities according to its strategic purposes. After the announcement of the Belt and Road Initiative, the state promoted use of Arabic script in Hui communities as part of its outreach to partners in the Islamic world. Signs containing Arabic script frequently appeared in Hui neighborhoods. For example, in Ningxia Hui Autonomous Region's capital of Yinchuan, all street signs display street names in Arabic transliteration alongside their presentation in romanized *pinyin* and Chinese characters. In part, these signs serve as official displays of the CCP's benevolence toward Islam and Hui culture intended for foreign audiences from the larger Islamic world. While a sudden reversal in 2017 saw the state begin an asymmetrical, nationwide campaign aimed at de-Islamification of public space, stripping Arabic script from street signs and business placards, up until the start this campaign official organs of the state reinforced the relationship between *jingwen* and Hui identity.[45] The CCP promoted the Hui autonomous region of Ningxia, and Yinchuan in particular, as a nexus for Sino-Muslim (especially Sino-Arab) cooperation.[46]

Proliferation of these multilingual signs was not limited to autonomous regions. On Niu Jie, site of Beijing's most famous Hui community, official buildings such as the community post office also displayed both Arabic and Chinese. Even in neighborhoods where urban redevelopment relocated the historically concentrated Hui population, some official buildings used

Arabic script formally. The Community Residence Center Offices (*shequ fuwu zhan*) on Douban Hutong in Beijing, a formerly vibrant Hui neighborhood with a famous mosque, displayed its sign in both Arabic and Chinese. Inside the office, however, none of the employees claimed to be Hui, and questions about why the sign contained Arabic script were met with puzzlement by those working at the desk.[47]

These official displays of Arabic adorned not only street signs but also propaganda posters, often heralding local neighborhood or municipal initiatives. Near the entrance to Jinan's Hui Quarter, on Gongqingtuan Lu, large wall-size posters placed there by the Luo Yuan Jie Dao Neighborhood Communist Party Worker's Committee depicted images of Jinan's glistening downtown. In bold red, both Chinese characters and Arabic script proclaimed the slogans "The City of Springs Is My Home! Creating a Clean City Relies on Everyone!" and "A Clean Environment Starts with Me!" Despite the prominence of the signs, no local residents claimed to be able to read the parts displaying Arabic script.[48]

Even though the local Jinan residents, who are the targets of the bilingual propaganda posters in the Hui Quarter, found the language inscrutable, the government still possessed incentives for displaying Arabic prominently in Hui neighborhoods. One man in Yinchuan who worked at the Ningxia Academy of Social Sciences explained that the promotion of Arabic language on signs in public places found throughout Ningxia was the result of a government initiative to showcase the Party's ethnic nationality policy (*minzu zhengce*) and highlight the official status of minority languages in an autonomous region. However, he admitted, the project made little impact because "most people have no connection to it" in their day-to-day lives.[49]

Moreover, prior to de-Islamification, various local and provincial government initiatives that actively promoted public displays of Arabic language on official signs were common. In 2015–16, such promotions were especially common in areas where the Hui were the titular autonomous minority and in prominent Hui neighborhoods like Beijing's Niu Jie. There, in the lobby of the headquarters of the Chinese Islamic Association, a sign listed the community outreach programs offered, among them, the "National Holy Qu'ran recitation competition."[50] Similar competitions were held in Jinan at the Dikou Zhuang Mosque.[51]

Some respondents echoed the state in their assertions that *jingwen* acts as the de facto minority language for Hui.[52] Many other respondents recognized the impact of Arabic and Persian language influences when describing distinctive patterns of speech present in conversations among Hui.[53] For instance, a man in his fifties who operated a Hui community charitable organization explained the need for Hui to speak and read Qur'anic Arabic by claiming, "Our ancestors are Chinese, mine included. So of course, we are influenced by Chinese traditions. But our ancestors are also Muslims, so we try to follow Islamic traditions."[54] Often respondents carefully distinguished this language of the Qur'an, which they viewed as the language tied to Hui cultural heritage, from modern standard Arabic (Alaboyu). A teacher at Yinchuan's Jing Xueyuan (Qur'anic Studies Institute) in his early thirties remarked that due to the importance of religious ritual, "almost every Hui can speak a little Arabic."[55] As such, he reasoned, it was the closest thing the Hui had to a "minority language."

However, one imam in Beijing clarified, "The Arabic we have isn't modern, conversational Arabic. It's Qur'anic Arabic."[56] Some respondents suggested that their primary vehicle for learning about Hui culture came through their studies of rudimentary Arabic language as a part of mosque school education.[57] A man in his early thirties from the Hui stronghold of Linxia who moved to nearby Lanzhou reinforced the centrality of the language of faith to Hui culture: "Hui culture all revolves around Arabic." Explaining this further, he discussed the way in which learning *jingwen* served as a vehicle for transmission of cultural values: "In Linxia, culture is taught in two places: at home and in the mosque. At home, we only learn the basics about Islamic beliefs and tradition. But at the mosque we learn about our culture through studying *jingwen*."[58] Likewise, the teacher at the Jing Xueyuan in Yinchuan reasoned that language courses at the school provided young Hui with means for learning about the history and development of Hui identity.[59] For these respondents, engaging in the study of Arabic provided a vital lifeline to a distant cultural heritage and fabled foreign ancestors. To study *jingwen* was to study one's own heritage.

Mosques proudly highlighted the classes in Arabic language as part of their program of community service. For instance, a billboard inside the courtyard of Madian Mosque in central Beijing celebrated its tradition of sponsoring language education and cultural promotion. "Previously, Madian mosque was famous for its system of *jingtang jiaoyu*," the sign informed visitors. "Now, even though there are no longer khalifa [*halifa*, students studying to be clergy], there are still Muslim studies classes."[60] Some respondents spoke of the importance of learning the language in a mosque setting. One imam in Yinchuan in his mid-forties proclaimed, "It's necessary that an *ahong* teaches you." He explained that otherwise, students might not understand the deep connections between language and faith.[61] Thus, through *jingtang jiaoyu*, the mosque provides a space for passing down knowledge of Hui heritage, culture, and religious ritual alongside language instruction.

However, where the institution of *jingtang jiaoyu* weakens, respondents attested to feelings of cultural loss. One woman in her fifties who ran a small convenience store in Jinan's Hui Quarter lamented the loss of *jingtang jiaoyu* at the city's Great Southern Mosque. Though the mosque offered classes in Arabic in the mid-1990s, she recalled, it had long since stopped, and now the community had very few resources it could draw on to teach Hui values. She complained that, as a result, "kids [didn't] know how to be Hui."[62] That the loss of mosque education contributed to a decline in knowledge and understanding of Hui culture was a common refrain in interviews. Respondents across all four cities cited the closure of *jingtang jiaoyu* during the Cultural Revolution as a blow that irreparably harmed religious and cultural knowledge in Hui communities.[63] Only once the relatively tolerant policies on religion allowed for the resumption of classes—usually for children on their school holidays—after the first few years of Reform and Opening did the community begin to recover from the damage wrought by years of neglect.

"WHEN I SPEAK WITH HUI, WE OUGHT TO SPEAK HUIYAN": HUI DIALECT AND DAILY LANGUAGE USE

Though mosque education provides a space for Hui to engage with Arabic language, not all Hui are able to do so. For instance, one interviewee in Beijing, a cab driver in her fifties originally from Shijiazhuang, upon learning about my research exclaimed, "If you study Hui, then you surely must be able to speak *jingwen*?" She excitedly mentioned that she had only recently begun to study the language herself and felt obligated to use it when conversing with other Hui. She professed, "When I speak with Hui, we ought to speak Huiyan. Like, just now, when I spoke to that waiter in the *baimaozi*, I said *Anseliangmu alaikong* [the Chinese transliteration of *Al salamu 'alaykum*, or Peace be with you] to him."[64] Like the cab driver, many Hui undertake Arabic-language learning only later in life and instead speak various Hui dialects influenced by Arabic and Persian loanwords.

Local dialects provide linguistic markers of Hui identity as Han do not use such vocabulary. As one respondent in Lanzhou remarked, in the multiethnic religious environments of community mosques, "language is how you can tell if someone is Hui, Bao'an, Salar, or Dongxiang."[65] However, as many respondents explained, these dialects resulted from the mixture of loanwords from various languages—Arabic, Turkic, and Persian—blending with regional dialects. The owner of a small electrical appliance store in Yinchuan explained how that city's Hui dialect incorporated expressions derived from Arabic words: "For example, we won't talk about how someone 'passed away' [*qushi*]. We don't say the word *si* [death] because it's not respectful to the deceased. Instead, we use Arabic words for this."[66] A Xining businesswoman in her late thirties explained, "You can hear it. It's all Qinghai dialect, but if a group of people from Qinghai are talking, you'll know it just from talking. It's all the same language, but there are a few pronunciations that will allow you to hear you're a Hui, he's a Han. It's really pretty clear."[67] However, these dialects remained purely local; no unified Huihua existed. Rather, each community possessed a distinct local Hui dialect. The imam at Madian in Beijing reasoned, "In China, every place has their own local dialect [*difanghua*], and so every place has their own Jinghanyu [Islamic Chinese dialect], and they're all spoken differently. This makes it easier for people to understand and learn, but it also means that there are different pronunciations. Beijingers have Beijing Jinghanyu, and people from Hebei have their own."[68]

A display placard in a Xining museum described the particular features of a localized Huihua this way: "Qinghai Hui usually use Chinese, specifically Qinghai dialect. Within the *minzu* and in religious life, we preserve the use of Arabic and Persian vocabulary."[69] Nearby, a wall-size government-issued poster outside an elementary school on the north end of Ledu Lu adjacent to the Dongguan Mosque elaborated on the features of this Huihua. While the poster fell short of labeling these linguistic differences a "dialect," it highlighted the distinction between word usage in Hui and Han communities. In particular, it described how the Hui's observance of Islamic customs led them to favor certain words and avoid others, especially in regard to matters of eating and diet: "With regard to language, when speaking about food like poultry and livestock [Hui] avoid saying *fei* [fatty] and instead say *zhuang* [robust/strong]. They avoid saying *sha* [kill] and instead say *zai* [slaughter]. They avoid saying *rou* [meat] and instead say *cai* [dish] for example *niu cai* [beef dish] and *yang cai* [lamb dish]."[70]

However, Huihua differs from community to community, reflecting their different histories. An official, originally from Lanzhou, who worked at the Chinese Islamic Association in Beijing illustrated these differences by comparing the way imams in different communities pronounced the Qur'an. He claimed, "Beijingers have their own recitation of the Qur'an which sounds like Beijing Opera [*jingju*]. In the northwest, we're more influenced by Saudi Arabia. When you go there, you'll see. You can hear it."[71] In his estimation, unlike Beijingers, for whom assimilation had contributed to a distortion of the original language, Hui from the northwest recited the Qur'an faithfully, in a more accurate Arabic pronunciation.

Elsewhere, in Jinan, respondents noted that the local Huihua borrows more heavily from Persian and medieval Turkic languages than in other communities. A Jinan Hui scholar in his seventies explained that the large number of Persian and Turkic Muslims that originally founded the city's Islamic community strongly influenced the localized Huihua, which borrowed numerous loanwords from these languages more than from Arabic.[72] Another respondent cited the Jinan Huihua word *digaizi* (a term for non-Muslims) as an example of a loanword, claiming that it derived from *digr*, a word of Persian origin.[73] He noted that this word was one he heard used only by elderly Hui, and that younger Hui rarely used such vocabulary.[74] Despite the decline in usage of Persian or Turkic loanwords, the scholar maintained that the influence of these early Muslims could still be seen in local Hui surnames. As examples, he cited Ma (from Muhammad) and Fa (from Fathallah/Fethullah) as common local Hui names with Arabic and Turkic origins.[75]

"MUSLIMS NEED TO KNOW ARABIC TO PRAY": (IL)LITERACY AND IDENTITY IN HUI COMMUNITIES

The gap between the prominence of the Arabic in official displays and the ability of residents to comprehend the meaning of these words illustrates an important dilemma: while Arabic language is important to the practice of Islam and strongly associated with Hui identity, few Hui are able to speak or read it. Indeed, for many Hui this connection to Arabic seems no more than vestigial. Respondents claimed that the extent of their ability to speak Arabic was to recite the *shahada*.[76] An engineer in his early fifties in Jinan remarked that the Hui had gone through a high degree of linguistic assimilation due to association with Han Chinese. "Of course, the Hui aren't a Chinese nationality," he reasoned, "but they've been influenced to a really large degree by the Han, and they speak Hanyu [Chinese language]. So currently, I certainly can't speak Arabic."[77] Particularly among secular Hui, responses like this were common. Though their Muslim ancestors may have relied on Arabic to worship, those who did not regularly attend mosque saw little use in learning the language.

A number of respondents noted that some clergy may not fully understand *jingwen* even when they have learned to recite it.[78] For example, an *ahong* in his forties at a prominent mosque in Yinchuan remarked that his experience learning Arabic language was typical of many who became imams in rural communities. Rather than study Arabic formally in school, most of his education came from studying with imams in country mosques near Guyuan. Thus, he memorized the Arabic of the Qur'an and the hadith, but his understanding of the language was constrained by this context. The shopkeeper of an Islamic goods store in Yinchuan explained the consequences of this informal, rural education: "*Ahong* don't necessarily speak Arabic. They can recite from the Qur'an, but they can't use Arabic to communicate."[79] As such, being able to pronounce and read Arabic matters not for communicative purposes, so much as it does for signaling that the speaker has not been completely Sinicized, unlike more secular Hui.

In communities that lack minority autonomous status, gaining access to Arabic language requires pursuing alternative paths. Young men may choose to take up full-time formal study with an *ahong* at a mosque with the intent of becoming clergy. In these classrooms, students study the Qur'an and hadith from textbooks filled with bilingual commentary and learn to read and write Arabic. However, choosing this type of study comes at the cost of other education. In the town of Weizhou in Tongxin County outside of Yinchuan, these young *halifa* rose before sunrise to study at a local mosque before 6:00 prayers. The young men studied this Qur'anic curriculum all day in place of other schooling.

In recent years, the CCP has enacted further limitations on this type of education. A fifty-six-year-old professor of history in Yinchuan described some of the legal restrictions that made formal study of Arabic difficult for most Hui: "The government has rules and limitations. Mostly you're not allowed to attend mosque education until you're eighteen."[80] In some cases, private institutions provide education that skirts these obstacles. At the Islamic school for girls founded by a wealthy local woman in Weizhou, students study the Qur'an and Arabic language alongside the standard curriculum.[81] Schools like these may provide the basis for learning Arabic but suffer from lack of resources.

Opportunities to study at private institutions are rare, and increased restrictions and oversight on religious education present even greater obstacles. Since the conclusion of my fieldwork in 2016, government bans on Qur'anic study at mosques limited already scarce language-learning resources.[82] Even before such impositions, however, many respondents cited the lack of educational opportunities and resources for learning Arabic as a reason for illiteracy in Hui communities. The loss of local institutions dedicated to the promotion of Arabic language and Qur'anic study, like mosque schools devoted to *jingtang jiaoyu*, hindered the ability of residents to pass down Huihua. Only a handful of cities possess such institutions. For example, in Yinchuan, the city's status as the capital of a Hui autonomous region opens avenues to formal study of Arabic language that may not be possible elsewhere. The Ningxia Hui Autonomous Region's Jing Xueyuan affords college-age students the opportunity to study a Qur'anic curriculum and, by extension, the Arabic language, in a formal, degree-granting setting.[83] However, even with institutions like the Jing Xueyuan, residents of Yinchuan noted the paucity of options for language learning in public schools. An imam in Yinchuan remarked, "There aren't really many places to learn Arabic. Ningxia University has an Arabic department, and there's the Jing Xueyuan, but there aren't really that many options."[84] Those who do elect to study Arabic at a university level may do so only in a program designed for those going into the field of international business and finance.

Xining provides a more successful picture of how informal Arabic classes affect a community. A professor in his fifties remarked that unlike other provinces, Qinghai did not place legal restrictions on Arabic-language classes, and as a result these classes flourished in Xining.[85] The city's prominent Dongguan Mosque offered daily classes in Arabic, which draw large crowds that fill classrooms and spill out into the surrounding courtyard (see figure 3.1). The classes, which occur just prior to the start of the midday *zuhr* prayer, consisted of mostly retired men repeatedly echoing a single instructor as he pronounced the sounds of Arabic letters. As he spoke, he pointed to the words written on a chalkboard. On some days, when instructing upper-level classes, the instructor taught larger passages of the Qur'an. He intoned phrases like *bismillāhi r-raḥmāni r-raḥīm* (In the name of God the most gracious, the most merciful) a line at a time in sing-songy Arabic, encouraging students to repeat after him.[86] One retiree who attended these classes remarked that while they primarily catered to seniors, young people attended as well, though the classes generally served a wide range of the community.[87] As a tour guide at Dongguan Mosque explained, the classes were deemed necessary for the basic observance of faith: "We have this class because Muslims need to know Arabic to pray."[88] For pious Hui like the guide, speaking and reading Arabic is a definitive marker of Hui identity because it forms an integral part of the practice of faith. To traditionalist believers, without proper Arabic language the Hui will lose the very core of their identity: their observance of Islam.

Elsewhere fewer options to study Arabic exist. In Jinan respondents noted that, though a school in the Hui Quarter called itself the Hui Elementary School (Huimin Xiaoxue), it offered no classes in Arabic or Qur'anic education.[89] A retired volunteer worker at the offices of the Jinan Islamic Association explained that the city had a small Qur'anic school that was founded in 1984 and attached to the Great Southern Mosque to coincide with its reopening after being shuttered for over a decade during the Cultural

FIGURE 3.1. Men study at an adult Arabic-language class in the courtyard of the Dongguan Mosque in Xining.

Revolution. However, recently the school was suddenly closed and had not reopened.[90] Aside from mosques in the community offering a few informal weekly classes, the neighborhood provided few ways for residents to study Arabic. A woman who served as one of the *ahong* at the women's mosque explained that one of her responsibilities as a leader at the mosque was to run informal Qur'anic study groups. These classes, she told me, not only served the purpose of commenting on the Qur'an but also provided lessons on the basics of Arabic language and learning about government policies on religion and ethnic minorities.[91] However, these classes were sparsely attended. One imam in the neighborhood complained that, of late, young people showed little interest in learning, causing the age of attendees to increase and the size of classes to dwindle.[92]

Accordingly, for many Hui, Arabic has become a language of business rather than faith. Most young people who study Modern Standard Arabic do so in order to work for companies doing trade in the Middle East, usually serving as translators or intermediaries for Arab partners. Even in Yinchuan, the incentives for engaging in Arabic study have changed. A teacher at Yinchuan's Jing Xueyuan explained, "The purpose of the school is to train imams, but we also have students who become translators and do other jobs." Due to a surplus of students trained as imams, the teacher remarked, it was unlikely that all students would find gainful employment as clergy: "Only about ten to twenty-five percent of students become imams. Why? Because Ningxia has four thousand mosques and over eight thousand imams. So imams are numerous but mosques are not. Many graduates wouldn't be able to find a job at a mosque. So yes, there are some students whose fathers were imams and so they feel like they also have to become imams. But most students will try to find work as translators or doing business because it's easier to find [that kind of] work."[93] The teacher's remarks illustrate that students undertaking formal study of Arabic increasingly do so for economic reasons. In part due to the increased focus on economic and political outreach to majority-Muslim countries as part of the Belt and Road Initiative, students now elect to learn Arabic in order to take jobs in global finance or trade.[94] As a result, Hui draw distinctions between contemporary Arabic for the purposes of doing business with Arab states and *jingwen*.

Just as the ability to speak and read *jingwen* has declined across communities, residents across all case sites expressed concerns about the decline of localized Huihua. As changes in urban landscapes reconfigured Hui neighborhoods and dispersed concentrated Hui populations, concerns arose among residents about the preservation of these Hui dialects. A twenty-nine-year-old publisher in Beijing explained, with a tinge of regret, "It's like this. We Hui don't have our own language. What Hui use, what we speak in our daily lives, some words are from ancient Persian. Some words we use in our religion come from Arabic. So, in the midst of our lives, of course maybe we're able to use some of these words, but the majority of them we're unable to use. The people who really grasp Arabic, they're all about sixty years old, and they all have ties to Qur'anic language."[95] The man's discouragement about the loss of Persian and Arabic loanwords reflects a greater fear about the blow that losing distinctive local Hui dialects might deal to Hui identity writ large. As the daily use of specialized Hui vocabulary waned, only a few elderly community members were able to maintain connections to the Hui's linguistic, cultural, and linguistic heritage.

In another example, the Madian neighborhood in north-central Beijing was once a deep pocket of Hui culture. Residents reported, however, that the redevelopment of the neighborhood in the 1950s and again in the 1990s led to dispersal of the original residents and precipitated a decline in usage of the local Hui patterns of speech. An imam at the mosque in the neighborhood lamented, "Here at Madian, we had our own Hui dialect. It used Arabic words and Chinese words. But now, there's nobody who can speak Huihua. It's already been lost."[96] In the Chaoyang neighborhood of Beijing, during an interview with the owner of a *lamian* restaurant who had moved to the city from the Zhangjiachuan Hui Autonomous County in Tianshui City of Gansu, the owner's teenage son who was sitting in interjected that the local dialect, Tianshuihua, contained a number of words derived from Arabic. He admitted, however, that unlike the older people in the community, he knew only a handful of phrases in the dialect.[97]

That young Hui no longer use the Persian- and Arabic-tinged Huihua spoken by elders is one way in which language concerns activate age cleavages in the community. Younger Hui are educated primarily in standard Mandarin in secular schools; with reduced opportunity to study Qur'anic Arabic, they view proficiency in that language as a skill primarily possessed by the clergy and the elderly. Especially in communities where opportunities for mosque education are scant, older Hui express concern that younger generations lack the resources and the will to learn Arabic and local religious vocabularies. As such, some older Hui despair that younger generations lack an understanding of how to be truly Hui.

"THERE ARE A LOT OF PEOPLE WHO THINK WE SHOULDN'T STUDY CHINESE": LANGUAGE USE AND HUI IDENTITY CONTESTATION

The success of classes like those at the Dongguan Mosque and the scarcity of Arabic-education resources in cities like Jinan, reinforce the commonly expressed notion that Hui from the northwest, particularly those from rural villages, are more competent in reading the Qur'an in Arabic are thus more devoted to the faith. One thirty-two-year-old man Beijing who had moved to the city from Harbin highlighted the language difference between east and west. He argued that, unlike Hui in his northeastern hometown, "these Hui, which is to say those from places like Xibei, Yunnan, and Xinjiang, can read a little bit more. Also, they start to study at an earlier age than we do."[98] In Jinan, an imam at one of the Hui Quarter's mosques echoed these sentiments, estimating that fewer than 5 percent of the people who attended his mosque had any competency in Arabic.[99]

Respondents painted a very different picture of the status of *jingwen* in the northwest. They commonly cited the availability of methods to learn the language outside of publicly provided classes as one of the major differences between eastern and western Hui communities. Noting the differences in Arabic proficiency between cities and rural villages, a history professor in Yinchuan pointed out, "In the countryside almost every mosque will have a class that teaches young students." An imam in a mosque in the rural suburbs of Jinan contrasted the habits of young students in the northwest with those in his community: "In the northwest, they spend a lot more time studying Arabic. Over school vacations and holidays, they'll go to the mosque like regular school."[100]

Despite these perceived differences in Arabic proficiency, respondents across all locations admitted that, even if they could read Arabic letters, they could not understand the words they formed.[101] As such, comprehending the meaning of the text mattered less to Hui that the ability to recite it in a "more accurate" pronunciation, without the aid of Chinese characters. Thus, many of the divisions that arose concerning use of language in Hui communities concerned the appropriateness of using Chinese characters to aid in pronunciation of Arabic texts. Those urban Hui, particularly those in eastern China, said they recited the Qur'an using Chinese characters to approximate the sounds of Arabic words (see figure 3.2).[102]

One eighteen-year-old college student from Shanxi studying at a university in Jinan described this system: "[In my hometown] our Qur'ans all have Chinese characters beside the Arabic, but I've forgotten all the Arabic I learned when I was young. When I memorized [the Qur'an] I just memorized the Chinese characters."[103] A retiree from Tai'an, near Jinan, described how, in her youth, she learned how to recite Arabic phrases using Chinese to approximate the sounds: "I've forgotten how to say the *qingzhen yan*, but when I was young, I could recite it all. But what I recited was the Chinese style, and the pronunciation was different."[104]

While learning to recite the Qur'an through such a different means of pronunciation and study may ease the process of learning about faith for some Hui, others scorn the method. More conservative Hui often viewed this use of Chinese characters as a language aid as a marker of assimilation

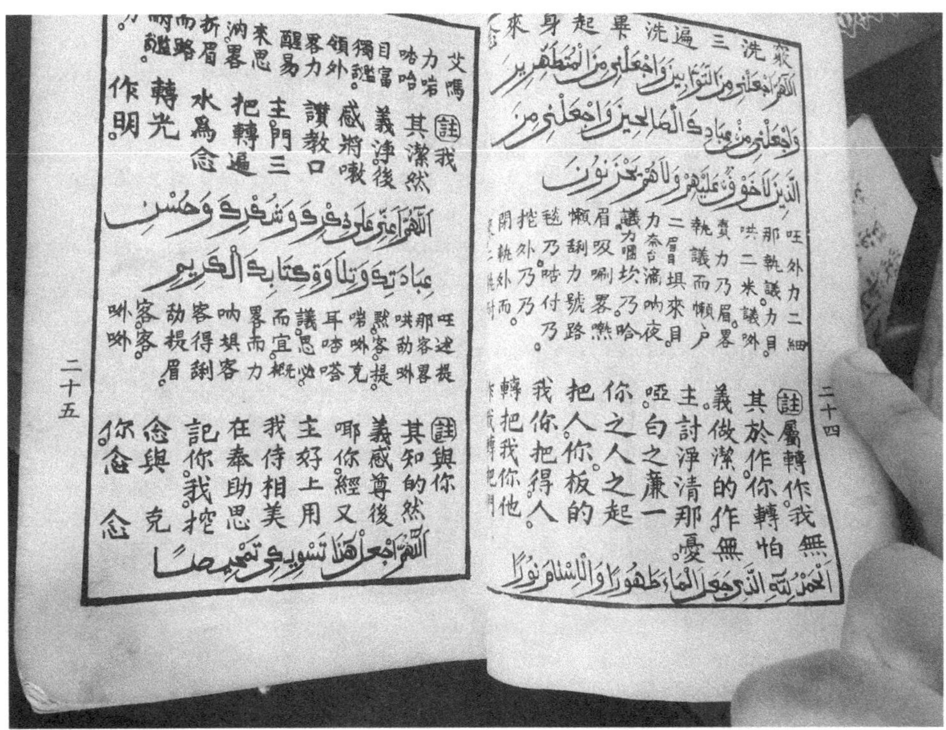

FIGURE 3.2. Qur'an with alternating Chinese and Arabic. Hualong Hui Autonomous County, Qinghai.

or insufficient commitment to Islamic heritage. For the more devout, often more rural Hui, the use of Chinese to read the Qur'an signaled secularization and Hanification (expressed as *danhua*, or Hanhua). A forty-eight-year-old teacher in Xining who was born in the nearby town of Huangyuan to a Salar father and Hui mother stated that many northwestern Hui "refuse to read the Chinese version of the Qur'an." When asked why, he replied, "There are a lot of people who think we shouldn't study Chinese, that it's just the rubbish language that's left over from a heathen religion. So it's possible that this attitude can create some problems."[105] As these rural Hui migrate to cities seeking work, they express frustration with their urban co-ethnics' lack of Arabic proficiency. An eighteen-year-old migrant from rural Qinghai, recently arrived in Jinan, cited this as one of many reasons the city's level of Islamic observance fell short of matching his hometown's.[106]

While religiously devout, rural Hui who migrate to urban spaces look at their dedication to learning Arabic as a mark of superior devotion to faith and evidence of a purer expression of Hui identity, secular, urban Hui, particularly those in eastern China, view this commitment less favorably. In Jinan, many longtime residents of the Hui Quarter described recent migrants from Qinghai and Gansu as unwilling to allow their children to study Chinese. Pointing to a difference in attitude between local Hui and recently arrived Hui who came to Jinan to open noodle shops, one shop owner maintained, "Many of the people who sell *lamian* can speak Arabic. That's because of how things are different in the northwest. There they teach their kids how to read and speak Arabic from a very young age. They forbid them to read and write in Chinese characters because they only want them to use Arabic."[107] Another longtime Jinan resident, a thirty-six-year-old factory worker, echoed these observations about the perceived difference between Jinan and the northwest. He remarked, "They [northwestern Hui] oppose everything to do with the Han, including using Chinese characters, and so they don't let their children study Chinese. There was a period of time, before Liberation [*jiefang*, the end of the Chinese Civil War in 1949], when the attitude was to not allow study of Chinese characters."[108] Though such statements were largely rooted in hearsay, Jinanese Hui internalized these cleavages that juxtaposed a supposedly more pious group of Hui from the northwest with their own perceived laxity in embracing their identity, as evidenced by a lack of proficiency in Qur'anic Arabic.

Increasingly, the prioritization of learning Islam over more standard education has come to be seen as a choice made by rural Hui who lack other educational opportunities. Children who struggle in the public school system may be channeled into mosque education when other career options have failed. A retiree in his sixties from Xining explained, "Some parents who have children don't do that well in school may send their kids to study the Qur'an. Mostly they go to Yinchuan or to Linxia to study where there are more formal schools. But if the kids do well in school, then parents encourage them to go to college to keep learning."[109] Linxia in southern Gansu, long a Hui stronghold and the birthplace of numerous Sufi orders and Muslim saints, attracts numerous northwestern Hui seeking religious education. With its plentiful resources, including Islamic bookstores and numerous mosques, the city functions as an intellectual hub for religiously observant Hui.[110]

However, negative stereotypes follow those that travel to Linxia or elsewhere to pursue Islamic education. Indeed, popular perceptions of those who elect to pursue a course of religious study frequently emphasize their failing public schools. Urban Hui tended to look at those Hui educated in rural mosques who had Arabic literacy but less formal education in Chinese as lacking the intellectual capability to succeed in other paths. Secular

Jinanese Hui looked down on recently arrived migrants, regarding their lower socioeconomic status and level of education as indicative of their being religious fundamentalists or rural bumpkins. In response to such perceived educational deficits of *jingtang jiaoyu*, one imam in Xining said he made special efforts in teaching the mosque's *manla* to ensure they were functionally literate in Chinese as well as in Arabic. He emphasized, "Of course we teach them Arabic and how to read the Qur'an. But there are also other subjects. Teaching them Chinese is also important."[111]

LANGUAGE AND THE INTERNAL BOUNDARIES OF HUINESS

These divisions over whether or not reading the Qur'an in Chinese is acceptable and whether or not teaching children to be literate only in Arabic is backward are illustrative of the ways in which language draws internal distinctions between Hui. Respondents' remarks frequently highlighted regional and sectarian differences based on language use. Residents in Jinan and other eastern cities repeatedly cited proficiency in reading and pronouncing *jingwen* as a marker that set migrant Hui apart from locals. Likewise, Hui from more conservative Islamic traditions disparaged those who used Chinese to read and recite the Qur'an as practicing syncretistic or degraded Islam that belied their Hanification. Many such judgments also displayed inherent reflections on social class. Migrants who prioritized study of the Qur'an in Arabic often were characterized as economically and socially backward by those more secular Hui who placed less importance on such matters. These judgments reflected not only attitudes about religious and regional matters but also inherent judgments about educational and economic status. Thus, the subject of what should be considered proper language use begets a multiplicity of expressions of Huiness. Despite the state's attempts to promote and standardize minority languages, disparities in the availability of Arabic-language-learning resources across China and economic incentives to educate children in a state-sponsored compulsory curriculum rather than through *jingtang jiaoyu* have renewed contestation over the boundaries and content of Hui identity.

In cities like Xining, where the Hui are one of many different Islamic minority groups, including small communities of Salar and Dongxiang, these questions may be bracketed into debates about Islamic piety and sectarian difference. In cities like Jinan, however, these differences may be equally as salient as those between Hui and the majority Han.

Whether or not Hui should consider Arabic a mother tongue and whether Hui should prioritize learning spoken and written Qur'anic Arabic form important internal distinctions among Hui. As Hui migrate from the countryside to the city, interaction between Hui from different regions and social environments activates a number of cross-cutting cleavages and ultimately draws internal boundary lines within the Hui community. Associating Arabic-language competency with lower literacy in Chinese and lower social status overlays the issue with class distinctions and activates economic cleavages. Attributing proper Arabic pronunciation to the superiority of one Islamic school over another activates sectarian cleavages. In overlapping these notions about the necessity for Hui to speak Arabic or the acceptability of speaking a Chinese-Arabic pidgin with cross-cutting cleavages that precipitate judgments about level of education, social class, or religiosity, Hui increase the salience of internal rather than external boundaries.

Internal migration increases contact between these disparate groups of Hui, and interaction between them brings these internal divisions concerning language into sharper relief. By highlighting differences in attitudes about the position of Arabic in Hui identity, the CCP's attempts to use language to promote integration and standardization achieve the opposite. Rather than smoothing over linguistic differences, these policies increase contestation and create divisions concerning everyday language use.

CHAPTER FOUR

CONSUMING

Islamic Purity and Dietary Habits

Real *qingzhen* restaurants use only clean ingredients.

—A TWENTY-SIX-YEAR-OLD HUI HOTEL RECEPTIONIST, XINING

ACROSS THE TABLE AT TONGXIN CHUN, THE FAMOUS ISLAMIC RESTaurant in Yinchuan, my interviewee, the twenty-something son of the owner, took drags of his cigarette as he told me about his understanding of a *qingzhen* lifestyle. As the table's automated lazy Susan whirred around, laden with numerous local delicacies made with mutton and beef, he said, "In a lot of Huis' understanding, it's just not eating pork that makes them Hui. In Yinchuan there are a lot of Hui like that. 'I'm Hui, so I don't eat pork.' But if you ask them 'What about God? What about speaking Arabic? What about praying?' They won't understand. What about fasting for Ramadan? They don't understand. They only understand 'I don't eat pork, so therefore I'm Hui.'"[1]

Throughout my fieldwork, many respondents echoed these sentiments explicitly linking Hui identity to the observation of *qingzhen* dietary codes. In their view, a strict observance of *qingzhen* served as the primary connection to their ethnic identity. A Hui adjunct professor in Jinan remarked, for instance, "What I understand about being Hui, in terms of Islam, is that the most important thing is to not eat pork. Besides that, I really don't know much."[2]

The strength of the Islamic taboo on pork and alcohol and the visibility of *qingzhen* branding in Hui communities makes the observance of a proper halal diet one of the most noticeable features of Hui identity. The practice of buying *qingzhen* foodstuffs and eating at *qingzhen* restaurants is not just an act of religious observation but a means of ethnic differentiation. The Hui prohibition on eating ritually unclean items stands in especially stark contrast to the majority Han, who observe few, if any, dietary restrictions.[3] Accordingly, the Chinese state seeks to promote and control the *qingzhen* food industry in order to showcase ethnic diversity and celebrate displays of ethnic differentiation that accord with its narrative of ethnic unity. Doing so allows the state to cast the development of the halal food industry as yet another benchmark in the state's quest for inclusivity and progress.

However, inattention to the actual substance of creating a standardized *qingzhen* food certification process undercuts the state's efforts to solidify and control the discourse over the form and expression of a *qingzhen* lifestyle. Instead, the lack of clear standards concerning *qingzhen* food opens up space for contestation of Hui identity and drawing of internal boundary lines. Hui from different regions, socioeconomic statuses, and levels of religiosity question how to properly observe and maintain a *qingzhen* diet and, by extension, Hui identity itself. Questions about whether Hui should consume alcohol or smoke while observing a *qingzhen* lifestyle, or if these practices should instead be considered haram (forbidden by Islamic law), divide Hui. While some respondents insisted that real Hui would fastidiously observe Qur'anic restrictions on diet, others were laxer. For instance, a teacher in Jinan in her late twenties, when asked what it meant to keep a *qingzhen* diet, shrugged and told me that she simply avoided eating pork and nothing more.[4] The strictness of one's observance of these dietary codes serves as a measuring stick for the strength of one's identity, with more strict adherents labeling lenient observers as *danhua*, or diminished as Hui.

ETHNICITY AND EATING: DIETARY PRACTICES AND BOUNDARY MAINTENANCE

The power of food consumption to create distinct boundaries between self and other is especially strong in situations where religious faith makes impositions on dietary routines. Islam's taboos on a number of ingredients, especially pork and alcohol, serve as bright and clear dividing lines between those who belong to the faith and those who do not. In Islam, cleanliness provides a foundation for belief and is regarded as "half of faith." Thus, practicing Muslims regard maintaining a halal diet as not only a practical matter but also a means of ensuring a greater sense of spiritual purity.[5] Consuming halal food serves as a clear marker of Islamic identity. Though the incredible breadth of items that may be considered halal limits entrepreneurs' ability to establish it as a coherent brand, consumers treat halal as a brand that vouches for the quality, safety, and appropriateness of a product, especially in those Muslim communities surrounded by non-Muslims.[6]

Keeping a halal diet is a practice of consumption that requires the purchaser's attention to specific qualities of the food, but also an act of ritual and devotion to the faith. Employing separate means of preparing and consuming food so as to avoid contaminating or making other items ritually "unclean" causes strong ideas of division between self and other to take root. The distinction between haram and halal "divides up the world for Muslims and relates to practically everything imaginable."[7] For instance, despite the fact that many Hui consume alcohol, jurisprudence in all Sunni schools of law unequivocally forbids drinking, regarding alcohol as impure (*najasa*) and considering anything it touches as contaminated.[8] However, despite the seemingly binary nature of halal and haram, gray areas exist. Any number of items, including tobacco and shellfish, fall somewhere between the two ends of the spectrum.[9]

EATING "PURE" AND "TRUE": HUI IDENTITY AND THE CENTRALITY OF *QINGZHEN* FOOD

In Hui communities the concept of *qingzhen* lies at the heart of debates concerning diet and identity. Though the term is frequently translated as "halal," and Hui often use the terms *qingzhen* and *halal* (*halali*) interchangeably, some scholarly discussions draw distinctions between them. Several studies employ the more literal "pure and true" to define *qingzhen* in a way that encompasses more than just dietary codes and describes a more complete lifestyle.[10] Gillette contends that to Hui respondents in Xi'an, *qingzhen* "transcended simple dietary restrictions" to govern matters such as how to prepare food, whom to share social spaces with, how to interact during business transactions, and how to conduct religious rituals.[11] As such it became a clear means of distinguishing Hui from others. Gladney interprets *qingzhen* as a framework that orders the moral universe and governs the lives of believers. Viewed this way, *qingzhen* is better understood as ritual and moral purity and authenticity that dictates how Hui should eat, pray, marry, trace their descent, and live their daily lives.[12]

In daily usage, however, the term usually refers to dietary matters and implies that food is permissible for Muslims to eat, due to either the ingredients used or the manner of food preparation. Starting in the early 2000s, as a result of extensive promotion by both local governments and Hui entrepreneurs, *qingzhen* became a byword for halal. In seeking to promote *qingzhen* as an international halal brand, these actors solidified the word's associations with food preparation, establishing it as an easily replicable, recognizable signifier.[13] In fact, the connections between halal and *qingzhen* run deeply enough that some companies vending *qingzhen* items attempt to harness the associations between the words to educate non-Hui consumers via their marketing and e-commerce and other online platforms.[14] As a consequence of these sustained marketing efforts, *qingzhen* has become a category of food on par with other regional styles, such as Sichuanese and Hunanese. Hui frequently contrast *qingzhen* with *Hancan* (Han food).

However, as a practical matter, very little consensus exists around what should be considered *qingzhen* and what must be avoided. Despite its regular use as a signifier of food that is safe for Muslims to eat, some non-Hui Muslims—especially Uyghurs—regard the designation of *qingzhen* with skepticism due to this unevenness of standards.[15] Even Hui disagree about basic aspects of observance. Respondents I spoke with differed over whether simply avoiding pork sufficed for maintaining *qingzhen*, or if proper observance required eating only food blessed by an *ahong*. Questions about whether alcohol and cigarettes count as *qingzhen* divide Hui.

Given that dietary restrictions play such a central role in the daily lives of Hui communities, the relationship between mosque and marketplace is usually close. In China's largest cities, small businesses and restaurants catering to Hui clientele frequently adjoin or surround community mosques and provide local Muslims with everything needed to maintain a strictly halal community.[16] In Xining's Chengdong District, behind the famous Dongguan Mosque in a narrow alleyway appropriately named Qingzhen Alley (Qingzhen Xiang), vendors sell fresh produce, *qingzhen* meat, fried street snacks, and other Islamic sundries out of small, tented stalls or from flatbed carts attached to the back of pedal bikes.[17] Removed from these mosque- and market-centered communities, Hui identity wanes. Many urban Hui living outside of concentrated Hui enclaves complained about the arduousness of maintaining a *qingzhen* diet while residing in predominantly Han neighborhoods. One longtime resident of Beijing's Dongcheng District in his seventies lamented that being distant from a predominantly Hui community made even simple acts like buying groceries difficult. "On Niu Jie it's easy to eat *qingzhen*," he opined. "You can close your eyes and eat anything and not worry. It's all clean and healthy. In this neighborhood its difficult. There aren't places to buy beef or mutton. There aren't *qingzhen* restaurants."[18]

Before the enactment of de-Islamification policies in many Hui communities at the start of 2018, Hui entrepreneurs created a cottage industry surrounding the purveyance of halal food.[19] Signs for *qingzhen* restaurants frequently used green and white or yellow (colors associated with Islam) and contained symbols related to Islam: stars and crescent moons, the silhouettes of Arabesque domes, and minarets. These signs were nearly always emblazoned with the word *qingzhen*, often placed alongside Arabic script that read *halal*.[20]

Popular understandings of the meaning of *qingzhen* reflect the triumph of ethnic branding campaigns. *Qingzhen* has become a byword in connection with quality and cleanliness. In recent years, scandals concerning consumption of tainted milk, food cooked in previously used cooking oil (known colloquially as "gutter oil," *digou you*), and cheap or unpalatable cuts of meat altered by chemicals and sold as premium cuts, created increased attention throughout China to food safety and cleanliness.[21] Several respondents claimed that eating a *qingzhen* diet allowed them a high degree of certainty in the safety and cleanliness of the product.[22] One woman interviewed in Jinan simply stated, "I think *qingzhen* food just is clean and pure."[23]

The association of *qingzhen* and purity is strong enough for some Hui respondents that they expressed sensations of physical discomfort when in the presence of non-*qingzhen* food. While walking through the Tongxin Lu meat and produce market in Yinchuan, a Hui professor remarked that the odor and sight of pork made him feel physically ill. "I know that this is all psychological, that it's all in my head, and that it's all through conditioning, but all the same I can't help it," he told me. "When I'm around pork, I get the feeling that I might throw up."[24] Such intense reactions to non-*qingzhen* for some Hui mean that the practice of eating only in *qingzhen* eateries or buying products exclusively from *qingzhen* markets arises not out of mere preference but out of necessity.

Even some Han attach associations of cleanliness to *qingzhen*. Niu Jie's reputation for butcher shops selling superior beef and lamb brought a middle-aged Han couple to the street from their northern suburb of Beijing, almost an hour and a half away. When asked what would justify such a long commute for grocery shopping, the man answered, "The people who live here on Niu Jie are all Muslim. They eat a lot of beef and mutton. So the beef and mutton here is very tasty [*haochi*] and safe to eat [*baozheng*]."[25] The belief in the superiority of *qingzhen* beef, even among Han customers, reflects the success of extensive efforts from both the CCP and Hui entrepereneurs to brand *qingzhen* products as an ethnic specialty product (*minzu techanpin*). The willingness of even Han to travel far for an ordinary and prevalent item indicates the pervasiveness of the association between quality and safety in the case of *qingzhen* food.

INTERNATIONAL EXPOS AND IMPOSTER *QINGZHEN*: STATE POLICY AND AMBIGUITY IN HALAL CERTIFICATION

The linkage between *qingzhen* food and Hui culture forms one of the most visible aspects of the government's attempts to present an official version of Hui identity. Many official displays of Hui culture showcase *qingzhen* food as a crucial element of the Hui community and celebrate the Hui's vibrant culinary traditions. Especially in northwest China, where Hui and other Muslim minorities are more numerous, local governments actively promote *qingzhen* food as an aspect of local culture. In part, the CCP achieves this objective by turning *qingzhen* items into a branded commodity that can be sold as "Hui specialties."

In Xining, the Qinghai provincial government went to great lengths to promote *qinghzen* foodstuffs and other goods during the annual Qinghai International Qingzhen Food and Ethnic Products Fair (Qinghai Guoji Qinghzen Shipin Jiminzu Yongpin Zhanlanhui). The carefully staged event broadcast an image of global interconnectedness, thriving commerce, and cutting-edge development. Signs posted outside the hall boldly displayed the motto for the event: "Innovation, Coordination, Greenness, Opening Up, Sharing" (*chuangxin, xiediao, lüse, kaifang, gongxiang*). The expo's main attraction, held in a hall the size of an airplane hangar, brought together vendors from eleven provinces throughout China, as well as thirteen foreign countries, including Pakistan, Turkmenistan, Malaysia, and Iran, selling everything from halal instant noodles to yak butter, hand-woven rugs, and intricate metalwork tea sets and statuettes. Elsewhere, individual counties of Qinghai erected booths and displayed their vision for future development efforts, including scale models of new convention centers, slick videos advertising new roads and highways, and other expressions of prosperity.[26]

In imbuing the *qingzhen* food industry with the sheen of prosperity and innovation and providing it a showcase, the provincial government painted a picture of inclusion in which minority culture and minority entrepreneurship are central to the province's development strategy. However, outside of these showy displays of support for *qingzhen* foods, the local government's commitment to developing standards for promoting the quality of *qingzhen* foodstuffs and eateries remains only superficial. Despite attempting to market *qingzhen* to consumers, the CCP makes very little effort to standardize the production of *qingzhen* goods or regulate their quality. Wavering quality occurs in part because no national standard exists for certification of *qingzhen* foods. The responsibility for policing and overseeing these industries falls to individual provinces, many of which implement their own certification processes. Though Ningxia pioneered an approach to *qingzhen* certification by publishing a written guide in 2010, and the five provinces of northwest China entered into a confederal agreement for certification in 2013, no single set of guidelines for certification exists on a national level.[27] The lack of a national oversight process results in uneven standards for halal food.[28]

The patchwork of regulations for food certification that results from the lack of a national standard offers opportunities for the state to consult and cooperate with local Hui communities in developing policy. Laws governing halal food and restaurant certification have been among the most prominent and successful examples of Muslim autonomous communities implementing Islamic law. *Qingzhen* certification laws were the only laws enacted by the government of Linxia Hui Autonomous County that found roots in the Qur'an. However, even though Islamic autonomous units such as the Ningxia Hui Autonomous Region possess some means of enacting law in accordance with Islamic law, these areas still face limitations.[29] While provinces often develop *qingzhen* certification standards through some form of collaboration with local Islamic associations, most certification processes were developed by bureaucrats in the state-run industries rather than religious experts.[30] As such, standards vary in their stringency of observation of Qur'anic standards.

In Yinchuan, for example, *qingzhen* restaurants are policed through a fairly standard system of certification and inspection. In order to display a *qingzhen* sign, restaurants must ensure that all food served in the restaurant has been purchased from *qingzhen* vendors, all kitchen staff preparing food are Hui, and at least half of the wait staff serving diners are Hui.[31] Vendors selling *qinghzen* meats must display certificates attesting to the authenticity of their products. These certificates list the name of the imam responsible for overseeing the slaughter of the animal and, in some instances, contain QR codes that patrons may scan with their phone in order to receive the imam's contact information.[32]

Elsewhere, however, a lack of similarly stringent enforcement may cause problems with authenticity. A rash of fake *qingzhen* products and poseur *qingzhen* restaurants plagues Hui communities and makes many Hui skeptical about the provenance of the food served there. These concerns are heightened as businesses relocate in the midst of urban renewal. Providers of *qingzhen* goods may be among those displaced as neighborhoods transform. With the dispersal of concentrated Hui communities, vendors may no longer find their businesses economically viable. As the physical spaces that define Hui neighborhoods change, so too must the consumer habits of residents living in these spaces. On Dikou Lu in Jinan, the renovation of the neighborhood's Hui community centralized a number of *qinghzen* butcher shops and restaurants. Whereas many of the vendors had been previously dispersed, the new market allowed for them to be concentrated in a single space. While this change made shopping easier for residents, it also brought in new vendors from outside the community.[33] Several interviewees told me that the influx of new restaurants and the opening of new market spaces like these came with a proliferation of impostor halal restaurants. A growing market for *qingzhen* goods, they explained, created opportunities for Han entrepreneurs to capitalize on the demand from the Muslim population.[34]

The proliferation of fake *qingzhen* eateries causes anxiety for Hui that they might unwittingly violate the dictates of their dietary code. With so many establishments posing as *qingzhen*, the likelihood of consuming improper or unclean food increases. A Hui shopkeeper in her mid fifties in Jinan's Hui Quarter explained that many of the neighborhood restaurants proclaiming to be *qingzhen* were actually run by Han. The problem, she noted, began with landlords seeking to help their tenants increase their profits. "A lot of landlords don't pay attention to who they rent to," she said. "They rent to a lot of Han. Their methods for preparing food are definitely not *qingzhen*, but these shops still put up signs that say *qingzhen*. The landlords give them these signs." When asked if the tenants would go as far as to put pork or other taboo items in their food, she replied, "They wouldn't dare do that. But they don't pay attention to whether or not their meat is properly *qingzhen*. And they also go home and eat pork and handle pork. This is unavoidable. But they come back to the restaurant afterward and so it's not properly *qingzhen*."[35] Even in Yinchuan, a respondent informed me, Han entrepreneurs may use forged documents or borrow a Hui friend's documentation to cheat the system and gain a *qingzhen* certification.[36]

Similarly, impostor restaurants may take advantage of the universality of *qingzhen* branding symbols to present products that appear to be certified *qingzhen*. At the new food court on Xining's Limeng pedestrian shopping street, *qingzhen* and non-*qingzhen* vendors occupy different floors but follow a similar color-coding scheme: green signs for *qingzhen*, red signs for non-*qingzhen*.[37] This kind of color-coded system recurs throughout China and usually allows patrons to easily identify *qingzhen* establishments. However, in some instances, slick entrepreneurs seek to take advantage of such strong color associations with food and use green for the signs on their own restaurants in hopes of luring diners who fail to notice the lack of a *qingzhen* certification. In Yinchuan, a forty-year-old Hui professor leading me on a tour of the market pointed to one such restaurant sign, green with red characters, advertising Hangzhou-style meat buns (*baozi*). "The people who run that restaurant are Han, but if you're not looking closely, it looks like a *qingzhen* restaurant," he observed.[38] Similarly in Xining, a Han butcher on the bustling Mojia Jie market street branded his store as vending "green meat products" (*lüse rou pin*), a common label on halal butcher shops. The shop, however, lacked a *qingzhen* label. When asked if the meat he sold was *qingzhen*, he admitted the sign was intended to convey that message. Further, he confessed that he selected the colors of the sign and the name of the shop to evoke *qingzhen* and Islamic dietary standards. In the end, he reasoned that, because his meat was slaughtered by local Hui, it was fundamentally the same as branded *qingzhen* meat. He explained why he could not label his store as *qingzhen*: "If we Han put out a sign that says *qingzhen* there would be Hui who would oppose it."[39]

The prominence of these impostor halal restaurants leads many devout Hui to express skepticism about the cleanliness of even supposedly *qingzhen* establishments. A twenty-one-year-old Hui butcher, originally from the nearby town of Wuzhong, working at the open-air market on Yuhuangge Bei Lu in Yinchuan explained that many Hui avoid even restaurants with halal signs: "There are a lot of *qingzhen* restaurants that we don't dare eat at. You go there and it's dark and the restaurants aren't necessarily that clean. Who'd dare to eat there?" When asked what made these ostensibly *qingzhen* eateries unfit for eating, he elaborated: "You know we Hui have strict dietary restrictions. You can't necessarily trust that the people working there are Muslims. Maybe the food isn't really *qingzhen*. A lot of Han open up *qingzhen* restaurants even though you're supposed to be Hui. A lot of Hui won't even go out to eat. Like my grandfather, who's eighty. He doesn't trust restaurants. He won't even agree to eat *lamian*. He doesn't eat outside of the house. A lot of Hui, when we travel, we carry our own pots and cooking gear." Asked to describe an acceptably clean and safe restaurant, the butcher named the family-run restaurant connected to his butcher shop. "You can go to our restaurant and see the difference," he insisted, adding, "Our restaurant is bright and clean, and everyone wears *baimaozi* or *shajin* [headscarf]. You can be sure it's *qingzhen*."[40] Given the ambiguities surrounding *qingzhen* certification, the young man sought other means of confirmation of purity relying on overt displays of Isalmic piety to serve as visual cues of a restaurant's standards of cleanliness.

This lack of oversight by some provincial governments and the high propensity for fraudulent *qingzhen* products compel some Hui ethnopreneurs into action, driving them to press for more thorough, more universal standards for certification of *qingzhen* products. In Xining, the Qinghai Qingzhen Food Production Association (Qinghai Qingzhen Shipin Hangye Shehui) seeks to resolve these ambiguities with the creation of an institutionalized standard for certification of foodstuffs. A representative from the Association, a visiting consultant from Malaysia, explained, "We want to create a standard that other places can follow. We want it to be a kind of brand that stands for halal." The consultant added, "People will see our certificate as a sign of quality, and the places that don't have them will fade away." Ultimately, the consultant remarked, the goal was to have the process become so widely accepted that the Association could petition to have it become adopted into national law, thus resolving any disputes about what is and is not certifiably *qingzhen*.[41]

THE BOUNDARIES OF BARBECUE: MARKET FORCES AND CONTESTATION OF QINGZHEN STANDARDS

Currently, the absence of a universal standard allows the definition of what is "necessary" or "proper" for the observance of a *qingzhen* diet to become the subject of internal contestation. Despite the centrality of *qingzhen* dining to the daily rhythms of Hui life, within the community different levels of religious observance and different notions about the very meaning of *qingzhen* spur internal debate.[42] Nowhere is this dilemma more pronounced than in debates about the sale of alcohol in halal establishments.[43] While the Qur'an prohibits the consumption of alcohol, provincial-level authorities in many provinces do not deem a prohibition on alcohol sales to be necessary for receiving *qingzhen* certification. As a result, the disjuncture between state policy and scriptural law causes renewed contestation regarding whether Hui should observe a taboo on alcohol.

In the absence of a definitive policy, market incentives may sway Hui merchants' decision about whether to sell or prohibit alcohol. Many conservative Hui view the sale of beer and liquor as a violation of the *qingzhen* dietary code. Strictly observant Hui treat this as disqualifying; if a restaurant elects to serve beer, it cannot truly be considered *qingzhen* because it is in violation of the laws of God. As a twenty-six-year-old receptionist at an Islamic hotel in Xining explained, "The only real *qingzhen* restaurants are the ones that forbid the sale of alcohol. Real *qingzhen* restaurants use only clean [*ganjing*] ingredients."[44] A forty-seven-year-old imam of a relatively large mosque in Yinchuan remarked that restaurants that sold liquor and claimed to be *qingzhen* "weren't truly halal restaurants." He told me that these types of restaurants "don't pay attention to *jiaofa* [religious doctrine, or *fiqh*]."[45] In rural Hui-majority communities, merchants realize that selling alcohol will lose them customers and money. In Weizhou, a small Hui-majority town in Tongxin County in rural Ningxia, a twenty-year-old student giving me a tour of the community remarked that previous merchants who attempted to open a liquor store found themselves quickly out of business due to lack of sales. Pious Weizhou citizens could not tolerate having such a presence in their community.[46] A university administrator in Xining echoed these sentiments in explaining why most *qingzhen* restaurants in that city refrained from selling alcohol: "If you served alcohol in a *qingzhen* restaurant it would be closed the next day because nobody would agree to come ever again."[47]

In response to demands for a dining experience that abides by strict Qur'anic interpretations of *qingzhen*, some entrepreneurs elect to embrace the prohibition on alcohol as a means of distinguishing their restaurant from the scores of competitors whose dietary cleanliness does not hold up. In so doing, these ethnopreneurs establish strict adherence to the guidelines as a brand associated with Hui identity. In Yinchuan, restaurants like the famous Tongxin Chun or the self-serve hotpot buffet on the top floor of Ningxia's Muslim Hotel choose to cater to Hui seeking a *qingzhen* meal without having to encounter alcohol, tapping into a niche market of devoutly religious diners.[48]

However, market demands may also encourage entrepreneurs to sell liquor. In Yinchuan and Jinan, most restaurants selling barbecue lamb kebabs also sell beer and *baijiu* (a Chinese liquor distilled from grain, very often sorghum). In this context choosing not to serve alcohol may put owners at a relative disadvantage. A thirty-five-year-old Yinchuan restaurateur who originally came from the predominantly Hui community of Wuzhong complained that he felt he had no choice but to serve alcohol in his restaurant. The space, which was connected to a large business hotel, served both Hui and Han patrons. He lamented that despite running a halal restaurant that served homestyle dishes from Wuzhong, he had to serve beer and *baijiu* in order to please his Han guests, though his personal reservations about the sale of alcohol made him hesitant to widely advertise this fact.[49] Another Hui restaurant owner who ran a traditional Hui restaurant adjacent to the Hui Culture Park in the Yinchuan suburb of Najiajhu noted that in the winter most of his clientele came from Yinchuan or nearby Yongning County to hold business lunches. These men, primarily Han, usually preferred to conduct business over beer or *baijiu*. Although he refused to sell alcohol, he was unable to stop guests from bringing their own bottles.[50] He regretted this practice he felt it was necessary to sustain his business.

Similarly in Jinan, demographic changes in the city's Hui Quarter affected the market for *qingzhen* food. Many longtime Jinan residents remarked that in the aftermath of the first wave of demolish-and-replace urban renewal in the early 1990s, the makeup of the neighborhood changed. Longtime local residents dispersed to live outside the quarter. In their place, newly arrived Hui from the northwest began to fill apartments in the neighborhood, opening up new restaurants and stores.[51] In particular, the arrival of restaurants and stalls selling lamb kebabs appealed to a wider customer base. One Jinanese Han respondent explained that the city's Hui and Han quickly adopted eating kebabs as a summer pastime, paired with a long-standing Shandong summer tradition of drinking local keg beer.[52] For most Jinanese residents, the Hui Quarter is synonymous with eating barbecue and drinking draft beer out of plastic kegs.[53]

Absent national regulations that provided definitive answers on points of contention such as the permissibility of the sale and consumption of alcohol, the standards for *qingzhen* developed heterogeneously, often in response to local market demand. While Hui entrepreneurs in cities like Xining have succeeded in creating a *qingzhen* brand that emphasizes strict adherence to Islamic guidelines, the market in Jinan dictates that prohibiting alcohol sales cuts against the economic interests of restaurateurs.

The tendency of some Hui to decry restaurants that serve alcohol as being inauthentically *qingzhen*, or as evidence that a community is Hanified, illustrates the degree to which the degree of religious observance, region, or social class creates internal boundaries within Hui communities. Despite the government's celebration of *qingzhen* food and its attempt to make it a unifying symbol of Hui culture, the lack of any clear standard for certification leaves matters of diet up for contestation and highlights the heterogeneity of Hui communities throughout China.

RECONTESTING *QINGZHEN* ONE BOWL AT A TIME

Food undoubtedly plays a pivotal role in marking the boundaries of Hui identity. The combined efforts of Hui entrepreneurs and the state turned *qingzhen* into an ethnic brand through strategic promotion. The prominence of *qingzhen* largely defines Hui culture and identity in the public sphere. For most Han and even some Hui, observing *qingzhen* dietary habits represents the defining feature of Hui ethnic identity. Symbolically *qingzhen* carries unmistakable connotations, about not just the sanitary and culinary quality of the food it describes but also the lifestyle of those who consume it. The symbolic power of *qingzhen* and the ease of its replicability as a brand provide ethnopreneurs with potentially lucrative opportunities to attach their business to the booming *qingzhen* food industry. Yet, as the remarks of many interviewees attest, the prominence of *qingzhen* also presents opportunities for counterfeit or knockoff halal food items.

The efforts of groups like the Qinghai Halal Food Production Association to standardize or create uniformity in *qingzhen* food certification point to an interesting dilemma arising from an era of mass-market branding and global consumption. Without a nationwide standard for *qingzhen* certification, consumers can't be certain of the provenance of the goods they consume. However, as illustrated in this chapter, the differences in the degree of dietary rigor and devotion to the faith across Hui communities throughout China make establishing a single, standard system for *qingzhen* certification difficult. Currently the patchwork system of halal certification leaves much to the individual consumer. As the *qingzhen* brand continues to spread across the country, even to communities that historically lack a sizable Islamic population, the dialogue between different groups of Hui concerning the precise meaning and standards connected with *qingzhen* food consumption will inevitably continue.

However, putting a nationwide standard into place necessarily involves yet another, different authority: the state. While establishing a set of standard practices for the certification of halal food may settle legal questions on the matter, it does not guarantee popular acceptance. In fact, placing the external constraints of state institutionalization around the processes of contestation of such crucial elements of Hui identity may deepen the concerns of some Hui about the disjuncture between the official state guidelines and those derived from the Qur'an.

Thus, even something so foundational to Hui identity as maintaining halal dietary codes becomes the subject of significant in-group variation. While some Hui express their belief that any food not containing pork can be considered *qingzhen*, others accept only food that has been processed according to strict Qur'anic standards, overseen and certified by a religious authority. As China's urbanization continues to draw rural Hui to urban centers, spreading *qingzhen* food to previously unreached markets and bringing Hui from different regions into constant contact, contestation about the precise meaning and regulations surrounding *qingzhen* will continue.

Differences in the level and manner of the observance of *qingzhen* now also mark important distinctions *among* Hui, potentially creating internal boundaries and sparking debate about which is the most valid or correct way to maintain a proper diet. Though changes in China's urban landscape may bring disparate parts of the Hui community closer together than ever before, the gulf between the ways in which these Hui from different backgrounds experience and understand the daily practices of production and consumption of goods associated with living a Hui lifestyle—to say nothing of the interpretations of the Islamic principles underlying them—remains as wide apart as ever.

CHAPTER FIVE

PERFORMING

Islamic Faith and Daily Rituals

> Without Islam, we're not Hui.
>
> —A FORTY-YEAR-OLD HUI IMAM, XINING

AS THE SUN SET ON A JUNE EVENING IN 2016 AT THE YANGJIAZHUANG Mosque in Xining's Chengdong District, members of the mosque community began to gather in the courtyard. On this night, like every other during the month of Ramadan, the congregation waited patiently as daylight waned to break the day's fast. Children played in the twilight, darting back and forth across the courtyard, while their parents busily handed out light snacks. One elderly man, seated on a stone bench near the edge of the courtyard, pressed a date into my hands, explaining that Muslims, following the Prophet Muhammad's own example, always broke their fast by eating dates. Others ate slices of melon or pieces of flatbread. After a few moments, the *adhan* (call to prayer; translated into Chinese as both *azang* and *bangke*) sounded, calling the congregation to the first of this evening's many prayer services. Once prayers ended, the community would join together to eat a communal *iftar* meal, prepared by the women of the mosque. After the joyous feasting concluded, the adults would reconvene in the large prayer hall to perform the evening's *dhikr* (a ritual act, usually in the form of group recitation, for the remembrance of God), where several elderly men of the community would lead the congregation, reciting from the Qur'an in sing-songy Arabic.[1] As we waited for the evening's celebration to begin, several congregants proudly remarked that Yangjiazhuang was the only community in Xining that ate the *iftar* together. In other mosque communities, families gather to eat in their homes, but at Yangjiazhuang the *iftar* was a community affair for the larger family of faith.[2]

Ritual performances like the *iftar* meal at Yangjiazhuang provide powerful opportunities to build the bonds of community. These celebratory moments of "collective effervescence" bring members of the community together to engage in the shared performance of identity.[3] Events like these are pivotal for building and maintaining a sense of groupness by defining the boundaries of Hui identity.[4] However, these practices have evolved in the face of urbanization and internal migration, sparking renewed contestation of the content of Hui identity and shifting boundary markers.

PERFORMANCE, ETHNICITY, AND STATE CONTROL IN URBAN SETTINGS

Public ritual performance holds an important place in an authoritarian state's toolkit as a means of generating support, compliance, and legitimacy.[5] Performance of public rituals allows participants to engage in symbolic behaviors that produce collective experiences and to feel bound by a sense of common belonging. Frequently, these public performances deliver messages about closely held values or integral aspects of shared identity.[6] At the same time, events like these provide states with a vehicle for broadcasting policy goals and objectives, disseminating legitimating narratives, or presenting a politically favorable national self-image.[7] Moreover, the state's ability to track participation in these events provides authoritarian regimes with a means to monitor obedience and reproduction of the official tropes and narratives.[8]

Authoritarian states possess particularly strong incentives to directly control or supervise those public performances that invest symbolic meaning in ethnic identity. During the implementation of state-building and development programs, authoritarian states often attempt to exert control over the expression of ethnic identity under the premise of promoting modernization.[9] Public rituals such as holiday celebrations or opening ceremonies provide opportunities for the state to showcase narratives about ethnic diversity or tolerance in ethnic relations.[10] These performances often portray minority ethnic groups as key contributors to and beneficiaries of the state's civilizing projects, symbolically enlisting them in the work of state-building.[11] Finally, by controlling the public performance of ethnicity, the state can limit the forms ethnic identity may take.[12] Such carefully managed portraits of ethnic identity intend to illustrate the state's benevolence and minority allegiance to the state.

Despite states' best efforts, however, such large-scale staged presentations of identity may fail to make the desired impact. Though official performances may broadcast a message aimed at creating moments of "collective effervescence" that intend to solidify the bonds of community, audiences may attach their own understandings to them or may simply choose not to pay attention at all.[13] Thus, while performance provides opportunities for unification, it may also lay the ground for fragmentation and contestation.

This multiplicity of interpretations of the meaning and significance of public rituals indicates the important role that unofficial, daily practices play in reproducing the boundaries of identity.[14] Informal, symbolic practices undertaken in private may hold more meaning and engender greater feeling of attachment to the community than large-scale, official displays.[15] Unlike tourist entertainments, galas, or parades in which participants knowingly engage in performance, small acts of performance or ritual may pass without fanfare or audience. In these moments, performers may take the significance of their actions for granted, or even lack awareness they are performing at all.[16] However, carrying out daily habits with the knowledge that throughout the community others simultaneously engage in similar acts allows ordinary people to feel a sense of shared identity, despite not being in direct contact with other community members.[17]

These dispassionate or routine performances do not inspire the excitement of more vibrant and colorful expressions of belonging, but instead act as a form of "national genuflection." The effervescence of such moments "is not measured in moments, but in lifetimes."[18] These habits of walking, sitting, dressing, or conversing invoke shared meaning between members. Such actions convey messages about norms of appropriateness or reflect deeply held cultural values that foster a sense of shared belonging among participants.

Daily and synchronized enactments of ritual give structure to "time-geographies" of the regular interactions between people and create a sense of "cultural rhythm or social pulse" that members of a community partake in.[19] Everyday habits reproduce structures that create predictability and reduce anxieties associated with unfamiliarity.[20] For example, to Muslim immigrants to the United States, establishing a daily ritual surrounding prayer and Islamic observation in the home helps to ease the challenges of adapting to living in a predominantly non-Muslim country.[21]

As another example, habits related to dress and clothing, despite being inherently functional, provide the most visible examples of the kind of day-to-day rituals that sustain identity.[22] Participants in the Han Clothing Movement seek to revive traditional culture by donning a style of clothing they see evocative of a distinctively Han identity.[23] Likewise, clothing may provide a powerful means of differentiation, both between and within identities.[24] Many subdivisions of groups, such as the White Miao, take their naming conventions from the color of clothing they wear.[25]

While authoritarian states may attempt to enforce an official version of ethnic identity that aligns with the regime's broader goals, these informal actions may clash with or contradict such efforts. Even ostensibly mundane practices may hold deeper cultural or political significance. Examining how ordinary residents in urban Hui communities perform ethnic identity in their daily lives will further illustrate the importance of these actions for maintaining a sense of communal belonging.

PERMISSIBLE DIFFERENCE AND CULTURAL CONTESTATION: A CASE STUDY OF PERFORMING IDENTITY IN HUI COMMUNITIES

In the entrance hall of the Minzu Museum (Minzu Bowuguan), located on the campus of Beijing's Minzu University of China (Zhongyang Minzu Daxue), a wall-size tapestry depicts all of China's *minzu*, brightly dressed in their finest traditional costumes, standing together in harmony. At the center, in contemporary Western dress and carrying a backpack, is a young man representing the Han.[26] Exuberant scenes like this one serve as physical illustrations of the CCP's embrace of ethnic diversity. Policy permits ethnic minorities to wear traditional costume or perform traditional songs and dances, provided they reinforce the harmony and unity that all *minzu* experience while living in China's system of *Zhonghua minzu*.

In showcasing this ethnic unity, such displays serve as a manifestation of China's official doctrine on ethnicity: China's *minzu* are colorful, distinct, and diverse. The tapestry presents a family of peoples unified in their love of and devotion to the larger Chinese nation. China's ethnic policies thus allow minorities to partake in carefully managed displays of ethnic culture.[27] The CCP creates official and acceptable forms of expression of ethnic identity that the regime may supervise and control in order to present a picture of interethnic tolerance and family-style cooperation among the various minority ethnic groups.[28]

In order to perpetuate this image, the state promotes minority festivals, religious worship, ethnic costumes, and other performances—frequently in the form of highly choreographed song and dance routines at a televised, annual Chinese New Year Gala.[29] These public displays of minorites participating in the Chinese state reinforce narratives about the tolerance of the

CCP toward ethnic diversity, while also solidifying *Zhonghua minzu* around a Han-centric core.[30] Through active sponsorship of displays of minority culture, especially festival celebrations, the CCP exercises a kind of "superscription" with which it asserts control in interpreting the meaning of the ritual on display.[31]

However, rhetorical attempts on the part of the state fail to create a unified, standardized expression of identity in fact. Ritual instead serves as grounds for further, renewed contestation and fragmentation of in-group consensus concerning the appropriate level of piety and observance and the proper content of Hui religious devotion.

PERFORMANCE OF PRAYER AND PERPETUATION OF HUI CULTURE

"Permitting" weekly prayers provides the state with an opportunity for involvement in displays of ethnic difference. This cooperation between Hui communities and the CCP is on public display during weekly Friday prayers at the Dongguan Mosque in Xining. The city government mandates that—among mosques belonging to Xining's dominant Yihewani sect—only the Dongguan may hold Jumu'ah (Friday afternoon prayers; referred to as Zhuma in Chinese) prayers. Consequently, the prayers attract enormous crowds. A mosque employee, who served as a tour guide for visitors, estimated that on Fridays as many as sixty thousand routinely attended.[32] Crowds fill the mosque's internal courtyard and spill out into the wide boulevard in front of the mosque, packing the sidewalk and the two eastbound lanes of traffic for the length of at least two city blocks. The local government even helps the mosque deal with logistics: to ensure safety and avoid roadblocks, the city deploys police to stand in the street near the mosque and direct traffic.

Unsurprisingly, Zhuma prayer services at the Dongguan Mosque attract international attention and serve as a showcase of ethnoreligious cooperation touted by both the local government and the local Hui community. Prayer services represent the most visible collective expression of Hui culture in Xining and are also a tourist attraction. Every Friday, onlookers, including foreign and Han tourists, and Hui women from the community who do not attend prayers at the mosque, gather on the opposite side of the street, holding up cameras to capture images of the crowd.[33]

For the CCP, the public performance of prayer in Hui communities reaches audiences both at home and abroad. Domestically, images of Hui holding large prayer services aided by supportive and accommodating local police projects an image of a mutually beneficial relationship between ethnic minorities and the state. Such a message targets both Han and minorities alike to suggest that the CCP's benevolent and protective governance allows all *minzu* to prosper. Further, to onlookers all over the world, the scene suggests the CCP's success in fostering a diverse, tolerant, and multicultural China. Hui audiences also vary. One respondent, a Hui taxi driver from Xining in his mid-twenties, spoke favorably of the large crowds on Fridays, claiming, "Qinghai Hui are just more devout."[34] Another, a middle-aged Salar man originally from Xunhua City, proudly asserted that Muslims all over the world spoke approvingly of the Dongguan's Friday prayers. He suggested that the local community—Hui and Salar alike—provided a model for piety, even for those visitors from Muslim-majority countries. For many participants, the crowds that gathered each week at the Dongguan broadcast a clear message about the piety of Xining's Hui to the larger Islamic world. However, these messages also found an audience within China. The respondent made explicit contrasts between the scenes of devotion on display at the Dongguan Mosque and what he perceived to be insufficient devotion in communities in eastern China. In this light, the performance of prayer in Xining became an expression of how to properly model religious faith, something he felt Hui communities to the east had lost touch with. He lamented, "If you go to the mosque [in eastern China], almost nobody will be there to attend prayer. Mostly, it's just older people and retirees. Last year I went to Taiyuan, and there was almost nobody at their mosque. They have such a big, beautiful old mosque, but it was almost totally empty. Nobody came to pray."[35]

Thus, for multiple sets of actors, these public performances of ritual present important opportunities for establishing boundaries of Hui identity. In these moments, audiences—Han, Hui, and international—witness a highly managed effort by both the state and Hui actors to set the boundaries of Hui identity. By using the city's resources to provide a single location for holding prayer services and promoting the ceremony as a large-scale, community-building experience of "collective effervescence," the state sets parameters on religious and cultural expression and articulates a sanctioned, monitored version of Hui culture.

The state's superficial commitment to promoting religion does not always translate into policies that accommodate the actual practice of religion. On the contrary, residents of Hui enclave communities in cities like Jinan, where Han form the preponderant majority of the population, frequently cite practical limitations in excusing their sporadic prayer attendance. In rural communities, employers tolerate breaks or allow time off from work to accommodate prayer, but Hui in Jinan allege that in large cities employers are not so accommodating. Many respondents argued that employer inflexibility forced them to make a choice between work and faith and complained about sacrificing the practice of daily prayer in order to save their jobs.[36] For example, the owner of a small tea shop in Jinan cited the difficulty of dutifully praying five times a day while facing the demands imposed by employers. He reasoned, "We're supposed to pray every day, but if you don't work near a mosque that's not easy to do. On Fridays, if you leave work to pray, your work unit [*danwei*] might fire you. You have to provide for yourself. God isn't too serious about these things."[37] A baker in his forties, also a lifelong Jinan resident, contrasted the faithfulness of local Hui to recently arrived migrants, claiming, "The Hui from the northwest go to pray more often than a lot of locals. For them, Islam is absolutely a part of their daily lives. But we local Hui are very business-minded [*shangye hua*]. We're really concerned about work and don't have a lot of time to go pray."[38] A thirty-two-year-old magazine editor in Beijing remarked that because he worked on Fridays he rarely found time to leave the office to attend weekly prayers at 2:00 p.m. As compensation, he often went to the mosque alone to pray after his workday was over.[39]

Obstacles like these that hinder the ability to observe daily prayer services present migrant rural Hui with substantial challenges when trying to adjust to their new urban surroundings. Rural migrant Hui often disparage their urban counterparts' lack of devotion to daily prayer. A front-desk worker at the Muslim Hotel (Musilin binguan) in Xining's Chengdong quarter recently arrived from nearby Minghe stated that, to be "qualified" (*hege*) as Hui, it was necessary to pray five times a day.[40] In Jinan, a nineteen-year-old chef in a *lamian* shop, recently arrived from rural Qinghai, groused, "[Jinanese Hui] just know 'I'm a Hui,' but they don't know about anything else." Unlike the Hui in his hometown, Hui in Jinan rarely attended daily prayers.[41] Another respondent in Jinan labeled these infrequent mosque attendees "yearly Hui," explaining, "There are Hui that pray regularly, and there are a group called *nian HuiHui* because they only pray once a year on Kaizhai jie [Eid al-Fitr]."[42] For these pious respondents, ethnic identity adhered to religious faith. Disparaging those who attended only on religious holidays by calling them *nian HuiHui* suggests that, in their eyes, without a regular practice of faith, a person could not claim to be Hui.

Contestation occurs over not just the frequency of prayers, but also their content. In particular, the practice of commemorating deceased saints and relatives (*jinian wangren*), where families invite an imam to visit their home, lead prayers, and recite the Qur'an on the anniversary of a relative's death (see figure 5.1), may spark controversy within the community. Many respondents,

FIGURE 5.1. Pilgrims offer incense at Da Gongbei in Linxia.

particularly those followers of China's various Sufi orders (*menhuan*), named these commemorations as one of the major rituals of faith in which ordinary members of the community frequently engaged.[43] They identified such rituals as an important part of holiday ceremonies.[44] Adherents cited these practices as originating within Chinese Islam and as linking Islam to traditional Chinese culture. As one imam in Beijing insisted, such blending of Islamic and Chinese tradition was not only permissible but inevitable: "Confucius taught that people all ought to act benevolently. We Muslims say that God is the most benevolent."[45] In Xining, one imam expressed the view that, as a product of cultural fusion, Hui culture necessarily incorporated elements of traditional Chinese ritual. Hui, he contended, needed to observe both their Chinese and Islamic roots: "The reason that the Hui are a *minzu* is because of our religion. Without Islam, we're not Hui."[46]

These discussions of the Hui as having equally Chinese and Islamic heritage align with the state's call for the Hui to value patriotism on an equal footing with religious devotion, often expressed through the maxim "Love your country, love your faith" (*ai guo, ai jiao*).

While such commemorations play a critical part in maintaining a sense of Hui identity for those adherents who practice them, others in the Hui community—particularly those members of the non-Sufi, reformist Yihewani school of Sunni Islam—regard them as syncretic, and ultimately in contravention of proper Islamic practice.[47] Two respondents from Lanzhou remarked that these readings of the Qur'an for one's dead relatives were influenced by the Confucian practice of ancestor worship and were essentially blasphemous.[48] Memorializing the dead in this manner broke the foundational commandment of Islam, that Muslims should worship no other besides Allah. Despite the fact that debates over the appropriateness of veneration of the dead occur in Muslim communities throughout the world, these men saw the practice as evidence of unacceptable Sinicization.[49] To these men, and others like them, Hui who burned incense in memory of ancestors did so because of the corrupting influence of Han after generations of assimilation and loss of identity.

In Xining, the growth in the number of adherents to Salafi Islam (Chinese: Sailaifeiye) provokes further challenges over whether Hui should adhere to Islamic rituals developed in China or look to emulate the Muslim community in the Middle East. Some respondents in the community express annoyance at the Salafi's haughty lectures about the syncretic nature of local traditions or the "purity" of Salafism. For example, a twenty-five-year-old taxi driver who claimed to be Yihewani expressed his disdain for Salafi, describing them with the pejorative term Santai (literally "three raises," a reference to the three times Salafi raise their hands during prayer). "[The Santai] come into our mosques and they tell us we're not following Islam correctly, and we ought to do things like them. They don't respect our differences," he grumbled.[50]

The reshaping of urban landscapes and populations causes conflicts like the one described by the taxi driver to occur more frequently. As the influx of rural Hui into urban communities continues, Hui with completely different standards for piety and practice encounter one another, causing disagreements over how often and in what manner Hui ought to pray to continue and intensify.

ISLAMIC GARMENTS AND WEARING HUI CULTURE

Measuring faithfulness and devotion often entails other practices besides merely going to the mosque to pray. Many respondents cited dressing in a manner consistent with Islamic religious dictates as a key indicator of Hui identity. Head coverings worn in Hui communities cover a range of styles.

In general, men wear either a knitted skullcap or a pillbox-style rounded cap, both referred to as *bai maozi*. Women's head coverings come in a far more diverse array. Cultural, social, political, and other influences mediate choices about whether and which kind of head covering to wear. Despite standardized descriptions of ethnic costume in both scholarly and official accounts, the choice remains highly personal.[51] Some women wear headscarves referred to as *shajin*; increasingly, women in religiously conservative Hui communities wear hijab-style veils (*gaitou*) resembling those worn in Malaysia or Indonesia that cover the hair, ears, neck, and shoulders. Older women may wear more boxy cloth prayer hats, usually in shades of pale blue or purple, that cover the hair but leave the ears and neck exposed. Such garments are local to China and are viewed as old-fashioned. Less commonly, women may elect to wear niqab-style veils that cover the face below the eyes. And some Hui, especially those who are less religiously observant, may choose to forgo head coverings altogether.[52]

These differences in practice reflect competing understandings of how Hui ought to dress. By wearing—or choosing not to wear—traditional ethnic costume, or Islamic garments such as headscarves and *bai maozi* Hui perform ethnic identity. The state too stresses the connection between costume and distinctive ethnic identity. Official documents on *minzu* policy frequently use images of minorities in ethnic costume, suggesting the strength of China's diversity and tolerance. Indeed, the vibrant minority costumes on display are upheld as having "rich cultural connotations which convey deep meanings," and are thus vital purveyors of culture. State-produced depictions of "official" Hui costume usually show Islamic clothing, such as the long-sleeved garments and hijabs at the exhibit at Minzu University in Beijing. The museum also contains a collection of *bai maozi* as part of an exhibit on religious headgear.[53]

Despite these official displays of ethnic clothing, many urban Hui respondents remarked that limitations placed on them in the workplace prevented them from routinely wearing hijabs or *bai maozi*. While the CCP did not enforce a nationwide policy on veiling at the time of my fieldwork in 2015–16, the Party had already begun to restrict wearing religious garments in cities within Xinjiang.[54] None of the municipal governments of my case sites imposed such extreme limitations as formal bans, nor did they actively campaign against wearing religious head coverings. My respondents suggested that—outside of Hui-run businesses—employers frowned upon wearing such attire. As a rule, respondents said, work units tended to prohibit their employees from wearing religious garments.[55] The owner of a store in Jinan cited these workplace limitations as a major reason why most local

Hui chose not to wear hijabs, even if they felt religiously obligated to do so. She expressed frustration with those recently arrived migrants who acted dismissively toward those who did not cover their head: "A lot of people who have moved into this neighborhood might be Muslims, but they don't really behave like Muslims should. Maybe they don't think I dress properly. They'll ask 'Why don't you wear a hijab? How can you really be a Muslim if you don't wear a hijab?' And I say, 'I know I should wear one, but I don't.' But here we just don't wear them except to go pray. In fact, a lot of work units will forbid you to wear a hijab, so people don't wear them."[56]

The restrictions against headscarves imposed by work units require Hui to weigh economic against cultural incentives. The store owner's explanation that Hui fear they might suffer economic consequences for choosing to wear head coverings reflects the kinds of anxiety that inform these decisions. Worries about cultural estrangement provide a counterbalancing set of apprehensions, leaving respondents like the shop owner caught between the threat of sanction from secular institutions and scorn from the more pious members of the religious community. In response, Hui feel they must prioritize either their economic interests or their cultural and religious heritage.

Observing the incompatibility between these choices, a twenty-four-year-old public school teacher from Xining explained the choice to wear a hijab as a choice between two lifestyle paths. Those who wore them limited their prospects for attaining higher education or engaging in professional employment and instead tended to marry young and work low-wage jobs.[57] Framed in these terms, many respondents portrayed the choice to wear a hijab or *bai maozi* as a choice to limit economic opportunity. As a response to such economic realities, a thirty-seven-year-old restaurant owner from Yinchuan told me that wearing a prayer hat or a hijab was reserved for special occasions: "I feel that wearing a hijab is becoming more formalized. Many people who work in cities, like entrepreneurs and other jobs like this, they seldom wear them. In Yinchuan there are few people who wear hijabs or prayer hats."[58] As a result, urban residents working in professional jobs rarely wore traditional religious dress. One woman in her early twenties who grew up in Jinan noted that migrant Hui from the northwest were far more likely than locals to regularly wear prayer hats or hijabs. "Nobody in my family wears [a headscarf]," she claimed.[59] To secular Hui like her, who rarely attend mosque, wearing a religious head covering—regardless of style—may seem like an alien practice rather than a part of their own cultural heritage.

Many respondents used wearing hijabs or prayer hats as an outwardly visible measure of devotion. The Qur'an provides an ambiguous set of standards surrounding dress and veiling.[60] Only broad instructions from a number of passages provide sartorial guidelines for both men and women. In one passage (33:53), the Qur'an advises, "When you ask his wives for something, do so from behind a screen: this is purer both for your hearts and for theirs." Elsewhere (33:59), the Qur'an dictates, "Tell your wives, your daughters, and women believers to make their outer garments hang low over them so as to be recognized and not insulted." And in yet another passage (24:30–31), the Qur'an lays out more specific guidelines for both men and women, including the mandate that women "should let their headscarves fall to cover their necklines" except in the presence of husbands, fathers, and other family members.[61] These competing instructions, as well as those handed down through different traditions of hadith or added by rulings from rival schools of Islamic jurisprudence, result in a wide array of interpretations about what the Qur'an requires in terms of dress.[62]

These divisions are echoed in the Hui community. A number of respondents associated manner of dress with level of faithfulness and associated wearing Islamic clothing with being more authentically Hui. Dressing in Islamic fashion, one respondent assured me, was a minimum qualification for being Hui.[63] One man, who sold yak butter products in the Hui Quarter in Xining, explained how wearing a hat served as a means of broadcasting ethnic identity. Citing the fact that I had initially inquired whether his product was sanctioned by Islamic dietary law, he remarked, "Just now, when you came in, you didn't know that I was Hui and so you asked about whether or not this was *qingzhen*. But if I was wearing a *bai maozi* you'd certainly know that I was Hui." He concluded, "If you wear a *bai maozi* it just shows that you're a Hui."[64]

Other interviewees expressed a similar religious obligation to wear a headscarf or dress in a more conservative fashion.[65] During one interview, a twenty-nine-year-old woman in Xining apologized for meeting me wearing only a loose *shajin*. Normally, she said, she wore a niqab, covering everything but her eyes. Reflecting further on the matter of appropriate dress, she told me, "The Qur'an explains how people are supposed to dress. They're not supposed to wear tight clothes or show hair or show the skin on their shoulders."[66] Unsurprisingly, these respondents pointed to those Hui who routinely donned hijabs and prayer hats as exemplifying the proper manner of dress and behavior. Especially when speaking to migrants from rural Hui communities, invocations of the fact that greater numbers of Hui wore white hats and headscarves in the village served as proof of superior faith. Many of these respondents looked with disapproval on the scarcity of Hui wearing white hats in urban communities. A middle-aged entrepreneur from Yinchuan asserted the superior devotion of Ningxia Hui on the basis that they wore Islamic dress with greater frequency than Hui from elsewhere.[67] These remarks associated a decline in visual expression of Hui identity by wearing religious headcoverings with a waning of Hui identity. Those who didn't wear headcoverings were presumed to have lost touch with their faith, and therefore to have become Hanified.

ISLAMIC HOLIDAYS AND THE PERFORMANCE OF HUI ETHNICITY

Islamic holidays like Eid al-Fitr (Kaizhai jie) and Eid al-Adha (Gu'erbang jie) offer the state an opportunity to promote an official, sanctioned version of Hui culture. For many Hui, Kaizhai jie marks the only occasion in a calendar year that obligates mosque attendance. These celebrations bring members of the community together to engage in the practice of faith and extend the bonds of the Hui community. In large cosmopolitan communities, such as Beijing's Niu Jie, Kaizhai jie prayer ceremonies attract Hui from every region of China and every sect or school of thought.

Accordingly, the state accommodates official observance of the holiday in many ways. On the morning of Kaizhai jie on Niu Jie in Beijing, traffic police erected barriers in the middle of the street, turning the avenue into a pedestrian thoroughfare. The Beijing Cuisine Association (Beijing Pengren Xiehui) hosted the Ninth Beijing Halal Culinary Culture Festival (Beijing Qingzhen Meishi Wenhua Jie), for which it erected a row of white tents that lined the avenue opposite the mosque, housing vendors selling snack foods. The morning's festival atmosphere gave the city government a channel for broadcasting its own message: over the avenue a bright red banner, hung especially for the occasion, read, "Raise high the great banner of Socialism with Chinese Characteristics! Build a prosperous, civilized, harmonious, and livable new Xi Cheng District!" Signs for the food festival likewise declared, "Spread nationality policy and promote interethnic cooperation."[68]

Similar celebrations take place throughout the country, and local governments play a role in staging large-scale holiday observances. The large crowds that gather at these celebrations present the state with a vital opportunity to endorse and display its control over the expression of Hui culture and Islamic faith. Respondents in Xining remarked that attendance at the Dongguan Mosque grew exponentially for morning prayer services on holidays. Some estimated that the number of worshippers on these occasions surpassed 200,000.[69] In Yinchuan, the government of the Ningxia Hui Autonomous Region declares Islamic holidays public holidays and gives civil servants three days of vacation time to accommodate worship.[70] Even in relatively isolated communities, such as Jinan's Hui Quarter, Kaizhai jie draws larger crowds than regular weekly prayers. A twenty-two-year-old woman from Jinan described a similar scene at Kaizhai jie observances at the city's Great Southern Mosque: "Last year for Kaizhai jie, I went [to the mosque] and there were so many people. Not just local Muslims from Jinan, but people from all over the country all attended."[71]

The holiday provides an important opportunity for the state to join with and promote mosques' efforts to build and strengthen the Muslim community. As one imam in Jinan explained, on Kaizhai jie the local mosque committee engaged in acts of charitable donation and distribution of goods like cooking oil and fried oil cakes (*you xiang*) to the neighborhood's poor.[72] In facilitating and overseeing the celebration of the holiday, and providing logistical support for the prayer services, the state gains the ability to monitor its tone and transform the celebration into a platform for its own agenda.

However, state support for celebrations remains uneven. While local governments in some areas promote public holiday events, elsewhere a lack of support prevents full participation within the community. A fifty-two-year-old Hui receptionist at a weekend English prep school in Jinan complained that local holiday celebrations lacked vibrancy because residents received no time off from work to celebrate. "Right now, the government doesn't give a holiday," she observed. "It's not like in the northwest, like in Xi'an or Shaanxi or Gansu, where everyone can take a vacation. We here in Jinan don't get a vacation."[73] Her remarks reveal distinct regional divisions that adhere to cultural rather than physical geographies. In taking leave from work to observe Muslim holidays, northwestern Hui established themselves as different from locals. In Jinan, however, residents faced a choice: they might take time off to observe the holiday, but doing so might cost them their job.

For many respondents, the most important observations of the holiday occur outside the purview of the state. Away from the pomp and circumstance surrounding official holiday celebrations, the most important aspects of Kaizhai jie involved informal gatherings with family to eat a large meal and to express holiday greetings. For many, these informal, family-oriented observances of holiday traditions represent a more relevant expression of Hui culture, and indeed matter more than the official, carefully messaged, state-sanctioned events. Multiple respondents, when asked to identify holiday activities, immediately mentioned gathering with family to fry oil cakes and cook large meals to share.[74] On Niu Jie, after the morning prayers ended, attendees spilled out into the streets, filling the neighborhood's many halal restaurants to celebrate with family and friends.[75] Even for those relatively secularized Hui who skip prayers at the mosque on Kaizhai jie, the act of celebrating the day by eating fried oil cakes provides a connection with a sense of Hui identity and a feeling of belonging in the Hui community.

Recent migrants complained that traditional holiday celebrations in urban communities lacked the vivacity of the countryside. One imam in Yinchuan remarked that Kaizhai jie celebrations in the city weren't as "festive" (*nuanhuo*) as those in his rural hometown of Pingluo because in the countryside entire villages came out to celebrate together, whereas in Yinchuan celebrations were small and private.[76] A professor at Yinchuan's Jingxue Yuan (Institute of Qur'anic Studies) shared these sentiments. In the countryside, he explained, celebrations of Gu'erbang jie (Eid al-Adha, derived from the Persian name, Qurban) took place in single-story courtyard houses where the community could gather together to slaughter sheep and cattle and roast whole goats to share with neighbors, in keeping with Islamic tradition. In the city, where everyone lived in cramped apartments, no communal space existed for gathering to celebrate the holiday together.[77]

SOMEWHERE BETWEEN *SHAJIN* AND SECULARISM: NEGOTIATING PERFORMANCES OF HUI IDENTITY IN CITIES

Though holiday events like the prayer services on Kaizhai jie provide a state-sponsored—and state-monitored—forum for performance of Hui identity and bring together members of disparate and diverse backgrounds, they do not always serve to unify the community in a single moment of collective effervescence. In fact, such ceremonies often achieve the opposite effect, by turning performances into sites of contestation. Certainly these public celebrations fill city streets and provide visible expressions of Hui culture and target numerous audiences, both in China and abroad. The CCP uses these celebrations to project an image of tolerance and benevolence to other ethnic minorities as well as to foreign observers. In Hui communities these performances broadcast the strength of Hui faith to the global Islamic community. However, such signals also target other Hui, sending messages of how Hui identity ought to be observed. As such, these displays seek to mark what the performers deem the proper boundaries of Hui identity.

As these performances open the process of boundary contestation, they contribute to the fragmentation of Hui identity as much as they do unity and integration. Limitations on the ability to wear headscarves at work or to take time off for weekly prayers force some Hui to weigh religious observance against economic self-preservation. Migration highlights the way in which Hui from different ages, classes, and regional and professional backgrounds weigh these choices differently. Many Hui on urban work units feel unable to sacrifice their employment in order to observe religious norms, while more pious Hui view this choice as evidence of secularization and lack of seriousness about being Hui.

Differences of opinion over the significance of wearing a hijab or prayer hat or how often to pray illustrate the fact that rituals do not impart universally accepted meanings, but instead may be a cause for contestation and debate. Previous studies of religiosity among the Hui observe that these discrepancies in mosque attendance and regularity of prayer often overlap with distinctions in which rural Hui are held up as more pious and urban Hui as more secular.[78] However, as migration brings Hui from different geographic regions and social environments into contact, other cleavages, such as social class, level of education, and age, also become salient as urban environments foster the kind of interaction that renews contestation of Hui identity.

Internal migration only amplifies differences between different groups of Hui and perpetuates further contestation. By bringing Hui from different regions and different social environments together, mass migration sparks new discussions about the proper ways to be Hui. Debates over how to properly practice and observe Islamic ritual are essential to defining the boundaries of Hui identity. This renewed contestation activates cross-cutting identity cleavages and draws intragroup boundaries, calling attention to the differences that exist within the Hui community. Even though the ethnic identity of Hui may provide common ground for these disparate groups, other identities may supersede it.

Migration also serves to revive interest in Hui identity. As more devout Hui come into contact with more secularized Hui, renewed interest in Islamic practice sometimes blossoms. The arrival of migrants from the northwest impacts the daily habits of residents of Jinan's Hui Quarter, and in many cases galvanizes local Hui to rediscover their religious and cultural roots.[79] Many residents observe that increased contact between Hui from the northwest and local Hui revitalizes mosque communities. The *qingzhen* baker in Jinan remarked that, after seeing how much more piously rural migrant Hui behaved than locals, he too began to go to the mosque more often in an effort to follow their example. To him, the presence of new Hui in the community offered him an opportunity to learn how to be properly Muslim for the first time.[80] Many others expressed the belief that these migrants model proper Islamic behavior and adhere more strictly to religious orthodoxy. Locals assert that northwestern migrants more regularly attend prayer services and often make up the majority of the attendees at daily prayers.[81] One interviewee noted that the arrival of migrants in the community led to increased visibility of Hui as the number wearing white prayer hats increased: "There are still some men who wear *bai maozi*, but over the past few years, I feel like the number of Hui wearing *bai maozi* around here has increased. There are also more who wear hijabs. When I was young, you never saw anyone else wearing a hijab. But these last few years there are quite a few."[82]

Moving to urban communities affects migrant Hui in their daily habits as well. Respondents in Yinchuan noted that, in a city comprised primarily of recently arrived migrants, the Hui community was defined by a blending of traditions.[83] For example, a Hui academic in his sixties remarked that as migrants moved into the city from elsewhere, more people within the Hui community began to celebrate the Chinese New Year. This, he contended, resulted from the dilution of the strength of Hui identity as migrants from rural Islamic strongholds in the countryside found themselves surrounded by Han in new urban settings.[84] Without the kind of community present in the countryside, rural migrants lapsed in their observance of faith and began to assimilate into Han culture. The Islamic goods store owner in Jinan also observed a loosening in the strictness with which recently arrived Hui observed dress codes: "I think these Muslims from the northwest also have become a bit more relaxed. In the northwest they cover their entire heads and don't allow any hair to show. But here you see women who still wear the hijab but have a little hair showing through because they think it's prettier to look this way. So they also have relaxed a little."[85]

Ultimately, ritual performance provides a vehicle for the creation of new understandings of the boundaries of Hui identity. These interpretations of Hui identity may draw on sources of authority other than those sanctioned by the state and may not conform to the template of Hui identity held up by the CCP.

As the contact between Hui groups triggers Islamic revival among some secular Hui and increased cosmopolitanism among some conservative Hui, new understandings about the essential nature of Hui culture emerge. This process of contestation and renegotiation happens outside of the control of the state, through informal processes. Though state policies seek to channel ethnoreligious expression into a state-sanctioned path, daily interactions in the context of urbanization and migration achieve the opposite effect. Rather than consolidation of Hui identity around the narrative of the state, debates over performance of Hui identity reveal the heterogeneity within the Hui community and illustrate the limitations of the state's ability to control how ethnic boundaries are set and maintained.

DRAWING LINES BETWEEN DEVOTION AND *DANHUA*

> We have people here from all over the country, and they're all in contact.
>
> —A THIRTY-SEVEN-YEAR-OLD HUI RESTAURANT MANAGER, YINCHUAN

ON A BLINDINGLY SUNNY DAY IN LATE MARCH, I SAT ON A LOW stool on the side of the road surrounded by fields of goji plants, the snow-capped peaks of the Helan Shan range looming in the distance. Beside me several residents of Nanliang Village, a small farming community about fifteen miles to the north of Yinchuan, sat stripping thorns and briars from the dead branches of goji bushes. The young man seated next to me, a twenty-something who wore a *bai maozi*, told me about his arrival in this suburb under the administration of Yinchuan from his hometown in southern Ningxia's overwhelmingly Hui Nanbushanqu (Southern Mountain District, comprising Guyuan Prefecture and Haiyuan County). At the age of ten he arrived at this suburban outpost with his family as part of a massive government-sponsored relocation of people from the rural south that began in the early 2000s. The entire community at Nanliang, which specialized in producing Ningxia's signature crop of goji berries, arrived from the same mountain village. He spoke softly, continuing to snap away at the branches with the clippers as he talked. "My hometown was very poor," he recalled. "The soil there is rocky, and it's not good for growing crops. Most people there herd sheep." When asked how his adopted community differed from his childhood home, he waved his hand toward the fields of bushes left bare-branched after the winter and answered, "Here, there are more opportunities. We grow goji berries and corn."[1]

The young man's story is but one among thousands just like it. Since the 1980s China's urban population has grown by some 500 million people. Projections estimate that by the year 2030 the urban population will swell to just over a billion. In part, economic incentive drives this mass movement of people from the underdeveloped countryside to more prosperous cities. However, government policies encouraging relocation to cities also increase the rate at which migration occurs.[2] Often the two forces work in tandem, as they do in the case of Hui migrants from rural communities in western China. A twenty-four-year-old Hui woman in Xining described the journey of migrants from nearby Hualong Hui Autonomous County:

> Lots of people from Hualong County migrate and open [*lamian*] restaurants. Right now, the government, the Qinghai government, really supports this kind of action. They give these young entrepreneurs a bit of money. They take this money to go and open restaurants, and really this spurs all of Qinghai's development. I'll give you an example. If you have a little money, but not enough to open a *lamian* restaurant, if I'm the government and I give you a little money, the money you have plus the money I give you together is enough for you to go open the restaurant. On the one hand, you spread publicity about Qinghai, and on the other hand you're driving your development. If you're from a small farm village, everyone, almost half the people, will go to open a restaurant and come back after they've saved up some money.[3]

Migration on this scale undoubtedly impacts social and economic life in both the rural communities from which migrants originate and the urban communities to which they relocate. Among the many consequences that this mass movement of people generates are changes in the way the boundaries of Hui ethnic identity are formed and maintained. As migration draws together Hui from different regions, class backgrounds, and degrees of education and religious piety, they contest ideas about how to define and set parameters around the content of the ethnic Hui identity. Though the state's policies on ethnic minorities attempt to standardize Hui identity by identifying a number of cultural traits and ethnic practices the state deems acceptable, the interactions between members of various Hui communities that occur as a result of migration belie the notion of a tidy, standardized version of Hui identity. Rather, Hui from different communities express thoroughly different understandings of how Hui identity ought to be chosen, talked about, consumed, and performed. As renewal projects transform urban landscapes and in-country migration changes urban populations, Hui from different class, regional, professional, and religious backgrounds encounter one another. Rather than sharpening the ethnic boundary lines that differentiate the Hui from other groups, this contact between Hui from all walks of life heightens the salience of internal boundaries by highlighting cross-cutting cleavages.

The inward focus of this debate facilitates the CCP's management of ethnic politics. Daily interactions undertaken in the context of urbanization and migration raise the salience of nonethnic categories of identity, including class, age, gender, region, and religious sect. Highlighting the differences between groups of Hui reopens the contestation of the boundaries of Hui identity. Because such contestation turns around matters of daily habit, it occurs in informal contexts outside the purview of the state. As Hui enclave neighborhoods disperse because of urban renewal or have their demographics transformed by an influx of Hui migrants, residents contest and renegotiate which markers ought to form the boundaries of Hui identity. The intragroup contestation of Hui identity focuses attention on internal boundaries and limits contentious politics to intragroup discourse.

Where contentious politics arise from the reopening of such identity contestation, they present limited opportunities for disruption of CCP authority. Though the state's categories and ethnicity policies provide the background against which these debates unfold, conflict rarely involves the state itself. Instead, disputes primarily involve Hui disagreeing with other Hui. The resulting debates about the most authentic form of Hui identity effectively displace tensions with the CCP and prevent widespread resistance or mobilization of opposition to the state. Anthropologist Dru Gladney refers to this manner of governance over ethnic politics, in which "people subscribe to certain identities, under highly contextualized moments of social relation" that are policed and constrained by the state, as "relational alterity."[4] By channeling contentious politics into intragroup debates, the CCP stands at arm's length from conflict, and thus effectively manages ethnic politics. As Hui haggle over how to properly express their cultural identity, the CCP monitors such contestation and operates with a relatively free hand in enacting policies regarding ethnicity.

These findings point to both a strength and a weakness of authoritarian regimes. Though containing contentious politics within the community may limit the ability of Hui to mobilize in organized resistance, the state's control remains tenuous. Attempts by the state to crack down on expressions of ethnic identity it deems undesirable may serve to increase the salience of ethnic identity and provoke greater resentment.

MIGRATION, ETHNIC BOUNDARIES, AND BELONGING

A frequently invoked maxim in the study of ethnic politics is that those who go looking for ethnicity will surely find it, imputing ethnic significance where it may not otherwise exist.[5] In looking at the practices that respondents attribute as defining Hui identity and describing how the importance of these practices is contested, their salience varies across a number of competing identity cleavages. I eschew the notion of any single, true expression of Hui identity and stress that class, gender, region, and other identities may be equally influential in shaping an individual's perceptions.

A tendency to prioritize ethnicity above other identities, falling back on essentialist understandings of ethnicity, reifying groups, and waving away nonethnic explanations, plagues migration studies.[6] Indeed, methodological nationalism and the assumed framework of the nation-state privilege ethnicity in migration scholarship and discount or ignore "non-ethnic 'pathways of incorporation'" such as class, age, gender, religion, and region.[7] However, closer examination reveals a far more complex picture.

In the course of migration, participants endure numerous social, cultural, and political challenges that impact self-conceptions of identity. Often, the arrival of a migratory wave of people spurs sociopolitical issues surrounding questions of integration and belonging at the point of destination. Migrants' daily experiences are thus marked by negotiations and struggles surrounding their very presence in the community. In the face of such scrutiny, migrant communities frequently strive to maintain a sense of difference from the local majority at the place of destination. Migrants' conceptions of their own identity often rely on idealized notions of their place of origin. These notions anchor identity and allow migrants to reproduce the community at the place to which they relocate.[8] Even if migrants share linguistic and cultural traditions with their co-ethnics at a particular location, notions of identity tied to the place of origin may prove to be overriding. Indeed, perceived closeness in cultural proximity to the majority group may influence elites in migrant groups to go to greater lengths to sustain boundaries that denote migrants' difference.[9]

However, migration may also incentivize integration of minority groups, blurring the boundaries that separate migrants from locals. Just as a diasporic group may engage in boundary maintenance to resist boundary erasure, migration may result in redrawing of boundary lines.[10] In these cases, migration may cause those who undertake it to completely reimagine how it self-identifies vis-à-vis different social hierarchies or relational contexts. These outcomes vary across contexts and reflect the ways in which migration reopens the inherently relational dynamics of identity (re)construction.[11] Migrant destinations become sites of constant negotiation.

In particular, contestation frequently occurs when migrants from a geographically dispersed or diaspora community arrive in communities already inhabited by a long-standing local community of co-ethnics.[12] As communities engage in these processes of contestation regional, sectarian, or social class identities may override commonly held ethnonational ones. Ethnolinguistic practices frequently become conflated with judgments about income, education, and progressiveness, and these likewise "fold into religious discourses of 'pollution' and 'purity.'"[13] Differences in speech, degree of religious observance, or manner of dress between locals and migrants come to stand for markers of "progress" or "backwardness," reinforcing prejudices and justifying exclusion. While these markers may continually shift and blur, they nonetheless enable processes of distancing and control.[14]

This politics of belonging has both formal and informal aspects, and contestation over who may be granted inclusion may just as easily occur in ordinary venues such as schools, places of worship, or neighborhood markets as it does in formal or legal institutions.[15] In some cases, even the bodies of migrants become sites for contestation of identity as styles of dress and self-presentation become markers used to draw insider/outsider boundaries.[16]

The condition of in-betweenness migrants occupy may be most acutely felt by children. Observations of migrant children often characterize them as "luggage" borne by their parents to new locations, making them a source of anxiety as the family attempts to preserve connections to places of origin while also integrating into the community of arrival. However, children of migrants play active, pivotal roles in the process, aiding their parents to adapt to unfamiliar local norms and institutions by attending schools, serving as translators, and making connections in the community.[17] However, while ease of access to these resources makes children of migrants a bridge between their parents and the community, the discrimination they face while within local public schools and other institutions may reinforce their own feelings of otherness.[18] By straddling these worlds, children of migrants paradoxically come to develop simultaneous feelings of belonging to and estrangement from their place of arrival.[19] Such estrangement may also occur at their parents' place of origin. Children of migrants often idealize such places that fail to align with the realities that meet them upon their return. Especially for those children of migrants who spent their formative years away from or grew up entirely outside of their parents' place of origin, the place they are told to think of as "home" may feel equally alien.[20] Children of migrants may thus develop identities that "put into question the location of 'home' and 'host'" communities or sit awkwardly between them.[21]

As a consequence, migrants may set up separate or parallel social networks to sustain a sense of identity rooted in their place of origin and cope with barriers to integration at their place of arrival. Such communities may contribute to notions of "internal ethnicity," which subdivide the larger community into smaller ones based on region, religion, or other facets of identity. As a result, associational clusters form around these internal ethnic group identities. Entrepreneurs in these internal ethnic communities frequently privilege members of their own group in matters of hiring or may cater exclusively to members of their own group as clientele. In response to these conditions, "ethnic economies" comprised of businesses run by members of a particular ethnic group emerge to cater to group members.[22]

The construction of migrant networks, practice of coping mechanisms, and debates across generational, gender, class, and other lines within the migrant community illustrate the complexity of migrant identities. Ethnicity captures only a single dimension of these realities. Better understanding of how migration impacts the lives and expression of identity of those who undertake it requires moving away from an analysis that presumes ethnicity holds a higher salience for migrants than other aspects of their identity. Examining cross-cutting cleavages presents a potential solution to the problems of overprioritizing ethnicity, analysis driven by essentialism, and the failure to account for multiplicity and variance in salience of identities. Focusing on where identities overlap or converge offers a more nuanced picture of how, when, and why ethnicity becomes salient vis-à-vis other social identities.[23]

CROSS-CUTTING CLEAVAGES, MIGRATION, AND CONTESTING THE BOUNDARIES OF HUI IDENTITY

In-group heterogeneity defines urban Hui communities throughout China. Recent rural-to-urban and west-to-east migration highlights these differences by bringing Hui from different locations, classes and social settings together in the context of an urban environment. Interactions between these Hui from different backgrounds spark contestation over which markers constitute the defining features of Hui identity and make such debates public (see table C.1).

The distinctions between different groups within the Hui community illustrate an unintended consequence of urbanization: the activation of

TABLE C.1. Activation of cross-cutting cleavages in Hui communities

COMMUNITY	REGION	TYPE OF COMMUNITY	CROSS-CUTTING CLEAVAGES ACTIVATED
Beijing	East	Isolated	Class Regional Education Age Sectarian Urban/rural
Jinan	East	Isolated	Class Regional Education Age
Yinchuan	Central plains/ Northwest	Titular autonomous	Class Urban/rural Regional Gender
Xining	Northwest	Multiethnic	Class Urban/rural Sectarian Gender

cross-cutting cleavages that result in drawing internal boundary lines. Despite all sharing the same official designation of Huizu according to China's *minzu* system, arguments about matters of marriage, childbirth, speech, diet, dress, and prayer underscore the internal cleavages that divide Hui communities.

BEIJING: THE DISPERSION AND CENTRALIZATION OF A PATCHWORK HUI COMMUNITY

As the national capital and one of China's largest cities, Beijing attracts residents from all walks of life. Economic opportunities draw a diverse array of migrants in search of a more comfortable standard of living.[24] Over the past twenty years changes in Beijing's demographics unfolded alongside large-scale transformation of its urban grid. During preparation to host the 2008 Summer Olympic Games, Beijing undertook an extensive urban renewal program that saw the demolition and transformation of many of the central city's *hutong* (narrow-lane alleys) neighborhoods.[25] Campaigns to transform the core of the city, both infrastructure and demographics, continue, as the city's summer 2017 "beautification" (*meihua*) campaign saw the displacement of scores of residents—many of whom belong to the so-called transient population of migrants—and the demolition of numerous structures deemed illegal.[26]

The consequences of these changes impact Beijing's Hui community just as they do the rest of the city. Formerly, the Dongsi and Madian neighborhoods stood out as distinct Hui enclaves surrounding prominent local mosques. After urban renewal, the mosques remain but many of the former Hui residents no longer live in the neighborhood.[27] Demolition scattered many of them, and the neighborhoods slowly lost their Hui character. An imam at the Madian mosque explained, "Due to *chai qian* and *gaizao* [transformation], most of the Hui in the area have moved away elsewhere [*banzou*]."[28] Another respondent, a seventy-year-old retiree who was a lifelong resident of a courtyard house in a *hutong* in Beijing's Dongcheng District, grumbled that many of his neighbors had been pushed out to the suburbs. "Some of them have even moved to Hebei!" he exclaimed incredulously.[29] The dispersal of Hui from once concentrated spaces diluted the distinctive character of the neighborhoods, leaving those who remained feeling isolated and disconnected from the community.

The changes in urban neighborhoods also drove many Hui away from their local mosques. Instead of worshiping in the neighborhood, many began to worship exclusively at the large and famous Niu Jie Mosque, while other mosques saw attendance drop. At the Dongsi Mosque in the eastern part of central Beijing, a middle-aged caretaker explained, "Before *chai qian* all of the buildings here were *ping fang* [single-story houses]. At that time many more people came to the mosque. Now, they all go to other mosques." When asked where congregants now went to pray, he offered Niu Jie as the most prominent location.[30] The dispersal of these neighborhoods contributed to a centralization of Hui culture around Niu Jie. As urban renewal scattered Hui from Dongsi and Madian, the community on Niu Jie became the city's primary remaining Hui enclave.

Even on Niu Jie the cost of living impacts the neighborhood's character. One respondent, a transplant from Gansu who worked for the Islamic Association, remarked that the rising cost of rent in the neighborhood made it harder for Hui to afford to live there.[31] A Han real estate agent in the neighborhood described the change: "Only a small number of [people who live here] are Hui. Before, this was Beijing's largest Hui neighborhood. But now, there are more Han. About seventy percent of [the people who live here] are Han."[32] *Chai qian* not only scattered Beijing's local Hui communities; it also brought in Hui from numerous other locations throughout China. According to several respondents, most of the Hui living in Beijing are now migrants from other places. The seventy-year-old retiree from Dongcheng bristled at the fact that his neighborhood, once a place where many Hui lived, was now home to outsiders. He ranted, "Beijing isn't Beijing anymore! When you go out onto the street you don't see Beijingers anymore."[33]

Niu Jie's rise to prominence as a predominantly Muslim neighborhood also attracts Hui from all over the country. Some local Beijingers testified that many of the residents of Niu Jie's tower apartments were outsiders (*waidi ren*) who came from locations as far away as Yunnan and Gansu and as close as Hebei.[34] Many seek out Niu Jie, hoping that the predominantly Islamic atmosphere will offer opportunities to make money. Such was the case for one Hui woman in her fifties, originally from Xinjiang, who operated a small novelties store. Locals, both Han and Hui alike, bought jade from Hotan and fruit—dried apricots and raisins—from her native Korla.[35] Many others in the neighborhood were, like her, recently arrived in Beijing to do business, contributing to its transient feel. While these outsider Hui infused the neighborhood with a wide range of cultural traditions from all parts of China's Islamic community, their temporary status in the community also made Niu Jie a place of constant change.

Given the multitude of Hui that come to Niu Jie, public spaces on the street often reflect the community's internal diversity. At times of worship, congregants from different walks of life often pray side by side.[36] Especially during holidays, such as the Eid al-Fitr ceremonies at the community's famous mosque, Beijing's Hui community displays its multifaceted composition (see figure C.1). Attendees come from all corners of China and mingle with Muslims of other ethnic groups: Uyghurs, Salars, Mongols, and others. Many foreign Muslims residing in the capital also attend. Worshippers represent China's various Sufi orders, as evidenced by the diversity of prayer hats worn by attendees, most notably adherents of the Jahriyya (Zhehelinye) *menhuan* (Sufi orders local to China) with their distinctive pointed, crown-like headgear. These Hui join together to worship, and afterward many amble across the street to fill Niu Jie's many famed *qingzhen* restaurants, feasting together in celebration.[37]

Such a multicultural and diverse community, however, does not always ensure smooth adaptation to life in the city. While Beijing may provide more opportunities to earn money, many migrants drew sharp contrasts between the level of secularization they experienced in Beijing and the more

FIGURE C.1. Worshippers fill the courtyard of Beijing's Niu Jie Mosque prior to the start of Eid al-Fitr ceremonies, July 2016.

traditional atmosphere of their hometown.[38] A thirty-three-year-old electronics salesman who moved to Beijing from Lanzhou gave a lengthy assessment of the differences he felt most clearly distinguished his hometown from the capital:

> Lanzhou Muslims are more conservative. Women all wear hijabs, especially after they get married. They don't wear short sleeves. In Beijing, women who are married and even elderly women don't wear [hijabs]. There are also differences in eating. In Lanzhou Muslims solely eat *qingzhen* food. If they go out to a restaurant to eat, it must be *qingzhen*. But in Beijing, none of the restaurants are *qingzhen*, but Muslims still go out anyway and eat haram [forbidden; *hefa*] food. If the food's not *qingzhen*, it's no problem; they'll just eat haram food. Or marriage. In Lanzhou, when you're looking for a partner, they've got to be a Hui,

> or someone who believes in Islam. Han, or Mongols who believe in Islam are permissible to marry—what's important is that they believe in Islam. In Beijing, there aren't any restrictions. Beijing Muslims' way of thinking is just more *kaifang* [permissive or excessively libertine].[39]

The salesman's view reflects the tensions that often arise between locals and migrants. While he expressed frustration with the relatively libertine attitudes of local Hui, another man, a lifetime Beijinger, commented on the severe and austere attitudes of migrants from the northwest. Many longtime Beijingers do not feel a sense of kinship or commonality with recent migrants. Indeed, respondents disagreed about the effect these migrants have on Beijing's culture. Some suggested that Hui coming to the city from Yunnan, Gansu, Hebei, or elsewhere were too transient to make a significant impact on the community.[40] A seventy-year-old Hui author and Beijing native dismissed the idea that these migrants might significantly impact local Hui culture. "Beijing isn't really a place that is easily influenced," he remarked. "Mostly people are assimilated into Beijing."[41]

Others see the impact of these migrants differently and frequently express concern for the loss of distinctly local customs and traditions. As migrants make up an ever-larger percentage of Beijing's Hui population, locals complain about the slow deterioration of Beijing Hui culture. One interviewee admitted, "Beijing doesn't really have any [local traditions]. There are very few protections here."[42] An imam at Madian sighed, "So many of our local traditions have already been lost."[43] The seventy-year-old resident of Dongcheng bluntly stated, "In some places, like Saudi Arabia, Muslims are very devout. They teach their children to attend prayer five times a day. In Beijing, the Huihui have all been Hanified. They only know the most basic things about Islam: don't eat pork. Besides this, they mostly don't think [being Hui] is important."[44] The retiree continued, explaining that younger Hui—including his own children and grandchildren—treated their ethnic identity as nothing more than a status listed on official documentation. Outside of official and formal declarations, these younger Beijing Hui rarely considered or engaged with their ethnic identity.

Transformation of both population and landscape asserts important influence on Beijing's Hui community. In physically moving people away from traditional Hui spaces, urban renewal leads to the diminishing salience of Hui identity in many communities. In others, like Niu Jie, the concentration of Hui culture around officially promoted spaces promotes contestation over numerous intersecting identity cleavages. The influx of migrant Hui from every corner of China to Niu Jie engenders a multifaceted and inclusive Hui community. However, these exchanges also highlight regional, class, and sectarian differences across a range of daily practices.

JINAN: CLASS DIVISIONS AND RELIGIOUS REVIVAL

In Jinan, the Hui Quarter is an island of Hui surrounded by a sea of ethnic-majority Han. Yet even in this environment dividing lines cut across the Hui community. Longtime Hui residents mark the increase in migrants to the city from Gansu, Qinghai, and elsewhere in the northwest as one of the most drastic changes of the past twenty years. However, not all residents welcome the arrival of these migrants, and some single them out as different. In this sense Xibei (the northwest) becomes not just a signifier of geographic region but a category of identity that suggests income level, education level, profession, sectarian affiliation, and other matters.

As such, distinctions of class, education, and region distinguish locals from migrants. Frequently Jinanese Hui seek to demarcate their own identities from those of Xibei Hui. Jinanese Hui highlight class and education differences when drawing distinctions between themselves and migrants. One man, the owner of a small tea shop in his fifties, remarked of migrants to the community, "They come from a place like Gansu where there are also other Muslims like Salar and Dongxiang. And of course, these areas are a little less educated and a little poorer."[45] He and others responded empathetically to these differences in class and education that separate Xibei migrants from locals, stressing the need to help these newcomers adapt to the markedly different social landscape of Jinan. Such gulfs in culture, habit, and worldview make migrants outsiders, even among fellow Hui, and make integration into the city a struggle.

Others were less kind toward migrants, some even holding prejudices against them. For instance, many viewed migrants' relative lack of formal education and lower social status negatively. A fifty-two-year-old Hui engineer who grew up in the Jinan Hui Quarter but moved away to the suburbs stated, "I really don't like going to the Hui Quarter. It's not like it used to be. A lot of new people have come into the neighborhood. Probably less than half of the residents there are locals now. It just seems like the people that live there aren't very well-educated or well-mannered."[46] Many would agree with him that a lack of sophistication defines Jinan's Hui Quarter, and they desire to avoid being associated with the quarter's residents. Rather than viewing recently arrived migrants in the neighborhood as models of Islamic piety, people like the engineer look upon them as rubes from the countryside or religious fanatics. As such, they express no desire to be grouped along with migrant Hui.

The fact that many Jinan Hui remained content in being culturally Hui while overlooking religion became a major source of tension with migrants from the northwest. While numerous locals prioritized abstention from pork and self-identification as Hui on official citizenship forms as the primary markers of Hui identity, such practices as frequently attending Zhuma prayers, wearing religious attire, or sending their children to study the Qur'an during school vacations were often brushed aside in favor of economic self-advancement. Taking off work to pray or wearing a headscarf were cited as obstacles to advancing in the workforce. Studying Arabic came at the cost of classes needed to ensure college admission. Devotion to these aspects of faith was often posed as choosing cultural and economic backwardness.

Migrants from more pious western communities expressed feelings of alienation from local Hui and displeasure at their perceived secularization and laxity. A man in his late thirties who had recently arrived from Qinghai to open a restaurant remarked, "My hometown is very small and maybe we're not as educated as Jinan." In contrast, however, he proclaimed, "In Qinghai there are a lot of Hui, so Jinan's Hui culture isn't nearly as strong as ours." Similarly, an eighteen-year-old who had recently arrived from Qinghai to work at a *lamian* restaurant glumly gave his impressions of Jinan: "People here just aren't as faithful."[47] These migrants expressed dismay at their local Hui counterparts' disconnect from religious roots. For these migrants, local Hui appeared lax in upholding the basic tenets of Islamic faith. An *ahong* at one of Jinan's mosques summarized these complaints concisely: "Well, the Islamic tradition in the west is stronger. They start going to the mosque, studying Arabic at an early age. Some of them, in places like Ningxia, when they're young, can speak and read Arabic but can't even write their own names in Chinese."[48] Responses like these repeated a common sentiment, that in the communities where migrants originated, the mosque stood as a pillar of daily social and cultural life, and thus migrants exhibited a deeper knowledge of and devotion to their faith than locals.

Local Jinanese echoed these views regarding the superiority of migrants' religious faithfulness. One man, a factory worker in his mid-thirties, testified, "People from Xibei, they teach their children at home. I've seen a lot of owners of *lamian* shops practicing the *qingzhenyan* [shahada] with ten-year-old kids, or teaching their seven- or eight-year-olds how to pray." Jinanese Hui, he claimed, rarely did the same.[49] A shopkeeper in her fifties remarked that the majority of people who showed up at prayer services on Fridays were migrants from Qinghai: "I think they're a big influence on the neighborhood.

They go to pray every Friday. Local Muslims aren't this observant. We're a little bit *danhua* ['watered down' or secularized]. But they regularly attend."[50] Indeed, Hui who grew up in Jinan frequently cited their own status as *danhua*, especially compared to recently arrived migrants. In some this response provokes defensiveness; in others it prompts annoyance with migrants.

This devotion to the faith caused friction in the minds of some locals. A number professed that their northwestern migrant neighbors struggled to integrate into the community. In part, locals claimed, migrant families prioritized Islamic over secular education; they hinted that the children of these migrants lacked functional literacy in Chinese characters but could read the Qur'an in Arabic. Viewed in this light, the piety of the northwestern Hui becomes stigmatized as a marker of backwardness and lack of sophistication. The tea shop owner frowned on such piousness and felt unfairly judged. "This is just my opinion, but I don't really think we should divide or separate into groups and say what we believe is right and what you believe is wrong," he declared, adding, "I think if you eat a *qingzhen* diet, don't eat pork, and believe in God, you're doing okay."[51]

XINING: RURAL MIGRANTS AND SECTARIAN DIVISIONS

While the arrival of migrants increases the salience of class and educational cleavages in cities like Jinan, in Xining migrants activate sectarian cleavages and perceived differences in level of religiosity. Several respondents boasted of the superior Islamic environment in the city. One, a taxi driver, scoffed at what he perceived as the comparative ignorance of eastern Chinese Hui regarding Islam. He emphatically boasted, "Qinghai Muslims are more devout. Muslims from the east like in Shandong don't know anything about Islam. They smoke and drink and everything. Some of them even eat pork!"[52] An elementary school teacher who grew up in Huangyuan, just outside the city, contrasted the religious atmosphere in Xining with other locations in China. Assessing the religious climate in Yinchuan, where he had spent some time, he remarked that he found the level of Islamic culture there wanting: "Especially in Yinchuan, people are very *danhua*. I say that because I went to Yinchuan, and after I arrived I could just feel it. The differences were enormous. The religious outlook there, as far we here are concerned, was maybe more *danhua*. If we're using contemporary terms here, maybe they're more modernized. But as far as we here are concerned, we're more conservative, because in addition to developing the economy, these circumstances are still good. I have money. I have standards. These standards are more numerous in regard to religious life."[53]

Accounts of those who have undergone the process of migration reinforce these ideas. Some respondents based their judgments on their own experiences living and working in *neidi* ("interior China," used by those in the northwest to refer to areas in the east). Others relied on accounts from family members. Still others drew on contact with *neidi* Hui who moved to Xining in search of new opportunities as a part of China's Great Western Development (Xibu Dakaifa) campaign, begun in 2000. Xining locals recounted that these new arrivals from *neidi* struggled to adapt to the higher religious standards of Xining. Xining locals disparaged these Hui migrants as clinging to Han traditions from back east and pointed to this as evidence of their Hanification. An entrepreneur in her late thirties remarked, "There are some people who are still a little rough from a religious point of view. For instance, those Hui whose hometowns are in Hebei and Shandong, who followed their parents to Qinghai as children. Their parents' religious faith was pretty lapsed, and so the children are also very lapsed. They all think they have to rush out and buy new clothes and a set of fireworks at Spring Festival, and things like that."[54]

Carrying on with such Han traditions earned *neidi* Hui scorn for engaging in ancestor veneration and other rituals deemed out of step with monotheism and Islam. By contrast, these respondents held up Xibei generally as a model and Xining as a standardbearer of Islamic devotion. They beamed with pride at the influence that Hui from Qinghai exerted when they moved into eastern communities. A high school teacher from Xunhua in his late fifities told me, "The people who live in *neidi*, they're very *danhua*, but when people from Qinghai go to the cities to *dagong* [do temporary work] they start to pray more often, and believe more deeply."[55] Another respondent, himself an *ahong*, noted that Muslim migrants planted the seeds of faith in long-dormant eastern Hui communities through their exemplary devotion: "[Migrants'] influence is really large. Maybe in those cities, before they arrive nobody goes to pray at the mosques, and after they arrive more people attend prayers. Or in some places there are communities where there is no mosque, and then after Qinghai Muslims arrive, the community builds a mosque."[56] By this reasoning, pious Qinghai Hui, through their movement and their devotion, viewed themselves as providing those with tenuous connections to their Hui heritage with a template for reviving their identity.

The pride about and emphasis on Islamic observance proclaimed by Xining's Hui illustrate the ways in which religion and religious observance provide a salient cross-cutting cleavage in Hui communities. Even though their eastern counterparts shared an ethnic identity as Hui, their insufficient devotion to Islamic practice, lax dietary standards, and insistence on observing custom regarded as Han distinguished them from locals. A visiting halal food industry consultant from Malaysia summarized this pride in religious faith concisely in his observance that Xining was, in his estimation, "the de facto Islamic capital of China."[57] Indeed, while nearby Linxia holds deep historical and cultural significance for Hui and claims the mantle of being China's "Little Mecca" (Xiao Maijia), the city also has a reputation for being impoverished and riven by sectarian conflict.[58] As such, some respondents in Xining looked down on the community, despite its historic roots. Commenting on their own city and drawing attention to its close relationship to the reformist Yihewani tradition, respondents proudly held up Xining as a center of Islamic modernity.

YINCHUAN: "OFFICIAL" HUI IDENTITY AND CULTURAL FUSION

As the capital of Ningxia Hui Autonomous Region and the seat of "official" Hui culture, Yinchuan provides an interesting counterpart to Xining, the perceived "de facto cultural capital" of Islamic China. The city spearheads much of China's cultural outreach to the Islamic world and is home to many state-sanctioned sites of Islamic culture. However, unlike Xining, a city with a strong Islamic flavor, Yinchuan's recent development leaves it, in many ways, in search of an identity. The Great Western Development Campaign, and the influx of migrants as a result of it, caused Yinchuan's population to balloon in recent years. One respondent, a restaurant owner in his late thirties, explained, "We have people here from all over the country, and they're all in contact."[59] Another interviewee, a Han woman working in a creative design firm preparing to marry into a Hui family, recalled her experience of moving to Yinchuan. "It's a very distinct experience," she began. "I'm also a migrant here. My grandparents moved here because my grandfather was a soldier. My grandfather was from Shanxi, and my grandmother was from Anhui. My mother was from Hunan. Even my friends who live nearby aren't purely from Ningxia. Most of them came from somewhere else."[60] Indeed, very few respondents were able to trace their roots to Yinchuan beyond a generation or two, whether they were Hui migrants from rural Guyuan or Wuzhong or Han migrants from Sichuan and Zhejiang. Such disparate origins made the city a space of cultural negotiation, fusion, and adaptation.

In a space where people from so many different backgrounds interact, regional identities gain increased salience. In particular, as migrants from impoverished regions of rural Ningxia move into the city, the urban-rural cleavage within the Hui community impacts what it means to properly claim

Hui identity. One woman, a Han convert to Islam working in a prayer goods store, described the impetus for Hui to leave their hometown in rural Guyuan or Haiyuan to relocate to more prosperous areas in the city:

> Migrants come in, they're mostly from remote and mountainous areas, and their lives are very difficult. One year's salary for a whole family is only about five thousand *kuai* [at the time about $757.22], and this five thousand *kuai* has to provide for the family's parents, their children, and the couple themselves. So, because it's very difficult, the government handed down a few policies that allow them to choose a place nearby in Ningxia that's a bit better and gives them a house that's built a bit better to provide relief. They have a big shed for growing produce, and they move from places that are hard to survive in to here, where they can survive.[61]

These migrants make an immediate impact on the city. As whole villages relocate from the Nanbushanqu, they change the cultural and demographic makeup of neighborhoods. A professor noted the effects of migration on neighborhoods typically regarded as Hui enclaves: "Migrants have come in and changed how people live in neighborhoods." He pointed to the example of the cluster of Hui businesses and restaurants near the southeastern end of the city, including the street of butcher shops and barbecue stalls surrounding the Nanguan Mosque, calling itself "Ningxia Niujie," that had cropped up when the mosque was renovated in the late 1980s. He concluded, "As Yinchuan has gone through *chengshihua* [urbanization] those neighborhoods have changed."[62] Migrants from rural Ningxia imbued the area with a more clearly Hui aesthetic as they attempted to sell the foodstuff and handiwork of their rural hometown as branded, ethnic products.

Once arrived in Yinchuan, these Hui migrants from rural Ningxia express their distance from their urban counterparts. One man noted that the faster pace of life in the city made it difficult for rural Hui to adjust. In contrast with his home of Wuzhong, he noted, "people [in Yinchuan] are more concerned with work. It's not like in Wuzhong, where people drink tea and chat. Wuzhong's more relaxed."[63] Without such connections city life seemed lonely and untethered to traditions. In part, respondents identified the isolating nature of city life as contributing to their feeling of alienation. An instructor at the local Qur'anic Studies Institute (Ningxia Jingxueyuan) who had moved to Yinchuan from Guyuan, described how such isolation made life difficult for recently arrived Hui from the countryside. "Here Hui are isolated from one another, and there isn't much opportunity for communication," he declared, adding, "Maybe in an apartment tower there might only be one or two Hui families. So people don't communicate as much."[64] Deprived of such resources, old practices and habits carried from the countryside faded, leaving residents feeling lost.

Along with the loss of community, many recently arrived rural Hui professed that the seemingly secular habits of their urban counterparts left them feeling out of place. Some complained that, unlike in their hometown, where almost everyone observed Islamic tradition, Yinchuan was marked by a more casual attitude about mosque attendance. The instructor at the Qur'anic Studies Institute contrasted prayer attendance in Yinchuan with his hometown: "In Guyuan religious belief is a little stronger." As testament to this fact, he claimed, "On Fridays, it doesn't matter whether you work in business, or you're a teacher, or whatever job: everyone goes to the mosque to pray. Maybe ninety percent of the town will attend. But in Yinchuan maybe only forty percent attend."[65] Another respondent noted that in rural areas, such as the nearby Hui stronghold of Tongxin County, standards of dress coincided more closely with Islamic standards for piety. She contrasted the habits of Yinchuan residents with those of Tongxin: "Yinchuan is a provincial capital, and it's also an important city for migration. Yinchuan's local traditions have also been influenced by customs from those who've migrated here from other parts of China. The changes have been significant. From our point of view, Tongxin is a pretty concentrated Hui area; it's almost a purely Hui county. So the religious atmosphere really stands out. Especially in regard to the way people dress, it's really different from Yinchuan."[66]

These differences in dress and diet and degree of religious observance and the lack of community lead migrants to conclude that urban Yinchuan Hui lack devotion to faith. "A lot of migrant [*yimin*] Muslims who come here find Yinchuan to be very *danhua*," remarked an academic in the local academy of social sciences in his late fifties.[67] Such jarring differences made it hard for recently arrived residents to cope.

Furthermore, rural migrants comment that close contact with Han results in compromising basic and foundational aspects of Hui culture, including abstention from alcohol and daily prayer. A restaurant owner originally from Haiyuan County discussed the ways in which local Hui felt the need to be flexible in their beliefs in order to adapt to life in majority-Han surroundings. Citing the fact that many Yinchuan Hui found themselves surrounded by Han, he described the social pressure that many faced: "For instance, if there are three of us that are friends, and you drink, and the other two of us don't drink, aren't we still friends? You understand. If we two aren't really persistent, then if five or six friends come, and they're all non-Muslims, they might say 'Today we're all getting along so well, let's hang out. But if you don't drink, it'll be awkward.' If you don't want to join in and go drink with them, then you have to be really persistent and uncompromising. I'm determined not to drink."[68]

Unlike their rural hometowns, which were overwhelmingly Hui, the new, secular, urban environs of Yinchuan presented challenges to maintaining religious and cultural practices. Working and living alongside Han meant having to learn how to maintain a Hui identity while not offending coworkers and neighbors and not limiting one's own personal and professional opportunities. Some inevitably drifted toward secularization or competing identities associated with work. As an example, the Hui professor of history explained how secular institutions and loci of social interaction outside of the mosque contributed to the erosion of salience of Hui identity: "In the city people are more open-minded. For instance, the things people can do for amusements are more numerous, like KTV [karaoke] or going to parties. So people may not identify as Hui quite as strongly. As for me, my identity as a scholar and an intellectual is more important. My identity as Hui is perhaps less important."[69]

The differences between urban and rural identity cross-cut ethnic identity cleavages in Yinchuan's Hui community. However, as rural migrants continue to move to the city, they increasingly exert influence on the formation of a local culture. Just as migrants feel the city's environment influences their participation in Hui dietary, religious, and cultural practices, so too do migrants influence change in the city. As the scholar from the Ningxia Academy of Social Sciences remarked, "It works both ways: [migrants] adapt to Yinchuan, but they also spur locals to think about being more [religiously] active."[70] As a result, interactions like these between pious, rural Hui and secular Hui not only became the basis of debate but also result in the solidification of new, localized identities.

"BECOMING PART OF A NEW YINCHUAN": CONTESTATION AND REMAKING THE BOUNDARIES OF A HUI IDENTITY

While migration may promote contact between different groups of Hui, the internal differences that emerge from such interactions may lead members of the community to reimagine Hui identity. Exposure to idiosyncratic local traditions that differ from their own may allow members of the community to extend the boundaries of the community beyond those with which they are familiar and embrace wider and more inclusive understandings of what it means to be Hui. As one retiree in Xining explained, "The faith is basically the same. All Muslims recite the *qingzhen yan*, 'There is no God but Allah and Muhammad is his prophet.' We all believe this. But everywhere there are Hui we have adapted some to the local culture."[71] Many respondents observed that the act of migrating from ancestral hometowns exerted a transformative effect on the lives of migrants.[72]

Others attested that living in urban spaces allowed migrants to become more open-minded. A university administrator in Xining argued, "The biggest change [for migrants] is freeing their minds and expanding their horizons, seeing more people. When they get to big cities, there's a huge change in their way of thinking."[73] A twenty-four-year-old woman in Xining, herself the daughter of migrants who had moved east to Zhejiang in her early childhood, echoed these sentiments and explained how a broader worldview could also impact migrants' home communities upon their return: "Because [migrants] go out to work, they also widen their horizons, open up their worldview, meet different people. This will also make changes. Some learn new things and transform their hometowns."[74] The university administrator noted that these changes were especially profound in regard to migrants' conceptions of household roles and responsibilities—particularly for women. He remarked, "It makes people a bit more open-minded [*kaifang*]. Especially for women. They come back and they want to go out and work. Traditionally women stay at home. But after working in the east lots of women want to work."[75] The Xining schoolteacher observed that changes in attitudes also frequently resulted in changes in daily habits and lifestyle choices. Citing changes that migrants frequently made to their attire upon returning from coastal cities, he said, "They might retain a few of their own traits from the city. For instance, habits about wearing a *bai maozi*, or women wearing *shajin* [hijab]. Maybe normally they'll go out to get together and they won't wear a *bai maozi* and instead wear Western-style clothes. Clothing and stuff like this is a pretty big change."[76]

These respondents suggested that time spent in large cities changed migrants' relationships with their hometown—particularly those who relocated during childhood. The exposure to different lifestyles and ways of thinking most profoundly influenced the children of migrants. Many respondents noted that the children of migrants who spent much of their youth in urban environments adopted habits from their urban counterparts. One imam remarked, "Yes, there are very clearly differences. For instance, the way young people dress. Muslims aren't supposed to wear short sleeves and women aren't supposed to show their hair. But you see lots of people these days that wear short sleeves and low-cut shirts and show their hair."[77]

Lifestyle habits like these choices in dress make the children who return from living away stand out as distinct from those grew up in rural areas. Further, this estrangement leads to a sense of in-betweeness, neither belonging to the cities in which they largely came of age or the rural communities to which they have returned. Traits developed outside of their place of origin mark them as semi-outsiders.

Among the most prominent of these traits is language. Rather than speaking the local dialect of their parents' village, these children grow up in environments where standard Chinese (Putonghua) is the most frequently spoken language. Respondents noted that these children lose many of the expressions and speech patterns of the village. In the case of Hui communities, children may no longer speak Huihua or use the Islamic terms derived from Persian or Arabic that punctuate their parents' speech. As a fifty-three-year-old professor who originally grew up in Xunhua stated, "[Migrants'] children also see so much more of the world. At the very least, their Chinese is standard."[78] Living in an urban environment also offers the children of migrants opportunities they might not otherwise have in the countryside. In particular, children's chances to receive quality education greatly increases. One Hui woman in Xining, a professor of sociology at a local university, observed, "Naturally, [migrants] greatly influence their own families. I think the thing they bring back is their influence on changes in their children's education."[79] Though greater education and more standard speech may open doors for these migrants, it may also arouse resentments about social class in their community upon return. Losing ethnic markers in speech or vocabulary may cause them to be seen as out of touch with Hui culture.

This place of in-betweeness generates new identities for children of migrants. Influenced both by the traditions of their parents' hometown and also by their interactions with others during their time away, these children may develop new understandings of how to model and engage with Hui identity. A respondent who managed his father's restaurants remarked that the children of migrant families were forging a new set of local traditions. To him, the interactions between these new generations of Yinchuan residents was responsible for forging "a New Yinchuan." Speaking of the impact of migrants on Yinchuan's overall cultural landscape, he mused, "There isn't really an inherent influence of migrants. Maybe these people's children, the next generation, they can become residents of a New Yinchuan. This includes residents of Old Yinchuan's children's children also becoming a part of New Yinchuan. Maybe it could be like that."[80] The idea of developing a "new" understanding of Yinchuanese or Hui identity speaks to the impact that internal migration exerts on cultural contestation. A high degree of mobility—both geographic and socioeconomic—among Hui opens new windows for exploring the content of Huiness. The children of migrants who grow up in these environments forge new boundary markers of Hui identity and form new understandings about the essential core of Hui identity.

MULTIPLE WAYS TO BE HUI: CROSS-CUTTING CLEAVAGES AND INTERNAL BOUNDARIES OF IDENTITY

In each of these communities—Beijing, Jinan, Xining, and Yinchuan—migration activates cross-cutting cleavages as Hui from different class, educational, regional, and religious backgrounds interact. The salience of these cross-cutting cleavages frequently overrides the encompassing ethnic identity of Hui and draws internal boundaries within the Hui community, making distinctions like *bendi* (local) and *waidi* (outsider), *xibei* and *dongbu* (eastern Chinese), or *qiancheng* (pious) and *danhua* subcategories into which Hui group themselves. When discussing which practices and traits established the boundaries of Hui identity, respondents seemed more eager to assert how their practices set them apart from—and in many cases marked them as superior to—others claiming Hui identity. Boundary-setting processes are inherently reflexive, and identifying which characteristics, traits, and practices make up an "us" requires a "them" for contrast. Over the course of my fieldwork, the more frequently evoked "them" in relation to discussion about Hui identity was not the majority Han but rather others seen as being differently—and perhaps improperly—Hui.

Examining internal divisions like these also illustrates various social challenges that arise in the context of migration. Renewed contestation of identity boundaries and the increased salience of internal boundary lines present challenges. The process of migration reveals many of these obstacles that both migrants and locals must face. As contestation reopens debates over which practices should stand as markers of group identity, migrants in particular may struggle to adapt to the differences between their place of origin and their current location. The feeling of disorientation may only intensify if those drawing contrasts are supposed co-ethnics.

EATING BITTERNESS: MIGRATION, ETHNICITY, AND SOCIAL CHALLENGES IN HUI COMMUNITIES

I sat at the table in the hotpot restaurant on the eighth floor of Yinchuan's Muslim Hotel (Ningxia Musilin Fandian), wisps of steam rising up from the ceramic pot filled with bubbling broth laced with chili oil, listening to my respondent, a middle-aged former imam currently working as the operator of a small electronics shop. He was extolling what he counted as the virtues of the Hui. "We Hui aren't very lazy," he began. Immediately he contrasted the Hui to other minorities, high-handedly declaring, "It's not like those Kazakhs and Uyghurs from Xinjiang who're so lazy. Hui are really able to *chiku* [to undergo hardship, literally translated as 'eat bitterness']."[81] He attributed this superior fortitude to the cleverness and ingenuity of Hui people. His confident boasts resembled many remarks I heard throughout my time in the field: unlike other *minzu*, Hui succeeded wherever they went, thanks to their adaptability. My respondent's invocation of the success of the Hui in adjusting to new surroundings and finding ways to integrate highlights the heterogeneity of Hui communities. His belief in the ability of his fellow Hui to overcome struggles disregarded the real and substantial obstacles that Hui migrants face.

Internal boundaries within Hui communities contribute to a number of these social, economic, and cultural challenges. While many respondents in Xining affirmed that leaving rural Qinghai provided migrants with better work opportunities and the ability to improve their quality of living, many also remarked that cultural chasms between urban and rural life made it difficult for migrants to adjust to life in cities.[82] One merchant selling yak butter in Xining described the cultural barriers that migrants confronted in eastern cities: "[Migrants] make a lot more money. Most people who make *lamian* come from Hualong County or Xunhua County. Most of them are farmers, but they go open restaurants in the east and they can earn a lot. When they come back they can afford a nice house in Xining, or a new car. It's made their lives a lot more comfortable. But they still lack *suzhi*."[83] Remarks like these point to an acute dilemma facing migrants: even after improving their economic circumstances, they face challenges fitting in. These educational and lifestyle obstacles also make integration into urban environments difficult. A Han professor in Yinchuan remarked of migrants from rural parts of Ningxia, "They're still integrating." She elaborated, "They still face some discrimination. They are not as educated or economically well off."[84]

These difficulties most profoundly affect the children of migrants, who grow up trapped between cultural spheres. Many respondents noted that the children of migrants spend the formative part of their youth living in large urban centers where they are stigmatized as different from local children. Then, upon returning to their parent's hometown, they experience similar feelings of distance. The twenty-four-year-old schoolteacher from Xining explained the difficulties that children who leave Xibei face upon their return: "The kids have some problems fitting in, because they've lived in Beijing or Shanghai for such a long time. The kids live there from when they're born until maybe they're seven or eight years old, maybe even into their teens. They go to school there. These kids return to Xining, and after they stay for a month or so, they just don't fit in. They want to go back, and they'll say 'I don't want to live here, let's go back home.' This is a big influence on the next generation."[85] Another respondent, a professor at a Xining university, connected the experiences of these children who grow up in eastern cities to a decline in religious observance: "[The children] grow up in cities and they don't want to be farmers. They want to come back and live in the city. This has some influence on faith. Their family has faith, but they grow up in areas that don't have strong faith. So, it's more difficult to maintain."[86] Such a decline in religiosity and an embrace of secularism may strike those remaining in their place of origin as an abandonment of not just Islam, but of Huiness as well.

Upon their arrival in larger cities like Jinan or Yinchuan, rural northwestern migrants struggle to adjust to social environments with different cultural practices and different standards for religiosity and piety than the hometown they left behind. Habits that might be ordinary in the context of their hometown may breach norms of appropriateness in the city. For instance, in November 2015 Jinan Capital City Television's leading nightly news and entertainment program, *Dushi Xinnübao*, reported that the public butchering of sheep on a street corner in a manner consistent with halal standards (wherein the animal is slaughtered by slitting its throat and draining all of the blood out of the meat) caused a stir because it frightened kindergarteners at a nearby school. The report, which did not specify the ethnicity of the vendors but heavily implied they were Hui, raised questions about the sanitary quality of the meat, as well as the emotional damage such events may have caused children who witnessed it.[87] While this process of slaughtering animals in a manner consistent with the dictates of Islamic law might be in keeping with normal practice in predominantly Islamic communities, in the overwhelmingly Han environment of Jinan such a practice might garner negative attention. Gulfs of understanding like these make it difficult for migrants to sustain the practices of daily life they bring with them from their place of origin and also prevent them from feeling fully integrated into their place of arrival.

Differences in cultural practices not only pervade interactions between locals and migrants but also color the interactions of migrants with social and administrative institutions. Such difficulties are particularly evident in cities like Jinan, where these institutions differ significantly from those in the communities that migrants leave behind. One imam in Jinan remarked that northwestern migrant Hui often have trouble adjusting to the cultural habits of the city and depend upon the mosque to help them learn how to settle in and integrate. Among other difficulties, he notes, migrants from the northwest are unfamiliar with local governance and administrative systems and therefore look to the mosque rather than the state to settle social and business disputes.[88] The factory worker in Jinan described the motivations that necessitate this intervention:

> It's called the Gansu Muslim Society for Connecting Migrant Muslims [Gansu Musilin Wailai Musilin Lianhe Lianyi Hui], and they are responsible for being a liaison for migrants. For instance, with the local government, if they're operating a business or if they have a conflict with other locals that needs to be settled. They go to the mosque, but in fact, if it were us locals in this situation, we wouldn't go to the mosque. In locals' opinion, the mosque is an *ahong*'s workplace, and it doesn't have anything to do with me. It's all completely separate. Only when my parents pass away, I'll go to find the *ahong*, or when it comes time to commemorate my parents, I'll go find the *ahong*. This is because of a secularized [*shisuhua*] way of thinking. But people from Xibei aren't like that. For people from Xibei, religion is the center of their whole life. Not only that, they frequently ask the *ahong* to be a mediator for their life's conflicts. They're convinced that the *ahong* has brought this way of thinking to the east, and they still think the *ahong* has a really strong and authoritative position here, so when conflicts arise in their lives, when they need an intermediary between people, they go find the *ahong*. But as far as local Hui are concerned, this is impossible. We go through the formal legal channels if we have a problem: offices, agencies, the police. Their first thought is the mosque. This is a difference in method.[89]

Discrepancies like these make matters of service provision and dispute resolution difficult and reinforce migrants' feelings of alienation from the local community. They also reinforce preconceived prejudices about migrants' lack of sophistication or cultural backwardness. The administrative and interpersonal headaches created by such situations grow even larger when they occur between migrant Hui and local Han.

Difficulties in adjusting to the societal conventions and differing means of overcoming obstacles and resolving problems like those described by

Jinan residents illustrate how differences in profession, region, and religious and class background divide Hui who claim a common ethnic identity. As migration draws disparate groups of Hui together in close contact in urban spaces cross-cutting cleavages grow in significance and become more readily apparent. As a result, urban spaces become the sites of renewed contestation of the boundaries of Hui identity.

CONTESTING HUI IDENTITY UNDER AUTHORITARIANISM

Observing the internally contentious politics brought on by migration and urban renewal within Hui communities yields several valuable theoretical insights. The Hui case presents opportunities for further development of theories about the role played by everyday practices in setting and maintaining boundaries of identity. Beyond this, the setting of these observations in the context of an autocratic state illuminates many of the mechanisms of authoritarian governance that stabilize and sustain regimes. Contestation within the Hui community over which practices should mark the boundaries of Hui identity illustrates the CCP's authoritarian management strategies in practice and provides important lessons about the nature of authoritarian legitimation and governance strategies.

The character of ethnic politics depends heavily on state capacity and the institutional dynamics set up by the state.[90] The conduct of ethnic politics unfolds as a dialectical process between the state and the people. The state's ability to shape this process depends heavily upon its capacity and the institutional dynamics it has created. Authoritarian strategies for conducting ethnic politics seek to centralize the authority of the state and limit avenues for wider societal participation to fit within "ill-defined" but predictable limits.[91] Authoritarian regimes consider ethnic politics a "red line" that must not be breached by dissenters, as doing so would threaten the ability to maintain the state's territorial integrity and national cohesion.[92] Successful management of ethnic politics by the state also presents autocracies with important opportunities to validate regime control. Occasionally, authoritarian regimes find utility in exploiting contentious ethnic politics to establish political order.[93]

Demobilization allows regimes to stop opposing voices from articulating alternative formulations of policy or governance.[94] Autocrats often achieve such suppression by stifling preconditions for collective action.[95] Using an indirect means of disrupting the method, timing, or resources available to dissenters may prove more effective and less costly to the state. Unobservable suppression tactics may even be carried out by nonstate actors.[96] Though harder to track, these tactics are no less effective in securing demobilization, as effective implementation of channeling by the state results in quieter, less threatening forms of protest.[97]

Viewed through the lens of authoritarian management, the CCP's ethnic policies—such as exemption from family-planning policy, preferential bonuses on college entrance examinations, housing subsidies for minorities, and the imposition of patriotic education classes in minority areas—may be seen as effective means of channeling China's ethnic politics to diffuse conflict between ethnic minorities and the state. The current CCP shows an overarching concern for the maintenance of regime-preserving stability.[98] Ensuring stable ethnic politics is therefore a core concern tied to the overall program of stability maintenance.[99] However, the "ethnic revival" of the Reform era poses many challenges to CCP leadership. The resulting "minority culture fever" (*wenhua re*) that accompanied the revival of state support for minority identification allowed for ethnic minorities to reestablish cultural institutions and develop a collective identity "outside the Han-centric mainstream." Construction of these institutions poses an acute threat to the CCP's structure of control. While a rise in ethnic secessionism spurred on by an increase in the salience of ethnic identity would perhaps threaten the territorial integrity of the PRC as constructed under CCP leadership, the threat such a movement might pose to the "on-going, Han-centric project of national identity construction" would pose a far thornier problem. Understanding these stakes, the regime attempts to highlight ethnic diversity and engage in cultural preservation in "forms of citizenship practice."[100]

In harnessing the enthusiasm for cultural differentiation, the CCP encourages citizens to buy in to becoming officially ethnic in a system that sets clear boundaries of appropriateness for ethnic politics, prevents disruptive contentious politics from targeting the institutions of the state, and ensures the CCP's continued ability to maintain control without resorting to outright repression.

In practice, the CCP uses development as a means of channeling ethnic politics into safe spaces for the regime, often by shifting the focus of contentious politics toward internal cleavages.[101] In this way, it implements suppression while avoiding use of violent force. James Leibold argues that although resistance in Tibet and Xinjiang provides a notable exception in which the regime's ability to exert control fails, the overall picture of China's ethnic politics "does not necessarily reflect patterns of communal conflict and violence" and thus stands as a "tenuous success" in channeling and demobilizing instability. Though Leibold's shaky equilibrium suggests fragility in the CCP's control, he argues that by (1) enhancing quality of life and ethnic consciousness, (2) enacting de facto ethnic-based segregation, and (3) promoting policies that create economic and spatial marginality for ethnic minorities, the regime successfully manages ethnicity.[102]

The CCP's mixture of providing economic incentives for minority participation in the state, constantly promoting messaging about ethnic unity, and stressing the Party's central role in providing a stable environment for the prosperity of all *Zhonghua minzu* reduces points of friction between minorities and the state. In so doing, the CCP ensures that its ethnic categories become a normal part of life. Debates about ethnicity that highlight class stratification, regional differences, or generational divides within the community draw conflict away from the regime and ensure that contentious politics turn around in-group arguments. The regime's control simply becomes the background against which these intragroup discussions take place. As Leibold asserts, "Managed diversity is the norm in China today."[103] Although built on tenuous foundations, the CCP's suppression tactics continue to prove effective. While the success of the CCP's channeling strategy rests on a fragile balance that requires precision to maintain, barring a seismic shift in China's sociopolitical or economic landscape the Party's practice of using internal divisions to exert indirect control remains tenable.[104]

The observations made over the course of my fieldwork in Hui communities provide further illustration of the CCP's attempts to channel ethnic politics in practice. The *minzu* system's state-sanctioned articulation of Hui identity provides a background against which the Hui community engages in the renegotiation of Hui identity through daily, informal interactions. Everyday habits and ordinary practice become the subjects of debate about what should be considered essential markers of Hui identity instead of the appropriateness, fairness, or representativeness of the CCP's ethnic policies.

These processes of contestation increase the salience of internal differences within Hui identity. Cross-cutting class, educational, or regional cleavages may lead Hui from different backgrounds to differ about forming a proper definition of *qingzhen,* determining whether Hui must wear religious head coverings, or choosing whether their children should learn Arabic. Expressions of Huiness range from secularized to religiously orthodox and from assimilationist to segregationist. Further, Hui residents often seek arbitration on these matters from figures outside of the state apparatus. Rather than forging a single Hui identity to allow "permissible displays of difference," migration may forge new understandings of the content of Hui identity that may not square with the formalized, state-sanctioned conceptions. But instead of resisting the state's established criteria, contestation over these matters unfold within the community itself. The state's program of economic incentivization, provision of resources for social and geographic mobility, and rhetorical promotion of the Hui as an equal and valuable contributor to the Chinese state reduce opportunities for conflict with the CCP.

This proliferation of conceptions of Hui identity does not weaken the state's ability to exert control, yet the CCP's control remains only tenuous. If the state persists in using heavy-handed tactics to suppress unauthorized or unwanted expressions of ethnic culture, it risks returning the focus to the external boundaries between Hui and non-Hui. Overregulation of ethnic identity focuses politics on state definitions or official measures. In so doing, the state provides opportunities for ethnic identity to become a vehicle for social mobilization and opposition. Stringent policing of ethnic practices may serve to flatten internal differences and raise the salience of ethnic identity above that of competing, cross-cutting identities. If the state attempts to quash any unwelcome displays of ethnic identity, it risks solidifying the common bonds of Hui identity and provoking a backlash that will hinder the CCP's objectives.

EPILOGUE

ETHNIC POLITICS DURING THE "PEOPLE'S WAR ON TERROR"

THE OBSERVATIONS DISCUSSED IN THE PRECEDING CHAPTERS reflect the nature of China's governance of ethnic politics in Hui communities during the period of my field observations, between June 2014 and July 2016. The years following my departure saw sweeping changes in the tone, substance, and intended goals of ethnicity policies enacted in Islamic communities throughout China. The dramatic shifts that accompanied the declaration of Xi Jinping's "People's War on Terror" (Renmin Fankong Zhanzheng) demand some additional reflection.

Recent demonstrations of force by the state in exerting control over ethnic identification illustrate the precariousness of the CCP's position. While the police measures implemented by the state within Muslim communities in the Xinjiang Uyghur Autonomous Region following the 2009 outbreak of ethnic violence in Ürümchi already greatly restricted ethnic and religious expression, new procedures taken in subsequent years increased state surveillance and repression. Following the March 2014 attack on the main train station in Kunming by eight Uyghurs, Xi's administration revived the Strike Hard Campaign against Violent Terrorism (Yanlidaji Baolikongbu Huodong Zhuanxiang Xingdong) and shortly thereafter declared the People's War on Terror in Xinjiang. Though relations between Hui communities and the state do not evidence the same level of conflict and tension as that of their Uyghur counterparts, a growing number of policies restricts expression of Hui identity. While the internal contestation within the Hui community allowed the regime to successfully mitigate the potential for Hui resistance, the years following the opening of the Strike Hard Campaign saw the state adopt a much more aggressive posture regarding all expressions of Muslim identity, including those made by the Hui.

The CCP enacted the most severe measures in Xinjiang. Retrospectively, the roots of the current program of repression date back as early as 2014, when the Party began to restrict the movement of migrant Uyghurs within Xinjiang. In 2015, alongside prohibitions on fasting during Ramadan and the wearing of religious garments, officials moved into Uyghur homes to monitor their hosts for behaviors deemed "extremist" in a program named *fanghuiju* (visit [the people], benefit [the people], and gather [the hearts of the people]). Officially, extremist behaviors included owning a Qur'an, engaging in regular prayer, and abstaining from alcohol consumption.[1] The appointment of Chen Quanguo as the region's Party secretary in 2016 intensified the severity of the campaign. Chen, who had earned a reputation for bringing order to minority regions during his tenure as Party secretary of Tibet, from 2011 to 2016, imported many of the same heavy-handed tactics to Xinjiang, dramatically increasing the size of the police force and building a security apparatus.[2] Between 2015 and 2017 the Party constructed extensive, sophisticated networks for surveillance of predominantly Muslim communities. These measures included the erection of numerous "convenience police stations" and security checkpoints, the installation of cameras equipped with facial recognition software, and the collection of biometric data.[3] Throughout this period the CCP also enacted a systematic removal of Arabic and Uyghur language from public signs and demolished community mosques and Uyghur graveyards.[4]

Most dramatically, in 2017 the state began the extralegal detention of Muslims it deemed potential extremists—predominantly Uyghurs and Kazakhs—in concentration camps.[5] By late 2019, the estimated number of detainees ranged between 800,000 and 2 million.[6] In early 2020, the leak of CCP internal documents referred to as the "Karakax List" revealed that reasons for being labeled "untrustworthy" and summarily detained included visiting abroad, getting a passport, visiting foreign websites, praying, having a long beard, or even having detained relatives.[7]

The crackdown on Islamic communities extends well beyond Xinjiang. The CCP began to export the tactics used there to Islamic communities throughout the country.[8] Within a year of my departure in July 2016, Hui enclaves throughout China began to experience crackdowns on ethnic and religious expression. The CCP intensified its scrutiny of Muslims, and the Party's greater restrictions on religious and cultural expression in Islamic communities across China came into clearer focus.[9]

In the early spring of 2018, the government of the Ningxia Hui Autonomous Region quietly implemented a de-Islamification campaign, removing Arabic from signs on restaurants and shops and mandating that mosques remove "Arabic-style" features like onion domes.[10] In a March 2018 editorial, the *Global Times*, the regime's major English-language newspaper, heralded the changes as necessary to combat the slow trickle of potentially corrosive extremism into the lives of ordinary citizens of Ningxia. The editor contended that "pan-halal tendencies appeared in some fields and religion starts to interfere with residents' social life" (*sic*), necessitating vigilance and dedication in response.[11] A few months later, in August, as Party officials in Xinjiang likened practicing the Islamic faith to being afflicted by a mental illness, protestors in tiny, rural Weizhou Township in Ningxia's Tongxin County met attempts by the governments to demolish the newly constructed Grand Mosque by occupying the mosque courtyard and forcing a stalemate.[12]

In autumn, the government of Linxia Hui Autonomous County in Gansu rolled out a series of policies aimed at "strengthening and improving Islamic Work under new circumstances." An official release announcing the changes echoed the usual boilerplate language of the CCP regarding ethnic politics, including emphasis on improving "national unity, religious harmony, and social stability." However, the document also compels the local government to "find weak links" and encourage the Islamic community to "follow the path of Sinicization, and resolutely prevent the 'Saudi-fication' or 'Arabization' of Islam." The policies ban pilgrimages or other religious activities for officials of the government, ban "high-pitched loudspeakers" in mosques that would "disturb the people" with religious activities, and beseeches the people of Linxia to step up their vigilance in daily surveillance.[13]

In early December, Ningxia Hui Autonomous Region announced that it would send representatives from its police forces to Xinjiang to study and learn from the security and "counter-terrorism" policies enacted by the region as part of the Strike Hard Campaign.[14] Later that month, police in Yunnan demolished three mosques in Weishan Yi and Hui Autonomous County, near the city of Dali. Authorities claimed these sites constituted "illegal religious structures" despite members of the mosque community claiming that they had sought to officially register for over a decade.[15]

Communities outside Hui autonomous areas also felt the imposition of restrictions. As the campaign of Sinicization expanded in 2018 and 2019, local Party officials in Zhengzhou, the capital of Henan, stripped domes and Arabic script from mosques and required imams to undergo mandatory ideology training.[16] By the middle of 2018, the Sinicization campaign had reached Jinan, where its simultaneous enactment alongside dramatic urban renewal drastically reshaped the Hui Quarter. As part of citywide "beautification" efforts, the city banned many of the neighborhood's outdoor barbecue restaurants and demolished a number of structures in a road-widening project. At the same time, my respondents in the city reported, the local government demanded that remaining restaurants remove Arabic script and Islamic iconography from their signs. Across the street from the Great Southern Mosque, one respondent told me, the local government razed the famous Yunting Restaurant—built with golden domes to resemble a mosque—as part of the campaign. Even the Great Southern Mosque received orders in late 2019 to strip away the green calligraphic Arabic script that adorned its entrance gate.[17]

Throughout the country, local governments enacted similar tactics in pursuit of Sinicization. When the city of Beijing announced plans to strip Arabic script from public signs on restaurants and shops in July 2019, the city's Committee on Ethnicity and Religious Affairs stated that the actions came as part of a "national directive."[18] Remarks from Party officials included in a batch of leaked documents from Xinjiang that surfaced in late 2019 evince the CCP's fear of Islam that drives the campaign. Speeches given by prominent officials, including Xi Jinping himself, called for strident actions to curb the expression of Islam—ostensibly to combat terrorism.[19] Among the many speeches and remarks prepared by various levels of the national and Xinjiang governments, the leaks contained remarks from Xi that conflated Islamic extremism with a "virus-like contagion" (*bingdu chuanbo de chuanranbing*) that would require a "period of painful, interventionary treatment" (*ganyu zhiliao zhentongqi*).[20] Though such extreme "interventions" by the CCP primarily impacted the Turkic-speaking Uyghur and Kazakh communities, reports emerging in early 2020 revealed that detentions in Xinjiang ensnared a number of Hui as well.[21]

Such aggressive measures and the rhetoric of the People's War on Terror echo in popular sentiment toward Islam. As the Party pursued policies of de-Islamification, an emboldened wave of popular Islamophobia swept across the Chinese internet.[22] Hui citizens reported being harassed in online forums and social media, where they were frequently accused of being terrorists or subjected to harsh stereotyping.[23] In 2017, the announcement from the popular food delivery service, Meituan, that their app would offer a halal delivery option, which would place halal food in separate delivery boxes, earned the company a flood of angry online responses.[24]

These events suggest a clear shift in the CCP's ethnic policies, with the Party moving away from the implementation of policies that achieved the unobservable channeling of contentious politics into safe spaces, opting instead for more forceful, direct, and observable forms of suppression. Since the ascension of Xi to the top leadership post in the Party in 2012–13, the CCP has shifted its posture on dealing with minorities—especially Islamic minorities and those resistant to integration—toward an unmistakable preference for derecognition of minority status and assimilation. Calls for a fundamental restructuring of the *minzu* system began as early as 2004, when the Hui scholar Ma Rong claimed that the Party needed to end policies that gave special recognition to minorities, citing it as the reason a Chinese national consciousness had failed to cohere in minority areas. In a 2008 assessment of the system, Ma critiqued the current system and concluded that differentiation and classification of *minzu* "creates institutional barriers for the interaction and integration" and thus perpetuates disunity, resentment, and instability. The system of differentiation, he argued, placed equality for groups rather than individuals as its top priority, and thus would "inevitably politicize and institutionalize these groups and strengthen their group consciousness."[25]

Other public intellectuals followed Ma, including the policy scholar Hu Angang and the counterterrorism expert Hu Lianhe. Outlining a statist vision of integration, the pair stressed policies that placed the interests of the state before autonomy.[26] In a series of articles the two wrote together they maintained that China's *minzu* policies left it vulnerable to unfair and hypocritical criticism from "Western countries." Excoriating these states in a 2011 article, the pair contended that "Western states" relished using nationality questions and invocations such as "human rights" and "national self-determination" to break apart socialist countries. The authors therefore dismissed concerns about minority rights as "detrimental external international pressures." They also echoed Ma's assertions that China's *minzu* policies left it vulnerable to instability, and they called for a "second generation of *minzu* policies" (*di'erdai minzu zhengce*) to "encourage the blending together of all *minzu*" and to "construct stronger cohesion, where you are in me and I in you, and there is not distinction between you and me—an inseparable, prospering community of *Zhonghua minzu*."[27] Elaborating, the pair implored, "We must be adept and persevere in handling the issues of domestic ethnic groups (minzu) as social issues according to the law, and prevent specially treating the issues of ethnic groups (minzu) as political issues, for the sake of strengthening every citizen's *Zhonghua minzu yishi* [Chinese national consciousness] and awareness of the rule of law, removing all fertile ground and exploitable cracks [*turang he kecheng zhi xi*] where regional nationalisms [*difang minzu zhuyi*] may grow, strengthen *Zhonghua minzu yishi*, and dilute the sense of belonging to classified communities of Han and other *shaoshu minzu* [ethnic minorities]."[28]

Xi's ascension to the Party's leadership in 2013 elevated the position of advocates for a second generation, including Hu Lianhe. Party leadership began to show increased concern for ethnic unrest as a catalyst for China's collapse, often citing the breakup of the Soviet Union as a cautionary tale.[29] State propaganda began to securitize ethnic and religious expression out of line with the state's narratives and emphasized the struggle against the so-called Three Forces (Sangu Shili) of terrorism, separatism, and extremism as "a zero-sum political struggle of life or death."[30] Xi himself began to express more explicitly assimilationist sentiments. In 2014, in the wake of the Kunming attack, Xi maintained that in response to "separatists" trying to "sabotage our ethnic unity," Chinese citizens needed to increase exchange and interactions. Citizens must "draw close like the seeds of a pomegranate that stick together," Xi contended.[31] The goal of this interaction, however, was to integrate all *minzu* into a singular notion of Chineseness rooted in "traditional culture." Xi's 2017 address to the CCP Party Congress illustrates this vision of unity. Speaking to the assembled cadres, Xi reminded them of the influence of China's traditional culture on the Party's own development: "Socialist culture with Chinese characteristics is derived from China's fine traditional culture, which was born of the Chinese civilization and nurtured over more than 5,000 years; it has grown out of the revolutionary and advanced socialist culture that developed over the course of the Chinese people's revolution, construction, and reform under the Party's leadership."[32]

Xi also stressed the importance of developing "cultural confidence" and called for measures to "promote the creative evolution and development of fine traditional Chinese culture" and ensure that religions in China be "Chinese in orientation."[33] By 2019, language stressing the importance of the "collective consciousness of the Chinese nation" (*Zhonghua minzu gongtongti yishi*) began appearing more frequently in Xi's speeches. The imperatives that he issued in these remarks over the course of his leadership closely mirror the recommendations of the policymakers tied to the United Front Work Development (Zhongong Zhongyang Tongyi Zhanxian Gongzuobu; UFWD), one of the country's staunchest advocacy groups calling for a revision of *minzu* policy.[34]

Throughout his leadership, Xi has reinforced such rhetoric with concrete policy measures. Reversing the trend toward a diminished role in ethnic politics for the UFWD in the post-Deng period, Xi oversaw the process of the UFWD's increasing oversight and tightening the reins of control over management of ethnic politics by the State Ethnic Affairs Commission (Guojia Minzu Shiwu Weiyuan Hui; SEAC). This restructuring culminated in March 2018, when the regime announced that the UFWD would assume control over the State Administration for Religious Affairs, giving it broad powers to regulate ethnic and religious behavior.[35] Coupled with the expansion of the UFWD through the creation of township-level branches, such a rearrangement of oversight signaled the group's ascension to a leadership position in the conduct of ethnic politics.[36] The primacy of the authority of the UFWD branches at a local level enabled them to become "laboratories of securitization and anti-terrorism work," especially in locations such as Xinjiang, where the group stands on the front line of the Party's efforts to implement more assertive measures of control over ethnic politics.[37] As a result, the Party's practice of ethnic politics in many areas now focuses on assimilation (*ronghe*) and unity (*yiti*) rather than the pluralism formerly pursued by the SEAC. Such emphasis on integrationist practices can be seen in the appointment of the leading advocate for a second generation of ethnic policies, Hu Lianhe, to a supervisory role over the newly created Xinjiang Bureau of the UFWD.[38]

While the regime's tightening of regulation of ethnic identity for Muslims illustrates an overall rise in stature of pro-assimilation policymakers, the persistence of preferential policies and minority-language instruction for some *minzu* belies the piecemeal implementation of "second-generation" measures. For example, the continued observance of preferential policies in matters of schooling and employment in Yanbian Korean Autonomous Prefecture in Jilin is evidence that second-generation integrationist policies remain far from universal.[39] Likewise, the persistence of Yi-Han education systems in Liagnshan Yi Autonomous Prefecture in Sichuan illustrates the CCP's willingness to allow bilingual and minority-language-based education to continue in certain communities. Indeed, rather than demonstrating drastic changes in minority education policy, the decline of Yi-language education in Liangshan reflects local dissatisfaction with the system's ability to adapt with the times to provide functional Yi-language literacy.[40] In both cases, preferential policies for *shaoshu minzu* persist in minority autonomous communities, with both governmental and popular support.

However, the aggressive posture taken by the state in regard to Islamic *minzu* suggests the beginnings of a more comprehensive shift in policy, starting in communities deemed potentially threatening to state interests. In these communities, "the phantom of instability" (*buwending huanxiang*) begets a "perpetual cycle" (*guaiquan*) of crackdowns and resistance.[41] In this way, Leibold reasons, "the mere perception of instability generates intensive surveillance and securitization which in turn generates more instability."[42]

By prohibiting religious expression—for instance, by banning beards and Islamic head coverings, restricting the use of written Arabic in public spaces,

FIGURE E.1. Screenshots of harassment of the CCP secretary of Wuhan, Ma Guoqiang, who is Hui, posted to Weibo at the beginning of the COVID-19 outbreak, January 2020.

limiting options for *qingzhen* diet in public institutions, and declaring certain rhetoric or kinds of religious observances illegal—the CCP risks arousing the enmity of segments of the Hui community. Campaigns like these also illustrate the failure of the CCP to deliver on the guarantees of *minzu tuanjie* (ethnic unity) and provide minorities with a shared stake in the state that forms the rhetorical core of its ethnic minority policies.[43] A deterioration of the regime's credibility as a good steward of ethnic relations and the perception that it cannot deliver the stable interethnic relations it promises also erode vital pillars of the regime's legitimating narrative.

The outbreak of the COVID-19 pandemic potentially represents the kind of "social earthquake" that could reshape the dynamics of China's ethnic politics.[44] During moments of disruption, social identities crystallize and distinctions between self and other heighten. When disruption overturns other sources of normality—such as work or recreation—people often seek ontological security in the relatively safe harbors of national or ethnic identities. In attempts to restore what they perceive as normality, individuals may exclude others they consider "outside" the community and whose presence serves as a reminder of the disruptive forces that overturn the usual conduct of life. Members of marginalized groups may find themselves excluded from solidarity in the face of unsettled times, or perhaps even scapegoated for the disruptions.[45]

Netizen harassment of the Hui official Ma Guoqiang on the social media platform Weibo during the COVID-19 outbreak in Wuhan in January 2020 best exemplifies this kind of othering. Ma, then acting as Wuhan's Party secretary, came under intense public scrutiny for his role in mishandling the initial outbreak, which contributed to the spread of the virus. In a January 27 press conference, as city officials admitted that their early mistakes worsened the spread, posters to Weibo excoriated Ma on the basis of his Hui identity. Some hurled slurs, using the homophone Huihui (回蛔, "Hui parasite") to other him based on his ethnic identity. Others spread the unfounded rumor that Ma's subsidization of mosques for his Hui co-ethnics left the city financially unprepared to handle the disaster (see figure E.1).[46] In directing such vitriol at Ma based on his ethnicity, citizens painted him as suspect and excluded him from the solidarity afforded those affected by the disease. Ma's harassment mirrors rising concerns about online harassment of Hui and other Muslims on China's most prominent social media sites.[47]

The online Islamophobic harassment of Ma illustrates the precariousness of the CCP's control over ethnic resentments. The regime's adoption of policies of Sinicization alter the dynamics on which the foundation of regime control rests. In securitizing Islamic and Hui identity the CCP may end up triggering precisely the kind of activation and mobilization it long sought to defuse. If it continues to crack down on what it considers illegal or extremist ethnic or religious expression, the CCP may revive the salience of the external boundaries that separate the Hui from others and redirect the focus of contentious politics toward the regime itself. While the regime's willingness to permit internal contestation allows it to, thus far, maintain control and prevent the outbreak of restive, contentious politics, its overzealous urge to root out any heterodox ethnic expression may cause its grasp on ethnic politics to slip away.

Appendix A

Interviewees

RESPONDENT CODE	AGE	GENDER	ETHNICITY	OCCUPATION	HIGHEST LEVEL OF EDUCATION
BJ01082815	33	M	Hui	Software editor	MA
BJ02082915	40	M	Hui	Imam	Jingxueyuan (Qur'anic Studies Institute)
BJ03083115	60	M	Hui	Mosque caretaker	High school
BJ04090115	45	M	Hui	Cemetery groundskeeper	Middle school
BJ05090115	45	M	Hui	Cemetery groundskeeper	Middle school
BJ06090515	60	F	Hui	Novelty shop owner	High school
BJ07090615	55	M	Hui	Retiree	High school
BJ08091215	29	M	Hui	Editor	MA
BJ09091615	57	F	Hui	Taxi driver	High school
BJ10091615	44	M	Hui	Real estate and finance agent	BA
BJ11091615	28	M	Hui	PhD student	PhD

BJ12091615	33	M	Hui	Entrepreneur	BA
BJ13092015	32	M	Hui	Office manager	BA
BJ14092415	40	M	Hui	Imam	Jingxueyuan
BJ15092615	40	F	Han	Architect	MA
BJ16100115	21	M	Han	Student	BA
JN17100615	32	F	Han	Information desk manager	BA
JN18100615	48	F	Hui	Factory worker	High school
JN19100815	38	M	Hui	Entrepreneur	High school
JN20101115	35	F	Han	Secretary	BA
JN21101215	45	M	Hui	Imam	Jingxueyuan
JN22101315	28	F	Hui	English teacher	BA
JN23101515	50	M	Hui	Imam	Jingxueyuan
JN24101515	22	M	Hui	Real estate agent	BA
JN25101915	29	M	Hui	Software developer	MA
JN26101915	49	M	Hui	Imam	Jingxueyuan
JN27102015	44	F	Hui	Banker	BA
JN28102215	52	F	Hui	Secretary/front desk staff	High school
BJ29102315	32	F	Hui	Visual artist	MA
BJ30102415	70	M	Hui	Retiree	High school
JN31103015	69	M	Hui	Volunteer at Islamic society	High school
JN32103115	52	M	Hui	Engineer	BA
JN33110115	42	M	Hui	Imam	Jingxueyuan

JN34110415	22	F	Hui	Airline worker	Technical school
JN35110515	38	F	Hui	Restaurateur	High school
JN36111015	44	F	Hui	Kindergarten teacher	BA
JN37111115	49	F	Hui	Imam	Jingxueyuan
JN38111115	61	F	Hui	Mosque manager	High school
JN39111115	26	F	Han	English teacher	BA
JN40111415	30	M	Han	Corporate spokesperson	BA
JN41112015	30	F	Han	English teacher	BA
JN42112215	60	F	Hui	Restaurateur	High school
JN43112415	55	M	Hui	Tea shop owner	MA
JN44112515	18	M	Hui	Student	BA
JN45112515	18	M	Han	Student	BA
JN46112515	36	F	Hui	PhD student/ adjunct faculty	PhD
JN47112615	18	F	Hui	Student	BA
JN48112615	19	F	Hui	Student	BA
JN49120115	26	M	Han	Coffee shop owner	BA
JN50120315	18	M	Hui	Cook/waiter	Middle school
JN51120315	40	M	Hui	Baker	High school
JN52120415	36	M	Hui	Factory worker	BA
JN53120515	37	M	Han	Entrepreneur	BA
JN54120715	55	F	Hui	Imam	Jingxueyuan
JN55120815	68	M	Hui	Restaurateur	High school
JN56120915	31	M	Hui	Fitness instructor	BA

JN57121015	31	F	Hui	Banker	BA
JN58121215	36	F	Hui	Homemaker	Middle school
JN59121215	62	F	Hui	Retiree	High school
JN60121215	62	M	Hui	Retiree	High school
JN61121615	55	F	Hui	Entrepreneur	High school
JN62122015	68	F	Hui	Retiree	Middle school
JN63122015	77	M	Hui	Author/historian	MA
BJ64123015	40	M	Hui	Islamic society official	MA
BJ65010716	70	M	Hui	Professor/author	MA
BJ66011016	40	F	Hui	Restaurateur	BA
YN67011716	26	M	Hui	MA student	MA
YN68012016	31	F	Hui	Professor	PhD
YN69012116	37	M	Hui	Imam	Jingxueyuan
YN70012116	26	M	Hui	Khalifa (clergy)	Jingtang jiaoyu (mosque education)
YN71012116	38	M	Hui	Khalifa	Jingtang jiaoyu
YN72012216	46	M	Hui	Entrepreneur	BA
YN73012316	33	F	Han	Cashier at Islamic goods store	Middle school
YN74012416	35	M	Hui	Restaurateur	High school
YN75012616	29	F	Hui	Government service worker	BA
YN76012616	37	M	Hui	Restaurant manager	BA
YN77012816	47	M	Hui	Imam	Jingtang jiaoyu

YN78012916	40	F	Hui	Butcher	High school
YN79012916	45	F	Hui	Butcher	High school
YN80020416	29	F	Hui	Government service worker	BA
YN81020416	24	F	Hui	Government service worker	BA
YN82020716	40	M	Han	Restaurant manager	BA
YN83021216	28	M	Hui	Restaurant manager/bakery owner	High school
YN84021316	37	M	Hui	Software engineer	MA
YN85021316	37	F	Hui	Restaurateur	BA
YN86021516	60	F	Hui	Islamic goods store owner	High school
YN87021816	27	M	Hui	Restaurateur	Culinary school
YN88022016	45	F	Hui	Restaurateur	High school
YN89022016	25	F	Hui	Restaurateur	High school
YN90022116	35	M	Hui	Education administrator	BA
YN91022216	21	M	Hui	Butcher	High school
YN92022216	57	M	Hui	Administrator, Ningxia Academy of Social Sciences	PhD
YN93022316	34	M	Hui	PhD student	PhD
YN94022416	46	M	Hui	Restaurateur	High school
YN95022916	35	M	Hui	Office worker	BA
YN96022916	33	F	Hui	Teacher	BA

YN97031716	50	F	Hui	Islamic goods store owner	High school
YN98031716	34	M	Hui	Hotel manager	BA
YN99031816	28	M	Hui	Restaurateur	High school
YN100032016	25	F	Hui	Hotel receptionist	Technical school
YN101032116	55	M	Hui	Imam	Jingxueyuan
YN102032116	33	M	Hui	Khalifa	Jingtang jiaoyu
YN103032216	61	F	Han	Professor	PhD
YN104032216	56	M	Hui	Professor	PhD
YN105032316	30	M	Hui	Instructor at Jingxueyuan	MA
YN106032616	32	F	Han	MA student/English teacher	MA
YN107033016	36	M	Hui	Business consultant	MA
YN108033016	32	F	Han	Business consultant	MA
YN109033116	21	F	Hui	Student	BA
XN110041116	48	F	Hui	Islamic goods store owner	High school
XN111041216	37	M	Salar	Islamic goods store owner	High school
XN112041316	48	M	Salar	Teacher	MA
XN113041316	30	M	Hui	Chemical engineer	BA
XN114041416	40	M	Hui	Imam	Jingxueyuan
XN115041516	52	M	Salar	Professor	PhD
XN116041516	55	M	Hui	Retiree	BA

XN117041616	43	F	Hui	Professor	PhD
XN118041816	40	M	Hui	Mosque tour guide	Jingxueyuan
XN119041916	28	F	Hui	Café waitress	BA
XN120042016	39	F	Hui	Small business owner	High school
XN121042116	24	F	Hui	Teacher	BA
XN122042216	53	M	Hui	Government service worker	BA
XN123042316	26	M	Hui	MA student	MA
XN124042516	51	M	Hui	Public charity operator	BA
XN125042616	50	M	Hui	Carpet store owner	High school
XN126042816	40	F	Salar	Islamic goods store owner	High school
XN128043016	27	F	Hui	MA student	MA
XN129050116	40	M	Salar	University administrator	MA
XN130050416	25	F	Hui	Teacher	MA
XN132050616	35	F	Hui	Small business owner	High school
XN133050616	29	F	Hui	Unemployed	High school
XN135050916	60	M	Hui	Retiree	High school
XN136051216	30	M	Han	Butcher	High school
XN137051216	30	F	Hui	Tea shop owner	High school
XN138051316	45	M	Malay	Halal food consultant	MA
XN139051616	24	M	Hui	Office worker	BA

XN140051516	28	M	Hui	Real estate agent	BA
XN141051616	25	M	Hui	Taxi driver	High school
XN142052116	35	M	Tu	Media production/ film director	BA
XN143052116	40	M	Hui	Professor	PhD
XN144052316	26	F	Hui	Hotel receptionist	High school
XN145052516	34	M	Hui	Small business owner	High school
XN146052816	59	M	Hui	Imam	Jingxueyuan
XN147052916	64	M	Hui	Imam	Jingxueyuan
XN148053016	59	M	Salar	Teacher	High school
XN149061416	46	F	Hui	Supermarket cashier	High school
XN150061516	40	M	Hui	Imam	Jingxueyuan
XN151061716	35	F	Hui	Antiques dealer	High school
YN152011816	63	M	Hui	Professor	MA
YN153011816	39	M	Hui	Professor	PhD
LZ01070714	30	M	Han	Office worker	BA
LZ02070814	30	M	Dongxiang	Office worker	BA
LZ03070914	35	M	Hui	Office worker	BA
LZ04070914	35	M	Hui	Office worker	BA

Appendix B

Mosques/Islamic Places at Case Sites

CASE SITE	MOSQUES/ISLAMIC PLACES
Beijing	Changying Mosque 常营清真寺
	Chinese Islamic Association 中国伊斯兰教协会
	Dongsi Mosque 东四清真寺
	Lanying Guang Mosque 蓝靛广清真寺
	MaDian Mosque 马甸清真寺
	Nandouya Mosque 南豆芽清真寺
	Niujie Mosque 牛街清真礼拜寺
Jinan	Beida Huaishu Mosque 北大槐树清真寺
	Dikou Zhuang Mosque 堤口庄清真寺
	Great Northern Mosque of Jinan 济南被大清真寺
	Great Southern Mosque of Jinan 济南南大清真寺
	Laozhai Mosque 老寨村清真寺
	Shandong Islamic Association 山东省伊斯兰教协会
	Women's Mosque of Jinan 清真女寺
Yinchuan	Central Mosque of Yinchuan 清真中寺
	Nanguan Mosque of Yinchuan 南关清真寺
	Najiahu Mosque 纳家户清真寺
	Ningxia Jingxue Yuan 宁夏经学院
Weizhou	Grand Mosque of Weizhou 韦州清真大寺
Linxia	Da Gongbei 大拱北
	Guo Gongbei 国拱北
	Huasi Gongbei 华寺拱北
	Lao Huasi Mosque 老华寺清真寺

Xining	Beiguan Mosque of Xining 北关清真寺 Dongguan Mosque of Xining 东关清真大寺 Nanguan Mosque of Xining 南关清真大寺 Shulinxiang Mosque 树林巷清真寺 Yangjiazhuang Mosque 杨家庄清真寺

Appendix C

Migration Inflow at Case Sites, 2006–2016

	BEIJING	JINAN	XINING
2006	203,019	155,143	125,701
2007	175,451	100,623	88,645
2008	184,770	121,721	37,664
2009	189,744	71,251	47,619
2010	185,101	71,589	24,998
2011	211,447	63,635	45,068
2012	190,510	60,208	27,867
2013	198,869	57,227	69,239
2014	166,600	36,075	25,762
2015	167,506	48,180	39,480
2016	160,739	47,405	37,661

Note: The Yinchuan Municipal Bureau of Statistics records only "natural change" in yearly population and does not keep records of migration inflows; Yinchuan's figures are thus omitted from this appendix. The Qinghai Provincial Bureau of Statistics subdivides yearly immigration figures into categories of "outside of the province" and "inside the province"; this table adds those two figures to present an overall total.
Sources: Annual reports of the Beijing Municipal Bureau of Statistics, Jinan Municipal Bureau of Statistics, and Qinghai Provincial Bureau of Statistics between 2007 and 2017.

Glossary of Chinese Terms

ahong 阿訇 imam, derived from the Persian *akhund*
Aiguo aidang 爱国爱党 "Love your country, love the Party"; a patriotic CCP slogan
Aiguo aijiao 爱国爱教 "Love your country, love your faith"; a patriotic CCP slogan
Alaboyu/Alabowen 阿拉伯语/阿拉伯文 Modern Standard Arabic Language
Anseliangmu alaikong 安色两目啊来空 Chinese transliteration of the Arabic greeting meaning "Peace be with you" (*Al salamu 'alaykum*)
azang 啊藏 the *adhan*, or Islamic call to prayer; also translated as *bangke*

baijiu 白酒 Chinese distilled liquor made from sorghum
bai maozi 白帽子 Islamic prayer hat; lit., "white hat"
bangke 邦克 the *adhan*, or Islamic call to prayer; also translated *azang*
Beida Huaishu Xiaoqu 北大槐树小区 neighborhood of Jinan's Tianqiao District
Beijing Pengren Xiehui 北京烹饪协会 Beijing Cuisine Association
Beijing Qingzhen Meishi Wenhuajie 北京清真美食文化节 Beijing Halal Culinary Culture Festival
bendi 本地 local; usually used to describe people, in contrast to *waidi*
bingdu chuanbo de chuanranbing 病毒传播的传染病 "virus-like contagion"; phrase used in remarks to Party members by Xi Jinping to describe Islam
Bosiyu/Bosiwen 波斯语/波斯文 Persian language

Chai Na'er? 拆哪儿 "Demolish Where?" (Beijingers' sarcastic name for China)
chai qian 拆迁 lit., "demolish and replace"; urban renewal where existing structures are destroyed and residents move to new housing
Chantou-Hui 缠头回 "Turban-hui," an antiquated term referring to Turkic-speaking Muslims of Xinjiang, usually understood as referring to Uyghurs

Chengdongqu 城东区 District of Xining, Qinghai
chengzhenhua/chengshihua 城镇化/城市化 urbanization
chunzheng 纯正 purity, as in "ethnic purity"

dagong 打工 to do temporary work; often involves wage labor for migrant workers
Da Han zhuyi 大汉主义 Han Supremacy or Han Chauvinism
danhua 淡化 lit., "watered down"; often used in reference to secularized Hui
Dehenglong 德恒隆 village in Hualong Hui Autonomous County, Qinghai
di'er dai minzu zhengci 第二代民族政策 Second Generation Minzu Policies; advocated by Ma Rong, Hu Lianhe, and Hu Angang, among others
difanghua 地方话 local dialect
difang minzu zhuyi 地方民族主义 regional nationalisms
digaizi 底盖子 a term in Jinanese Huihua for non-Muslims, derived from the Persian *digar*
digouyou 地沟油 lit. "gutter oil"; previously used, dirty cooking oil
Dikou Zhaung 堤口庄 Neighborhood of Jinan's Tianqiao District
dingzihu 钉子户 lit. "nail houses"
Donguan Dajie 东关大街 street in Xining's Chengdong District
Dongxiang-Hui 东乡回 an antiquated term for Dongxiang
Dongxiangzu 东乡族 Dongxiang, a Mongolic-speaking Muslim minority in Gansu and Qinghai
Douban Hutong 豆瓣胡同 neighborhood in west-central Beijing

fanghuiju 访惠聚 "visit [the people], benefit [the people], gather [the hearts of the people]"; campaign begun in Xinjiang in 2015
fanke 番客 lit. "foreign guests"; used as early as the Ming dynasty, often to describe Hui and other Muslims in China
fumin qiangguo 富民强国 a "rich and strong country," a phrase from CCP propaganda

Gaige Kaifang 改革开放 Reform and Opening Campaign, begun under Deng Xiaoping in 1978
gaitou 盖头 religious head covering, usually used in reference to hijab
Ganqing 甘清 A portmanteau of Gansu and Qinghai; usually refers to the southern part of Gansu and eastern parts of Qinghai
Gansu Musiilin Wailai Musilin Lianluo Lianyi Hui 甘肃穆斯林外来穆斯林联络联谊会 Gansu Muslim Society for Connecting Migrant Muslims, located in Jinan
gaolou 高楼 high-rise (lit., "tower" style) apartment buildings
Gedimu 各地亩 a non-Sufi, Hanafi school of Islam, originating in China; derived from the Arabic *qadim*, or "the ancient ones"; also sometimes referred to as "old teaching" (*lao jiao*, 老教)

gongbei 拱北 mausoleums built to house the tombs of Sufi Muslim saints
Gongqingtuan Lu 共青团路 street in Jinan's Shizhong District
Gu'erbang jie 古尔邦节 Eid al-Adha (also known in some places as Qurban), the celebration of Abraham's voluntary sacrifice of Ishmael
Gulanjing 古兰经 Qur'an
Guojia Minzu Shiwu Weiyuan Hui 国家民族事务委员会 State Ethnic Affairs Commission of the People's Republic of China
Guomindang/Kuomintang 国民党 Nationalist Party of the Republic of China
guozu 国族 national people, belonging to a "race state"
Guyuan 固原 city in Ningxia Hui Autonomous Region

Haiyuan xian 海原县 county in Ningxia Hui Autonomous Region
halali 哈拉里 transliteration of the Arabic word *halal*
halifa 哈理发 khalifa, or student at a madrassa; in northwest China these students may also be referred to as *manla*
Hanhua 汉化 Hanification
Han-Hui 汉回 an antiquated term for Chinese-speaking Muslims; today considered Huizu
Han Ketabu 汉克塔布 *Han Kitab*; a collection of commentaries on Islam written in Chinese by Hui literati during the Ming and Qing
Hanyu 汉语 Chinese language; refers to spoken dialect
Hanyu minzu 汉语民族 "Chinese-speaking nationality"; used in reference to both Han and Hui
Hanzi 汉子 Chinese characters
Hanzu 汉族 Han ethnicity, sometimes referred to as "Han Chinese"
hefa 合法 forbidden; used by Hui as a transliteration of the Arabic *haram*
hege 合格 "qualified"; used by Hui to denote Islamic piety
Heze 菏泽 city in Shandong
Hualong Huizu Zizhuxian 化隆回族自治县 autonomous county in Qinghai
Huaxia 华夏 Chinese civilization
Huihua/Huiwen/Huiyan 回话/回文/回言 Hui dialect
Huijiao 回教 antiquated term for Islam; lit., "the teaching of the Hui"
Huimin 回民 colloquial ethnonym for the Hui ethnicity; used informally
Huimin Xiaoqu 回民小区 Hui Quarter, in both Jinan and Xining
Huizu 回族 Hui ethnicity; sometimes referred to as "Chinese Muslims"
hukou 户口 household registration
hutong 胡同 narrow-lane neighborhoods of traditional houses in central Beijing

jiaofa 教法 religious doctrine, or *fiqh*
jiaopai 教派 Chinese Islamic sects

jiating jiaoyu 家庭教育 home education; refers to teaching children informally about Islam
jiefang 解放 "liberation"; the CCP phrase for its victory over the Kuomintang and the end of the Chinese Civil War in 1949
jiejing 解经 exegesis, scriptural commentary on the Qur'an
Jinfeng qu 金凤区 district of Yinchuan
Jinghanyu 经汉语 local Hui dialect of Chinese
jingming 经名 Islamic name; taken by Hui in addition to Chinese names
jingtang jiaoyu 经堂教育 mosque education
Jingwen/Jingyu 经文/经语 Qur'anic Arabic
Jingxueyuan 经学院 Qur'anic Studies Academy
ji'nian wangren 纪念亡人 ceremonial commemoration or veneration of the deceased

Kaizhai jie 开斋节 Eid al-Fitr, the celebration of the end of Ramadan
Kaligang 卡里刚 community in Hualong Hui Autonomous County, Qinghai (referred to in Tibetan as Khargang, ཁ་སྒང)

Laocheng Qu 老城区 Jinan's Old City Quarter
laojiao 老教 used to describe non-Yihewani schools of Chinese Islam, including, but not limited to, the Gedimu and Sufi lineages
laorenjia 老人家 the head of a Chinese Sufi order (or *menhuan*); not to be confused with an imam (*ahong*)
Laozhai cun 老寨村 village in Jinan
Ledu Lu 乐堵路 street in Xining's Chengdong District
Linxia Huizu Zizhizhou 临夏回族自治州 autonomous prefecture in Gansu
liudong renkou 流动人口 lit., "transient population"; describes migration from rural villages to cities
lüse roupin 绿色肉品 lit., "green meat products"; usually connotes halal food, but occasionally used by impostors selling fake halal meat
Lusha'er 鲁沙尔 township in Huangzhong County, Qinghai (known in Tibetan as Rushar, རུ་གསར)

manla 满拉 students at madrassas; more frequently used in northwest China; elsewhere in China, these students may be referred to as *halifa*
meihua 美化 beautification; references urban renewal campaign undertaken in Beijing in 2017
menhuan 门宦 Chinese Sufi orders
Minkaohan 民考汉 minorities educated in standard Mandarin
Minkaomin 民考民 minorities educated in their minority language
minzu 民族 ethnic group; translated by the CCP as "nationality"

minzu jingshen 民族精神 minzu spirit, a phrase invoked by Chinese Republicans in the early twentieth century
minzu shibie 民族识别 ethnic classification project first undertaken by the CCP in the 1950s
minzu techanpin 民族特产品 ethnic specialty products
minzu tuanjie 民族团结 interethnic unity
minzu xuanchuan 民族宣传 ethnic propaganda
minzu zhengce 民族政策 ethnicity policy
Mojia Jie 莫家街 street in Xining's Chengdong District
Musilin穆斯林 Muslim
muyu 母语 lit., "mother tongue"; native language

Najiahu 纳家户 village in Yonging County, Ningxia Hui Autonomous Region
Nanbu Shanqu 南部山区 area of southern Ningxia Hui Autonomous Region (refers mostly to areas of Guyuan, Zhongwei)
Nanliangxiang 南梁乡 village in Yinchuan
neidi 内地 "interior China" ; used by those living in the northwest to refer to areas in the east, usually the Chinese coastal heartland
niangao 年糕 a sweet snack sold by street vendors
nian Hui 年回 lit., "yearly Hui"; Hui who attend mosque only on holidays
Niu Jie 牛街 "Oxen Street" and surrounding neighborhood in Beijing
niurou lamian 牛肉拉面 handmade beef noodles, a dish associated with *qingzhen* food and Hui culture

pingfang 平房 single-story courtyard homes
Putonghua 普通话 standard Chinese, Mandarin

qiancheng 虔诚 **pious**
Qinghai Guoji Qingzhen Shipin Jiminzu Yongpin Zhanlanhui 青海国际清真食品及民族用品展览会 Qinghai International Halal Food and Ethnic Products Fair
Qinghai Qingzhen Shipin Hangye Xiehui 青海清真食品行业协会 Qinghai Qingzhen Food Production Association
qingzhen 清真 a set of lifestyle standards governing Hui daily life; lit., "pure and true"; often used to mean halal; mostly used in relation to food (e.g. 清真食品, 清真菜)
qingzhenyan 清真言 the *shahada*, the Islamic profession of faith
Qufu 曲阜 city in Shandong

Renmin Fankong Zhanzheng 人民反恐战争 People's War on Terror; declared by Xi Jinping in 2014
ronghe 融合 assimilation, to assimilate

Sailaifeye 塞莱菲耶 Salafi reformist movement of Hanbali Islamic thought; pejoratively called *Santai* by some other Hui
Sala-Hui 撒拉回 an antiquated term for Salar
salamu 萨拉姆 Chinese transliteration of the Arabic greeting *salaam*
Salazu 撒拉族 Salar; a Turkic-speaking Muslim minority in Gansu and Qinghai
Sangu Shili 三股势力 the "Three Forces" of terrorism, separatism, and extremism, as identified by the CCP
Santai 三抬 pejorative term for Salafis; lit., "Three Raises," a reference to the three times Salafis raise their hands during prayer
semu 色目 a category of ethnic classification for non-Mongol, non-Han citizens under the rule of Yuan dynasty; Hui were included in this category; approximately translates to "assorted categories"
Shadian 沙甸 township in Gejiu City, Yunnan
Shadian Shijian 沙甸事件 Shadian incident or Shadian massacre; an armed standoff between local Hui and the People's Liberation Army in 1975 in Shadian village in Yunnan in which at least 1,600 died
shajin 纱巾 headscarf, or other Islamic headcovering for women
shangyehua 商业化 business-minded, or commercialized
shaoshu minzu 少数民族 ethnic minorities
shexide 舍西德 Islamic martyrs, from the Arabic *shahid*
shisuhua 世俗化 secularization

Tianqiao qu 天桥区 district in Jinan
Tianshui shi 天水市 city in Gansu
Tongxin Lu 同心路 street in Yinchuan's XiXia District
Tongxin xian 同心县 couny in Ningxia Hui Autonomous Region

waidi/wailai 外地/外来 outsider, often used in contrast to *bendi*
Wansheng Jie 万圣街 street in Jinan's Tianqiao District
Weishan Yizu Huizi Zizhi xian 巍山彝族回族自治县 autonomous county in Yunnan
wei shibie minzu 未识别民族 unrecognized ethnic groups (e.g., those lacking official *minzu* status)
weiwen 维稳 "stability maintenance" initiatives undertaken by the CCP
Weizhou 韦州 township in Tongxin County, Ningxia Hui Autonomous Region
wending 稳定 societal stability
wenhua re 文化热 "minority culture fever"; describes the increase in minority identification after the start of Reform and Opening
woerzi 卧尔兹 sermon, from the Arabic *wa'z*
wudu 乌杜 Islamic ritual washing or ablutions
Wuzhong 吴忠 city in Ningxia Hui Autonomous Region

Wuzu Gonghe Guo 五族共和国 "Nation of Five Peoples," a system of ethnic classification under the Kuomintang

xiandaihua 现代化 modernization

xiaojing/xiao'erjing 小经/小二经 phonetic system using Arabic letters to approximate Chinese words

xiaokang shehui 小康社会 variously translated as "comfortable society" or "moderately prosperous society"

Xibei 西北 northwest China; usually includes provinces of Gansu, Qinghai, Ningxia Hui Autonomous Region, and Xinjiang Uyghur Autonomous Region

Xibu Dakaifa 西部大开发 The Great Western Development Campaign; comprehensive infrastructure and economic development program targeting western China, begun in 2000

xili 洗礼 Islamic conversion ceremony

Xi Xia qu 西夏区 district in Yinchuan

Xunhua Salazu Zizhi xian 循化撒拉族自治县 autonomous county in Qinghai

Yanlidaji Baolikongbu Huodong Zhuanxiang Xingdong 严厉打击暴力恐怖活动专项行动 Strike Hard Campaign against Violent Terrorism, often shortened to Yanda; crackdown campaign begun in 2014 conducted in Xinjiang, ostensibly to curb radical Islamic terrorism

Yantai 烟台 city in Shandong

Yidai Yilu 一带一路 Belt and Road Initiative

Yihewani 伊赫瓦尼 Chinese branch of the Ikhwan school of Hanafi Islamic thought; sometimes colloquially referred to as "new teaching" (xinjiao, 新教)

yimin 移民 migrant

Yisilanjiao 伊斯兰教 Islam

Yongning xian 永宁县 county in Ningxia Hui Autonomous Region

youhui zhengce 优惠政策 preferential treatment policies (for ethnic minorities, administered by the CCP)

youxiang 油香 fried oil cakes often eaten by Hui on holidays

Yuhuangge Bei Lu 玉皇阁北路 street in Yinchuan's Xingqing District

Zang-Hui 藏回 Tibetan Hui, particularly from Hualong Hui Autonomous County, in Qinghai

zang, luan, cha 脏,乱,差 lit., "dirty, disorderly, and dilapidated"; frequently used by Jinan residents to describe the Hui Quarter

Zhangjiachuan Huizu Zizhi xian 张家川回族自治县 autonomous county in Gansu

Zhehelinye 哲赫林耶 the Jahriyya Sufi order

Zhonggong Zhongyang Tongyi Zhanxian Gongzuobu 中共中央统一战线工作部 United Front Work Development of the Chinese Communist Party
Zhonghua minzu 中华民族 Chinese nationalities
Zhonghua minzu yishi 中华民族意识 Chinese national consciousness
Zhuma libai 主麻礼拜 Jumu'ah, Friday afternoon prayers
zuji 祖籍 ancestral hometown
zujiao yiti 族教一体 ethnoreligious integration
zuqun 族群 "ethnic groups"; a term advocated by second-generation ethnic policy proponents to replace *minzu*

Notes

PREFACE

1 A pseudonym.

2 See, for example, Oakes, *Tourism and Modernity in China*; Donaldson, *Small Works*; Ian Johnson, "In China, 'Once the Villages Are Gone, the Culture Is Gone,'" *New York Times*, February 1, 2014.

3 Tobin, *Securing China's Northwest Frontier.*

INTRODUCTION

1 Interview, JN43112415. Throughout the text I cite interviews by code numbers that correspond to each respondent. Appendix A gives a complete listing of interviewees by their assigned code numbers and lists demographic data, including ethnicity, age, gender, profession, level of education, and interview location.

2 Xibei refers to China's northwest in both cultural and geographic terms. While definitions of what constitute the region differ from person to person, it usually includes the provinces of Gansu, Qinghai, and the Xinjiang Uyghur Autonomous Region. Occasionally my respondents included Ningxia Hui Autonomous Region, and sometimes even Shaanxi Province. In this book, Xibei includes Gansu, Qinghai, Xinjiang, and—where my respondents did so—Ningxia.

3 Interview, JN43112415

4 Mark Abrahamson's commonly accepted definition of *enclaves* describes them as "places in which members of an ethnic, religious, or racial group, sharing common traditions, support specialized shopping venues, such as ethnic groceries or religious goods stores. Many of these shops are owned by co-ethnics who reside in the same community. Enclaves also tend to be relatively self-contained institutionally; that is, there are

usually institutions attached to the enclave that support people's distinctive ways of life, such as schools that teach in their native language or homes for the aged that accommodate cultural dietary preferences" (*Global Cities*, 60). In "Creating a Sense of Place," Mazumdar et al. note that these spaces produce "a strong tie between the lifestyle and the geographic space the residents occupy" (320).

5 Harrell, "Introduction."

6 Côté, "Internal Migration and the Politics of Place"; Hillman, "Introduction"; Cliff, "Lucrative Chaos."

7 Dreyer, "China's Vulnerability to Minority Separatism"; Kaltman, *Under the Heel of the Dragon*; Davis, "Uyghur Muslim Ethnic Separatism in Xinjiang, China"; Mackerras, "Tibetans, Uyghurs and Multinational 'China'"; Leibold, "Ethnic Policy in China"; Kolås, "Degradation Discourse and Green Governmentality"; Côté, "The Enemies Within."

8 Interviews, JN17100615, JN21101215, JN40111415, JN54120715.

9 Interview, JN54120715.

10 Interview, JN55120815.

11 McCarthy, *Communist Multiculturalism*, 14–15.

12 On these rebellions, see Kim, *Holy War in China*; Atwill, *The Chinese Sultanate*; Lipman, *Familiar Strangers*.

13 McCarthy, *Communist Multiculturalism*, 15.

14 For examples from the international press, see Andrew Jacobs, "Light Government Touch Lets China's Hui Practice Islam in the Open," *New York Times*, February 1, 2016; "The Hui: China's Other Muslims," *Economist*, October 8, 2016.

15 Gladney, *Muslim Chinese*, 97.

16 Gladney, *Muslim Chinese*, 13. Gladney's explanation of *qingzhen* is not universally accepted. On the meaning of *qingzhen*, particularly as it relates to halal standards, see also chapter 4.

17 Dillon, *China's Muslim Hui Community*.

18 Jaschok and Shui, *The History of Women's Mosques in Chinese Islam*.

19 Gillette, *Between Mecca and Beijing*.

20 McCarthy, *Communist Multiculturalism*, 130–66.

21 Erie, *China and Islam*.

22 I borrow the phrase *quiet politics* from J. Paul Goode's work on everyday nationalism in Russia. See especially Goode, "Nationalism in Quiet Times"; Goode, "Love for the Motherland."

23 Barth, "Introduction," 7.

24 Wimmer, *Ethnic Boundary Making*, 3.

25 Citrin and Sears, "Balancing National and Ethnic Identities," 147.

26 Brubaker, *Nationalism Reframed*, 13.

27 Brubaker, *Ethnicity without Groups*, 1–28.

28 Fox and Miller-Idriss, "Everyday Nationhood"; Goode and Stroup, "Everyday Nationalism"; Bonikowski, "Nationalism in Settled Times"; Skey and Antonsich, *Everyday Nationhood.*

29 In Chinese, *Feng pu ci te ci zhenzhu zhi zunming*, and in Arabic, *bi-smillāhi r-raḥmāni r-rahim.*

30 Field observations, Beijing, August 2015.

31 George and Bennett, *Case Studies and Theory Development in the Social Sciences*, 93.

32 At the time this manuscript went to press in late February 2021, the 2010 national census provided the most recent publicly available comprehensive national statistics on ethnicity.

33 The word *minzu* is a neologism first introduced to the Chinese language from the Japanese *minzoku* in the late nineteenth century. The CCP translates *minzu* as "ethnic nationality"; however, scholars contest the appropriateness of this term and, because of its ambiguity, leave it untranslated.

34 For a list of Islamic populations in China, see Zhou and Ma, *Development and Decline of Beijing's Hui Muslim Community*, 1.

35 Gladney, "Islam in China," 92–94.

36 The Song dynasty polymath Shen Kuo's tome *Meng xi bitan* (originally written by 1088) mentions a battle between the Song's armies and a group of HuiHui occurring near the Yellow River. Likewise, the *History of the Liao (Liao Shi)*, compiled by Toqtogha in 1344, draws on the records from the era of Yelü Yanxi, Emperor Tianzuo of the Liao dynasty (reigning approximately 1101–25), which recount the surrender of "the King of the HuiHui" to the general (and future Emperor Dezong of the Western Liao) Yelü Dashi in the third year of the Baoda era (approximately 1123–24). See Shen, *Meng xi bitan*, 36–37; Toqtogha, *History of the Liao*, 30:356; Pillsbury, "Muslim History in China," 16; Ma, "A Primary Investigation of the History of the Hui People," 89–91.

37 Yang and Yu, *Yisilan yu Zhongguo wenhua*; Haw, "The Semu Ren in the Yuan Empire," 40–44; Lipman, *Familiar Strangers*, 33.

38 Gladney, *Muslim Chinese*, 15.

39 Lipman, *Familiar Strangers*, xxiii.

40 Schluessel, *Land of Strangers*, 14–44.

41 Gladney, *Muslim Chinese*, 19; Lipman, *Familiar Strangers*, xviii.

42 Schluesselxx, *Land of Strangers*, 38.

43 Leibold, "Competing Narratives of Racial Unity in Republican China."

44 Mullaney, *Coming to Terms with the Nation*, 25.

45 Cieciura, "Ethnicity or Religion?," 115; Ha, "Hui Muslims and Han Converts," 331.

46 Cieciura, "Ethnicity or Religion?," 112–15.

47 Eroglu Sager, "A Place under the Sun," 3.

48 Lee, "Muslims as 'Hui' in Late Imperial and Republican China," 245–49.
49 Lee, "Muslims as 'Hui' in Late Imperial and Republican China," 249–51.
50 Mullaney, "Critical Han Studies," 10–11; Litzinger, *Other Chinas*, 4–8.
51 Mullaney, *Coming to Terms with the Nation*, 28–29.
52 For further discussion of the CCP's handling of the legacy of Ma Bufang, see Cooke, "Surviving State and Society in Northwest China."
53 Côté, "The Enemies Within," 10.
54 For further discussion of these events, see Lipman, *Familiar Strangers*; Kim, *Holy War in China*; Atwill, *The Chinese Sultanate*.
55 Chen, "Islamic Modernism in China," 117–24.
56 Cieciura, "The Crescent and the Red Star," 9.
57 Gao, "The Call of the Oases"; Lin, *Modern China's Ethnic Frontiers*, 113–24.
58 Cieciura, "The Crescent and the Red Star," 16.
59 Cieciura, "The Crescent and the Red Star," 19.
60 Su, "Harmony and Martyrdom among China's Hui Muslims."
61 Lipman, *Familiar Strangers*, 38.
62 Erie and Carlson, "Introduction to 'Islam in China/China in Islam.'"
63 Lipman, *Familiar Strangers*, 25–57.
64 Ben-Dor Benite, *The Dao of Muhammad*.
65 Hillman, "The Rise of the Community in Rural China"; Hille, Horlemann, and Nietupski, *Muslims in Amdo Tibetan Society*.
66 The Yihewani share a name with the global Ikhwan (commonly referred to as the "Muslim Brotherhood"), borrowed by the sect's founder, Ma Wanfu, in 1888. However, Lipman asserts that shortly after its founding the Yihewani distanced themselves from the Saudi, Hanbali branch of the movement and "dropped much of [their] fundamentalist program, at least parts that impinged on the world of politics." Thus, despite retaining an anti-Sufi outlook, by the early twentieth century the Yihewani "had become an ally of Chinese nationalism, a tool of an acculturating Muslim elite, and an important bridge between Muslim communities and the burgeoning Chinese nation-state" (*Familiar Strangers*, 205–9).
67 Erie and Carlson, "Introduction to 'Islam in China/China in Islam.'"
68 Gillette, *Between Mecca and Beijing*.
69 *Jiaozi* translates to "the education of children." Though not properly marked with street signs until 1934, the *hutong*'s name was passed down orally by Muslim residents as far back as the late Ming and would have referred to its position adjacent the Niu Jie Mosque and its teaching of Islamic education. See Li, "Zhuiyi Jiaozi Hutong," 78.
70 Gillette, *Between Mecca and Beijing*, 22–29.
71 Zang, "Ethnic Differences in Neighbourly Relations in Urban China," 197.
72 Cooke, "Surviving State and Society in Northwest China," 414–16.
73 Gladney, *Muslim Chinese*, 171–228.

74 Field observations, August 2015.
75 Aldrich and Waldinger, "Ethnicity and Entrepreneurship."
76 Cooke, "Surviving State and Society in Northwest China."
77 I borrow this phrase from John Comaroff and Jean Comaroff's outstanding *Ethncity, Inc.*
78 Gladney, *Muslim Chinese*, 173. Despite the fact that many of the owners of restaurants that produce the noodles come from Hualong Hui Autonomous County in Qinghai, these noodles have come to be associated with the city of Lanzhou in Gansu and are sometimes called "Lanzhou *lamian*." Internationally, however, the characters for *lamian* are perhaps better known for their Japanese pronunciation, "ramen."
79 Dillon, *China's Muslim Hui Community*, 153.
80 Field observations, Jinan, October–December 2015.
81 People's Republic of China, National Bureau of Statistics, "Sixth National Population Census of the People's Republic of China, 2010."
82 Mosques in these communities include Beijing's Niu Jie Mosque, Jinan's Great Southern Mosque, the Great Mosque at Najiahu, and Xining's Dongguan Mosque.
83 Lipman, "Ethnicity and Politics in Republican China."
84 Liang, *Niu Jie*; Zhou and Ma, *Development and Decline of Beijing's Hui Muslim Community.*
85 Wang, Zhou, and Fan, "Growth and Decline of Muslim Hui Enclaves in Beijing," 113.
86 Wang, Zhou, and Fan, "Growth and Decline of Muslim Hui Enclaves in Beijing," 114.
87 Haw, *Beijing*, 8.
88 Wang, Zhou, and Fan, "Growth and Decline of Muslim Hui Enclaves in Beijing," 116–19.
89 Interviews, BJ0308115, BJ07090615, BJ14092415.
90 Wang, Zhou, and Fan, "Growth and Decline of Muslim Hui Enclaves in Beijing," 112.
91 Interview, JN26101915.
92 Jinan Municipal People's Government, "Population of Jinan."
93 Boland-Crewe and Lea, *The Territories of the People's Republic of China*, 178.
94 A stela at the Great Southern Mosque claims that the mosque was built in 1295, replacing a mosque built two hundred years earlier in another part of town.
95 Yang and Yu, *Yisilan yu Zhongguo wenhua*; Yi, *Jinan Yisilan jiao lishi.*
96 People's Republic of China, National Bureau of Statistics, "Sixth National Population Census of the People's Republic of China, 2010."
97 Fairbank and Goldman, *China*, 25.
98 Garnaut, "Pen of the Jahriyya."
99 Bulag, "Seeing Like a Minority," 135.

100 Perdue, *China Marches West*, 20.
101 Perdue, *China Marches West*, 1–11.
102 Ma, "Fanhui or Huifan?," 2.
103 Lipman, *Familiar Strangers*, 286.
104 "Better City, Better Life" served as the motto for the 2010 Shanghai World Exposition.
105 Pullan and Baillie, "Introduction," 4–6.
106 See Weber, *Peasants into Frenchmen*; Scott, *Seeing Like a State*; Scott, *The Art of Not Being Governed*; Callahan, "Making Myanmars"; Migdal, "The State in Society"; Chen and Gao, "Urbanization in China and the Coordinated Development Model."
107 Scott, *Seeing Like a State*, 79. On "legibility" Scott remarks, "Legibility implies a viewer whose place is central and whose vision is synoptic."
108 McGarry, "'Demographic Engineering,'" 618–20.
109 Meer, "Muslim Diasporas and Their Framing(s)."
110 Starting in the 1980s, many Hui communities replaced older, "Chinese-style" mosques with newly constructed buildings in the "Arabic" style. For more on this wave of "Arabization" of Hui mosque architecture, see Gladney, *Muslim Chinese*, 55, 155, 166–67; Fan, "'Zai difanghua' yu xiangzheng ziben"; Gillette, *Between Mecca and Beijing*, 107–10.
111 Dutton, Lo, and Wu, *Beijing Time*, 10.
112 Hessler, *Oracle Bones*, 180.
113 Shin, "Residential Redevelopment and Social Impacts in Beijing."
114 Pan, *Welfare for Autocrats*, 14–20.
115 Wu, *China's Emerging Cities*, 66–86.
116 Field observations, Jinan, July 19–24, 2014.
117 Tian and Wong, "Large Urban Redevelopment Projects and Sociospatial Stratification in Shanghai"; He and Wu, "Neighborhood Changes and Residential Differentiation in Shanghai."
118 He and Wu, "Neighborhood Changes and Residential Differentiation in Shanghai."
119 Meyer, *The Last Days of Old Beijing*; Hessler, *Oracle Bones*, 174–87; Osnos, "Can China Deliver the China Dream(s)?"
120 Mertha, "From 'Rustless Screws' to 'Nail Houses,'" 234.
121 For more on the subject, see Smith Finley, "Now We Don't Talk Anymore"; Loubes, "Urban Changes in Xinjiang"; Rachel Harris, "Bulldozing Mosques," *Guardian*, April 7, 2019; Grose, "If You Don't Know How, Just Learn," 6–10.
122 Miller, *China's Urban Billion*.
123 Lee, *Against the Law*; Loyalka, *Eating Bitterness*; Zhang, "Migrant Enclaves and Impacts of Redevelopment Policy in Chinese Cities."
124 Iredale and Guo, "Overview of Minority Migration," 12–22.
125 Iredale and Guo, "Overview of Minority Migration."

126 Côté, "Horizontal Inequalities and Sons of the Soil Conflict in China"; Côté, "Internal Migration and the Politics of Place."
127 Burgjin and Bilik, "Contemporary Mongolian Population Distribution, Migration, Cultural Change, and Identity."
128 Interview, YN105032316.
129 Goode and Stroup, "Everyday Nationalism," 724–30.
130 Fox and Miller-Idriss, "Everyday Nationhood."
131 Fox and Miller-Idriss, "Everyday Nationhood," 537–38.
132 Fox and Miller-Idriss, "The 'Here and Now' of Everyday Nationhood," 575.
133 Brubaker et al., *Nationalist Politics and Everyday Ethnicity in a Transylvanian Town*, 381.
134 Bernard, *Research Methods in Anthropology*, 347.
135 Schmoller, "The Talking Dead."
136 Brubaker et al., *Nationalist Politics and Everyday Ethnicity in a Transylvanian Town*, 379. Indeed, as Brubaker et al. note, "ethnic nationalism emerges interactionally through the appropriation and transformation of discursive resources made available (in a non-ethnic frame) in the preceding turns of talk."
137 Dillon, *The Practice of Questioning*, 133–34.
138 Kvale, *InterViews*, 29–31.
139 Rubin and Rubin, *Qualitative Interviewing*, 13–14.
140 Brubaker et al., *Nationalist Politics and Everyday Ethnicity in a Transylvanian Town*, 380–84.
141 While critiques of the approach suggest that snowball sampling produces nonrandom, nonprobabilistic samples—especially in larger populations where the chain of referrals moves beyond the researcher's initial respondent—it offers a number of distinct strengths. In employing local knowledge to direct researchers' inquiries and relevant participants, the approach provides a sample of "natural interactional units" and provides researchers with strong insights about community networks. For this reason, it is a strong approach for studying sensitive subjects or hidden populations. For further reading, see Biernacki and Waldorf, "Snowball Sampling"; Heckathorn, "Comment"; Handcock and Gile, "Comment"; Bernard, *Research Methods in Anthropology*, 93.

1. "GOD IS A DRUG"

1 Rachel Harris observes that while the depictions of smiling minorities reinforce narratives about their happiness at being included in the homeland, the demand that they smile imposes emotional labor costs on performers. Demands for smiles as a show of loyalty therefore estrange performers from their own authentic emotions. See Harris, *Soundscapes of Uyghur Islam*, 185–87.

2 Field observations, Beijing, August 2015.
3 Brady, "'We Are All Part of the Same Family.'"
4 Gladney, *Dislocating China*; Schein, *Minority Rules*.
5 Information Office of the State Council of the People's Republic of China, "China's Ethnic Policy and Common Prosperity and Development of All Ethnic Groups."
6 In Arabic, the phrase is *lā 'ilāha 'illā -llāh*.
7 Madsen, "The Upsurge of Religion in China."
8 Translated in MacInnis, *Religion in China Today*, 10. .
9 Field observations, Laozhai, December 2015.
10 Brubaker et al. , *Nationalist Politics and Everyday Ethnicity in a Transylvanian Town*, 10–12.
11 Pan, *Welfare for Autocrats*, 9–14, 45–47.
12 Perry, "Chinese Conceptions of 'Rights.'"
13 Laliberté and Lanteigne, "The Issue of Challenges to the Legitimacy of CCP Rule," 10.
14 Feng, "The Dilemma of Stability Preservation in China," 7.
15 Laliberté and Lanteigne, "The Issue of Challenges to the Legitimacy of CCP Rule," 2.
16 Shue, "Legitimacy Crisis in China? ," 60; Wang and Zhao, "China's Peaceful Rise."
17 Pan, *Welfare for Autocrats*, 45–47.
18 Gladney, *Dislocating China*, 9.
19 Schein, *Minority Rules*, 81–83.
20 Mullaney, *Coming to Terms with the Nation*, 11–12, 45–64.
21 Gladney, *Dislocating China*, 9.
22 Mullaney, *Coming to Terms with the Nation*, 12–14, 69–91.
23 Schein, *Minority Rules*, 73.
24 Heberer, *China and Its National Minorities*, 16; Cheung, Lee, and Nedilsky, *Marginalization in China*, 12.
25 Gladney, *Dislocating China*, 20.
26 Tobin, "Worrying about Ethnicity," 66.
27 Callahan, *China Dreams*, 107; Xi, *Kexue yu Aiguo*.
28 Roberts, *The War on the Uyghurs*, 172–76.
29 Tobin, "Worrying about Ethnicity," 73.
30 Though often translated as "Chinese nationality," James Leibold's history of the term notes that *Zhonghua minzu*, in both its historical and current usage, carries not only political but also racial and biological implications (*Reconfiguring Chinese Nationalism*, 1–3).
31 Barmé, Goldkorn, and Jaivin, *Shared Destiny*, xxxii.
32 For more on this so-called second generation of ethnic policymakers, see Ma, "A New Perspective in Guiding Ethnic Relations in the Twenty-First

Century"; Leibold, "Toward a Second Generation of Ethnic Policies?"; Tobin, "Worrying about Ethnicity," 70–76.

33 Schein, *Minority Rules*, 73.

34 Mullaney, "Critical Han Studies"; Chen, *Multicultural China in the Early Middle Ages*; Gladney, "Representing Nationality in China"; Chow, "Imagining Boundaries of Blood"; Leiboldxx, *Reconfiguring Chinese Nationalism.*

35 Leibold, *Reconfiguring Chinese Nationalism*, 92–96.

36 Leibold, *Reconfiguring Chinese Nationalism*, 170.

37 Brady, "'We Are All Part of the Same Family,'" 162.

38 Brady, "'We Are All Part of the Same Family,'" 162–70.

39 Field observations, Lusha'er, July 2014. A note on transliteration of Tibetan place-names: I use the THL Simplified Phonetic Transcription of Standard Tibetan developed by David Germano and Nicolas Tournade. Tibetan names were verified via the SHANTI Place Dictionary and the KMAPS project at the University of Virginia (http: //places.kmaps.virginia.edu/).

40 Field observations, Lanzhou, July 2014.

41 Field observations, Xining, April 2016.

42 Field observations, Xining, July 2014.

43 Such is the finding of Gordon W. Allport's "intergroup contact theory." For further discussion, see Allport, *The Nature of Prejudice*, 260–81; Varshney, *Ethnic Conflict and Civic Life.*

44 Bracic, *Breaking the Exclusion Cycle.*

45 Mackerras, "Tibetans, Uyghurs and Multinational 'China,'" 225–27.

46 Feng, "The Dilemma of Stability Preservation in China," 7–12.

47 Hillman and Tuttle, *Ethnic Conflict and Protest in Tibet and Xinjiang.*

48 Li and Ji, "Still 'Familiar' but No Longer 'Strangers,'" 154; Su, "Meet China's State-Approved Muslims"; Beech, "If China Is Anti-Islam, Why Are These Chinese Muslims Enjoying a Faith Revival?"; "The Hui: China's Other Muslims," *Economist*, October 8, 2016.

49 Li and Ji, "Still 'Familiar' but No Longer 'Strangers,'" 167.

50 For further discussion of Islamic rebellions in the late Qing, see Lipman, "The Border World of Gansu"; Ma, "New Teachings and New Territories."

51 Dillon, *China's Muslim Hui Community*, 87–88.

52 Gladney, *Muslim Chinese*, 137–40; Su, "Harmony and Martyrdom among China's Hui Muslims."

53 MacFarquhar and Schoenhals, *Mao's Last Revolution*, 387.

54 Gladney, *Muslim Chinese*, 137–40; MacFarquhar and Schoenhals, *Mao's Last Revolution*, 387–88. Sources differ on the length of the engagement. Gladney states that the fighting lasted seven days, while MacFarquhar and Schoenhals record it as twenty-one.

55 Gladney, *Muslim Chinese*, 140; Turnbull, "In Pursuit of Islamic 'Authenticity,'" 48–49.

56 The Gang of Four was a faction of the CCP, comprised of Jiang Qing, Zhang Chunqiao, Yao Wenuyan, and Wang Hongwen, that gained de facto control of the Party's leadership structure in the late stages of the Cultural Revoluaiton (1966–76) and largely shouldered the blame for the calamities occurring during the campaign.

57 Su, "Harmony and Martyrdom among China's Hui Muslims."

58 Turnbull, "In Pursuit of Islamic 'Authenticity,'" 48.

59 Allès, Chérif-Chebbi, and Halfon, "Chinese Islam," 12.

60 Andrew Jacobs, "Light Government Touch Lets China's Hui Practice Islam in the Open," *New York Times*, February 1, 2016; "The Hui: China's Other Muslims"; Su, "Meet China's State-Approved Muslims."

61 Gladney, *Dislocating China*, 99–103.

62 Interview, XN150061516.

63 For more on Saudi influence on Hui communities and its influence on Sino-Saudi relations, see Al-Sudairi, "Adhering to the Ways of Our Western Brothers."

64 Field observation, Najiahu, February 2016.

65 Smith Finley, "Now We Don't Talk Anymore."

66 Field observation, Xining, July 2014.

67 Field observations, Ningxia Provincial Museum, February 2016.

68 Field observations, Najiahu Hui Culture Park, July 2014.

69 Cooke, "Surviving State and Society in Northwest China," 416. Cooke makes similar observations about the current presentation of Ma Bufang's life at the museum that now occupies his former place of residence in Xining. She contends that "the state has not yet resolved how to deal with this legacy."

70 Personal communication, Yinchuan, July 2014.

71 Field observations, Najiahu Hui Culture Park, July 2014.

72 Field observations, Najiahu Hui Culture Park, July 2014.

73 Field observations, Yinchuan, February 2016.

74 The term *qingzhen* literally translates to "pure" (*qing*) and "true" (*zhen*). Though it is often used as essentially interchangeable with *halal*, it may be used to describe lifestyle habits other than diet. Chapter 4 provides a more thorough discussion of the meaning and usage of the term.

75 Field observations, Jinan, November 2015.

76 Field observations, Yinchuan, March 2016.

77 On this phenomenon, see Schein, "Gender and Internal Orientalism in China"; Comaroff and Comaroff, *Ethnicity, Inc.*

78 Interview, JN39111115.

79 Interview, YN106032616.

80 Field observations, Yinchuan, February 2016.

81 Interview, JN32103115.
82 Interview, JN22101315.
83 Field observations, Weizhou, February 2016.
84 Gaubatz, *Beyond the Great Wall.*
85 Zhou and Ma, *Development and Decline of Beijing's Hui Muslim Community.*
86 Field observations, Jinan, July 2014.
87 Gaubatz, *Beyond the Great Wall*, 54–62.
88 Interview, BJ11091715.
89 Interview, BJ11091715.
90 Though often translated as "quality" or "intrinsic qualities," the word *suzhi* is a floating signifier that resists easy translation into English. As such I follow recent scholarship in choosing to leave it untranslated. The word, promoted by both state and popular discourse, implies a measurement of the quality of individual citizens, but may also be abstracted to assess larger groups and is frequently cited to explain or justify inequalities in social or economic hierarchies. See Zhang, "Governing (through) Trustworthiness," 569–70.
91 Interview, XN117041616.
92 Kipnis, "Neoliberalism Reified"; Han, "Policing and Racialization of Rural Migrant Workers in Chinese Cities"; Wilczak, "'Clean, Safe and Orderly'"; Zhang, "Governing Neoliberal Authoritarian Citizenship," 869; Gillette, *Between Mecca and Beijing*, 44–45.
93 Interview, BJ30102415.
94 Interview, JN41112015.
95 Gillette, *Between Mecca and Beijing*, 128–30.
96 Interview, JN39111115.
97 Interview, JN41112015.
98 Interview, JN22101315
99 Interview, JN23101515
100 Interview, JN53120515.
101 Hoshino, "Preferential Policies for China's Ethnic Minorities at a Crossroads"; Hansen, *Lessons in Being Chinese*, 3–24; Zhaxi, "Housing Subsidy Projects in Amdo"; Sturgeon, "The Cultural Politics of Ethnic Identity in Xishuangbanna, China'"; Park and Han, "A Minority Group and China's One-Child Policy."
102 Hoshino, "Preferential Policies for China's Ethnic Minorities at a Crossroads," 7.
103 Interview, JN18100515.
104 Interview, JN32103115.
105 Field observations, Laozhai, December 2015.
106 Interview, XN112041216.
107 Carrico, *The Great Han.*

2. CHOOSING

1 Interview, YN108033016.

2 Fox and Miller-Idriss, "Everyday Nationhood."

3 Haleem, *The Qur'an*, 2:221. The text of *sura* 2, *ayat* 221 reads, "Do not marry idolatresses until they believe: a believing slave woman is certainly better than an idolatress, even though she may please you. And do not give your women in marriage to idolaters until they believe."

4 Fox and Miller-Idriss, "Everyday Nationhood," 544.

5 Fox, "The Edges of the Nation."

6 Fox and Miller-Idriss, "Everyday Nationhood," 543.

7 Brubaker, *Citizenship and Nationhood in France and Germany*, 22.

8 Roeder, "Soviet Federalism and Ethnic Mobilization"; Marx, *Making Race and Nation*; Martin, *The Affirmative Action Empire*.

9 Anderson, *Imagined Communities*, 166, 168–70, 184.

10 Tilly, *Durable Inequality*, 52–77; Hirschman, "The Meaning and Measurement of Ethnicity in Malaysia."

11 Citrin and Sears, "Balancing National and Ethnic Identities," 147–49.

12 Cheung, Lee, and Nedilsky, *Marginalization in China*, 11.

13 Bai, "Identity Reproducers beyond the Grassroots."

14 Stevan Harrell remarks that while the *minzu* system provides an illusion of uniformity within groups, in reality actors face daily choices about identity; decisions ordinary people make about whether or not to reinforce or cross ethnic boundaries may result from processes of both intention and selection (*Ways of Being Ethnic in Southwest China*, 313–30).

15 Gil-White, "How Thick Is Blood?"

16 Anthias and Yuval-Davis, "Introduction"; Enloe, *Bananas, Beaches, Bases*; Yuval-Davis, *Gender and Nation*; McClintock, "Family Feuds"; Özkırımlı, *Theories of Nationalism*, 175–82.

17 Yuval-Davis, *Gender and Nation*, 11–22.

18 Anthias and Yuval-Davis, "Introduction," 9.

19 Yuval-Davis, *Gender and Nation*, 22–25.

20 Yuval-Davis, "National Reproduction and 'the Demographic Race' in Israel."

21 Fox and Miller-Idriss, "Everyday Nationhood," 542.

22 Landau, "Religiosity, Nationalism and Human Reproduction," 71.

23 McClintock, "Family Feuds"; Anthias, "Women and Nationalism in Cyprus."

24 People's Republic of China, National Bureau of Statistics, "Sixth National Population Census of the People's Republic of China, 2010."

25 See, for instance, Jinba, *In the Land of the Eastern Queendom*, 117–27.

26 Heberer, *China and Its National Minorities*, 16; Cheung, Lee, and Nedilsky, *Marginalization in China*, 12.

27 Harrell, *Ways of Being Ethnic in Southwest China*, 264–65.

28 Mullaney, *Coming to Terms with the Nation*, 123.
29 Schein, *Minority Rules*, 69–86.
30 Altner, "Do All the Muslims of Tibet Belong to the Hui Nationality?"
31 Chang, "Self-Identity versus State Identification of 'Tibetan-Speaking Muslims' in the Kaligang Area of Qinghai."
32 For the Naxi, see Yuan and Mitchell, "Land of the Walking Marriage"; White, "State Discourses, Minority Policies, and the Politics of Identity in the Lijiang Naxi People's Autonomous County"; Mathieu, "Lost Kingdoms and Forgotten Tribes." For the Zhuang, see Mullaney, *Coming to Terms with the Nation*, 120–34. For the Yao, see Litzinger, *Other Chinas*. For the Yi, see Harrell, *Ways of Being Ethnic in Southwest China*. For the Miao, see Schein, *Minority Rules*.
33 Harrell, *Ways of Being Ethnic in Southwest China*, 313–30.
34 Smith, "'Making Culture Matter,'" 162–63.
35 Goldstein et al. , "Fertility and Family Planning in Rural Tibet," 36.
36 Gladney, *Muslim Chinese*, 242–59.
37 Zang, "Hui Muslim–Han Chinese Differences in Perceptions on Endogamy in Urban China."
38 Ha, "Religion of the Father," 8–13.
39 Jaschok and Shui, *The History of Women's Mosques in Chinese Islam*, 143.
40 Gladney, *Muslim Chinese*, 229–60.
41 The CCP's early efforts to establish a Hui identity are the subject of extensive study from the Party, mostly notably the now famous volume *Huihui minzu wenti* by Ya and Li. See also Liu, "Yan'an shiqi de Huizu yu Yisilanjiao gongzuo," 26–29; Hua and Zhai, "Minguo shiqi de Huizu jieshuo yu Zhongguo Gongchangdang 'Huihui minzu wenti' de lilun yiyi."
42 Lipman, *Familiar Strangers*, xxii.
43 Israeli, *Islam in China*, 272.
44 Interview, YN83021216.
45 Gladney, *Muslim Chinese*, 62.
46 Interview, XN112041316.
47 Interview, XN116041516.
48 Interview, JN48112615.
49 Interview, JN27102015.
50 Interview, JN46112515.
51 Interview, JN46112515.
52 Interview, JN47112615.
53 Interview, XN129050116.
54 Interview, JN56120915.
55 Interview, XN119041916.
56 Interview, XN111041216.
57 Interview, JN52120415.
58 Interviews, JN28102215, JN36111015, JN46112515, JN48112615, YN8120416.

59 Interview, JN28102215.
60 Interview, JN48112615.
61 Interviews, JN52120415, YN68012016 YN75012616, YN80020416, YN8120416, YN106032616, XN134050716.
62 Interview, XN134050716.
63 Interview, XN128043016.
64 Ha, "Religion of the Father."
65 Ha, "Religion of the Father," 7–10, 65, 90.
66 Interview, BJ65010716.
67 Interview, XN122042216.
68 Interview, XN112041316.
69 Interview, JN44112515. The term *xili* is usually translated as "baptism." The respondent's use of the term is not standard, nor is *xili* commonly used in Hui Islam. Rather, the term *wudu* is used to refer to ablutions or ritual washing before prayer. In our conversation, the respondent specified that the *xili* he described was a ritual in which one became a Muslim, though he did not elaborate much further. Muslim conversion ceremonies in China, such as one I observed in Yinchuan in January 2016, do not use ablutions in ways that differ from normal prayer, and the respondent did not indicate that this ritual involved special acts of washing. I thus elect to leave the term untranslated to preserve his intended meaning.
70 Interview, XN143050216.
71 Interview, XN122042216.
72 Interview, XN111041216.
73 Interview, XN134050716.
74 Interview, BJ65010716.
75 Interview, BJ29102315.
76 Interview, BJ09091615.
77 Interview, BJ29102315.
78 Interview, BJ01082815.
79 Interview, BJ29102315.
80 Interviews, JN34110415, JN41112015, JN46112515.
81 Interviews, JN32103115, JN36111015, JN48112615.
82 Interview, JN42112215.
83 Interview, JN34110415.
84 Interviews, JN27102015, JN28102215, JN32103115.
85 Interview, JN32103115.
86 Interview, JN28102215.
87 Interview, JN36111015.
88 Interviews, XN144052316, XN143052116, XN119041916, XN111041216.
89 Interview, XN120042016.
90 Interview, XN139051616.

91 Interview, XN130050416.
92 Interview, XN117041616.
93 Interviews, YN68012016, YN69012116, YN73012316, YN75012616, YN76012616, YN900022116, YN107033016, YN108033016.
94 Interview, YN95022916.
95 Interview, YN94022416.
96 Interview, YN80020416.
97 Interview, YN108033016.
98 Interview, YN106032616.

3. TALKING

1 *Gongbei* (拱北) are mausoleum complexes that house the tombs of Sufi Muslim masters who served as the heads of their orders, and their disciples. The term *bai maozi* literally translates to "white hat" and refers to a number of styles of Muslim head coverings, including knit skullcaps and stiffer, rounded caps. Confusingly, some respondents referred to caps as *bai maozi* even if they were not white.
2 Field observations, Xining, April 2016.
3 Field observations, Yinchuan, January 2016.
4 Interviews, XN115041516, XN134050716, XN135050916, XN143052116, XN146052816.
5 Interviews, LZ03070914, LZ04070914.
6 Petersen, *Interpreting Islam in China*, 1–26.
7 Billig, *Banal Nationalism*, 87.
8 De Cillia, Reisigl, and Wodak, "The Discursive Construction of National Identities," 153.
9 Laferriere, "Ethnicity in Phonological Variation and Change"; Wei, "The 'Why' and 'How' Questions in the Analysis of Conversational Code-Switching."
10 Bonner, "Garifuna Children's Language Shame"; Koziura, "Everyday Ethnicity in Chernivtsi, Western Ukraine"; Vigil and Bills, "Spanish Language Variation and Ethnic Identity in New Mexico."
11 Jones and Merriman, "Hot, Banal and Everyday Nationalism"; Raento, "Political Mobilisation and Place-Specificity."
12 Mullaney, "Critical Han Studies." See Lenin, *The Rights of Nations to Self-Determination*; Lenin, *National Liberation, Socialism and Imperialism*.
13 Brady, "Ethnicity and the State in Contemporary China," 4.
14 Hansen, *Lessons in Being Chinese*, 1–24.
15 Hansen, *Lessons in Being Chinese*, 1–24; Postiglione, "Introduction"; Johnson and Chhetri, "Exclusionary Policies and Practices in Chinese Minority Education"; Shih, *Negotiating Ethnicity in China*, 163–96;

Tsung, *Language Power and Hierarchy*, 23–58; Grose, *Negotiating Inseparability in China.*

16 Postiglione, "Introduction," 4, 8–10.

17 Glasserman, "Making Muslims Hui."

18 Interview, XN115041516.

19 Borchigud, "The Impact of Urban Ethnic Education on Modern Mongolian Ethnicity"; Bilik, "Language Education, Intellectuals and Symbolic Representation"; Burgjin and Bilik, "Contemporary Mongolian Population Distribution, Migration, Cultural Change, and Identity"; Bulag, "Mongolian Ethnicity and Linguistic Anxiety in China"; Ojijed, "Language Competition in an Ethnic Autonomous Region."

20 Enwall, "Inter-Ethnic Relations in Mongolia and Inner Mongolia," 244, 254–56.

21 Borchigud, "The Impact of Urban Ethnic Education on Modern Mongolian Ethnicity."

22 Bulag, "Mongolian Ethnicity and Linguistic Anxiety in China," 753–55.

23 Helen Davidson, "Inner Mongolia Protests at China's Plans to Bring in Mandarin-Only Lessons," *Guardian*, September 1, 2020.

24 Atwood, "Bilingual Education in Inner Mongolia"; Jargalsaikhan, "Mongolia's Response to China's New Educational Policy in Inner Mongolia."

25 Kaltman, *Under the Heel of the Dragon*, 3–4, 15–17, 20, 35, 39, 66, 78–79; Lim, "China's Ethnic Policies in the Xinjiang Region."

26 Kaltman, *Under the Heel of the Dragon*, 17–29.

27 Grose, "Uyghur University Students and Ramadan."

28 Kaltman, *Under the Heel of the Dragon*, 17–29.

29 Hillman, "The Rise of the Community in Rural China"; Gladney, "Islam in China," 91; Andaya, *Leaves of the Same Tree*, 45, 168; Chang, "Self-Identity versus State Identification of 'Tibetan-Speaking Muslims' in the Kaligang Area of Qinghai"; Hille, Horlemann, and Nietupski, *Muslims in Amdo Tibetan Society.*

30 Ma, "Huizu yuyan jiqi fanying de minzu rentong xinli"; Song et al., "Cong Huizu yuyan kanqi minzu rentong."

31 Israeli, *Islam in China*, 60–63, 122.

32 Li, Ma, and Ma, "Cong Huizu yuyan jiedu qi minzu rentong."

33 Ben-Dor Benite, *The Dao of Muhammad.*

34 Jin, "Alaboyu jiaoxue zai Ningxia de lishi yange ji qi minjian tedian."

35 Ma, *Zhongguo Xibei Yisilanjiao jiben tezheng*, 38.

36 Ma, "Zhongguo Yisilanjiao de jiben tezheng," 103.

37 Lipman, *Familiar Strangers*, 49–51.

38 Ben-Dor Benite, *The Dao of Muhammad*, 13.

39 Lipman, *Familiar Strangers*, 215.

40 Interviews, LZ03070914, LZ04070914.

41 Interview, JN63122015.

42 Interview, JN51120315.
43 Interview, JN52120415.
44 Field observations, Yinchuan, January 2016.
45 I characterize this campaign as one intended to achieve de-Islamification. While the state contended that these efforts were to combat forces of extremism, Arabization (Shahua, or A'hua), and "pan-halalifcation" (*fan-qingzhenhua*), the enactment of such measures coincided with the rise of a sentiment that regarded Islam itself as dangerous. See Stroup, "The De-Islamification of Public Space and Sinicization of Ethnic Politics in Xi's China."
46 Ho, "Mobilizing the Muslim Minority for China's Development"; Chen, "Zhong-A Hezuo luntan li yi lai de zhongguo dui A meiti jiaoliu"; Qian, "'One Belt One Road' Initiative and China and the Middle East Media Exchanges."
47 Field observations, Beijing, September 2015.
48 Field observations, Jinan, October 2015.
49 Interview, YN92022216.
50 Field observations, Beijing, December 2015.
51 Field observations, Jinan, October 2015.
52 Interviews, JN32103115, XN125042616, LZ02070814, LZ03070914, LZ04070914.
53 Interviews, BJ02082915, BJ09091615, JN43112415, JN52120415, JN62122015, YN72012216, YN92022216, YN98031716, XN120042016.
54 Interview, XN124042516.
55 Interview, YN105032316.
56 Interview, BJ14092415.
57 Interviews, BJ09091615, BJ30102415, BJ65010716, JN52120415, YN109033116, XN137051216, XN151061716.
58 Field observations, Lanzhou, July 2014.
59 Interview, YN105032316.
60 Field observations, Beijing, September 2015.
61 Interview, YN7712816.
62 Interview, JN61121615.
63 Interviews, BJ65010716, YN86021516, YN88022016, YN104032216, XN122042216, XN124042516, XN143052116.
64 Interview, BJ09091615.
65 Interview, LZ02070814.
66 Interview, YN72012216.
67 Interview, XN120042016.
68 Interview, BJ14092415.
69 Field observations, Xining, May 2016.
70 Field observations, Xining, April 2016.
71 Interview, BJ64123015.

72 Interview, JN63122015.

73 As a nonspeaker of Persian languages, I was not able to independently verify this claim, though a combined search of Persian-English dictionaries at the University of Chicago's Digital Dictionaries of South Asia website gives the word *deegar* or *digar* (دیگر) as meaning "different; other; separate," lending credibility to the respondent's claim of *digaizi* as a Persian-derived term for people outside of the group. Regardless of accuracy, the respondent's citation of this word as a marker of speech signifying ethnic difference between local Hui and non-Hui holds significance. I thank Eric Schluessel for his consultation on this subject.

74 Interview, JN52120415.

75 Interview, JN63122015; confirmed by Interview, JN52120415. These names are also listed in Leslie's index of major Chinese Islamic surnames, though their origins in Persian, Arabic, or Turkic languages is not traced. See Leslie, *Islamic Literature in Chinese Late Ming and Early Ch'ing.*

76 Interviews, BJ09091615, JN44112515, JN52120415, JN62122015, YN69012116, YN74012416, YN109033116, XN113041316, XN116041516.

77 Interview, JN32103115.

78 Interviews, YN92022216, YN97031716, YN101032116, YN10532316, YN107033016 XN114041416.

79 Interview, YN97031716.

80 Interview, YN104032216.

81 Field observations, Weizhou, February 2016.

82 Chris Baynes, "China Bans Children in Muslim County from Attending Religious Events during Holidays," *Independent*, January 17, 2018; Feng, "'Afraid We Will Become the Next Xinjiang.'"

83 Field observations, Yinchuan, March 2016.

84 Interview, YN101032116.

85 Interview, XN115041516.

86 Field observations, Xining, April 2016.

87 Interview, XN135050916.

88 Interview, XN118041816.

89 Interviews, JN24101515, JN27102015, JN32103115, JN34110415, JN57121015.

90 Interview, JN31103015.

91 Interview, JN37111115.

92 Interview, JN23101515.

93 Interview, YN105032316.

94 Ho, "Mobilizing the Muslim Minority for China's Development."

95 Interview, BJ08091215.

96 Interview, BJ02082915.

97 Field observations, Beijing, September 2015.

98 Interview, BJ01082815.

99 Interview, JN2101215.

100 Interview, JN33110115.
101 Interviews, BJ08091215, BJ11091715, JN24101515, JN37111115, YN74012416, YN94022416, XN112041316, XN113041316, XN117041616, XN120042016, XN121042116, XN123042316.
102 Interviews, JN33110115, JN47112615, JN621212015, YN90022116, XN112041316, XN113041316, XN128043016, XN130050416.
103 Interview, JN47112615.
104 Interview, JN62122015.
105 Interview, XN112041316.
106 Interview, JN50120315.
107 Interview, JN61121615.
108 Interview, JN52210415.
109 Interview, XN135050916.
110 Dillon, *China's Muslim Hui Community*, 55–56.
111 Interview, XN150061516.

4. CONSUMING

1 Interview, YN83021216.
2 Interview, JN46112515.
3 This is especially true regarding meat, as a famous Chinese aphorism observes: "Any animal whose back faces the sun can be eaten" (*Beiji chaotian, renjie keshi*). Many Hui respondents mentioned this to me when describing a Han diet.
4 Interview, JN22101315.
5 Kuşçular, *Cleanliness in Islam*, 3–23, 65–73.
6 Wilson and Liu, "Shaping the Halal into a Brand?"
7 Denny, *An Introduction to Islam*, 278.
8 Denny, *An Introduction to Islam*, 171.
9 Denny, *An Introduction to Islam*, 419–21.
10 Gladney, *Muslim Chinese*, 7–15; Gillette, *Between Mecca and Beijing*, 114–25.
11 Gillette, *Between Mecca and Beijing*, 115–17, 119, 124.
12 Gladney, *Muslim Chinese*, 13–15.
13 Ha, "Specters of Qingzhen."
14 Brose and Su, "Marketing as Pedagogy."
15 Cesaro, "Consuming Identities," 229.
16 Gladney, *Muslim Chinese*, 175, 189.
17 Field observation, Xining, April 2016.
18 Interview, BJ30102415.
19 Huizhong Wu, "Sign of the Times: China's Capital Orders Arabic, Muslim Symbols Taken Down," *Reuters*, August 1, 2019, https: //www.reuters.com /article/us-china-religion-islam-idUSKCN1UQ0JF.

20 Dillon, *China's Muslim Hui Community.*

21 On food safety in China, see Michael Moss and Neil Gough, "Food Safety in China Still Faces Big Hurdles," *New York Times*, July 23, 2014; Klein, "Everyday Approaches to Food Safety in Kunming"; Liu, Pieniak, and Verbeke, "Food-Related Hazards in China"; Rimal et al., "Perception of Food Safety and Changes in Food Consumption Habits."

22 Interviews, BJ29102315, XN117041616.

23 Interview, JN46112515.

24 Interview, YN153011816.

25 Field observations, Beijing, August 2015.

26 Field observations, Xining, May 2016.

27 Sai, "Policy, Practice and Perceptions of Qingzhen (Halal) in China"; Hong et al., "Determinants of Halal Purchasing Behaviour,"410.

28 For more on China's halal food certification processes, see Sai, "Policy, Practice and Perceptions of Qingzhen (Halal) in China"; Brose, "Permitted and Pure."

29 Erie, "Muslim Mandarins in Chinese Courts," 1006–7.

30 Sai, "Policy, Practice and Perceptions of Qingzhen (Halal) in China," 4–6.

31 Interviews, YN78012916, YN79012916, YN87021816, YN88022016, YN89022016, YN91022216, YN99031816.

32 Field observations, Yinchuan, January 2016.

33 Interview, JN26101915.

34 Interviews, YN153011816, JN61121615.

35 Interview, JN61121615.

36 Interview, YN79012916.

37 Field observations, Xining, April 2016.

38 Field observations, Yinchuan, February 2016.

39 Interview, XN136051216.

40 Interview, YN91022216.

41 Interview, XN138051316.

42 Gillette, "Children's Food and Islamic Dietary Restrictions in Xi'an."

43 Gillette, *Between Mecca and Beijing*, 167–91.

44 Interview, XN144052316.

45 Field observations, Yinchuan, January 2016.

46 Field observations, Weizhou, February 2016.

47 Interview, XN129050116.

48 Field observations, Yinchuan, January 2016.

49 Field observations, Yinchuan, January 2016.

50 Field observations, Najiahu, February 2016.

51 Interviews, JN42112215, JN43112415, JN54120715, JN61121615.

52 Interview, JN49120115.

53 Field observations, Jinan, October 2015.

5. PERFORMING

1 For a complete discussion of the forms and purposes of *dhikr*, see Denny, *An Introduction to Islam*, 352; Harris, *Soundscapes of Uyghur Islam*.

2 Field observations, Xining, June 2016.

3 Durkheim, *The Elementary Forms of the Religious Life*.

4 Here I follow Rogers Brubaker, who observes that groupness "varies not only across putative groups, but within them; it may wax and wane over time, peaking during exceptional—but unsustainable—moments of collective effervescence" (*Ethnicity without Groups*, 4).

5 Goode, "Humming Along."

6 Durkheim, *The Elementary Forms of the Religious Life*.

7 Hwang and Schneider, "Performance, Meaning, and Ideology in the Making of Legitimacy"; Xi, "Media Events Are Still Alive."

8 Wedeen, *Ambiguities of Domination*.

9 Scott, *The Art of Not Being Governed*; McGarry, "'Demographic Engineering.'"

10 Li, "Minorities, Tourism and Ethnic Theme Parks."

11 Harrell, *Ways of Being Ethnic in Southwest China*; McCarthy, *Communist Multiculturalism*, 7.

12 Schein, *Minority Rules*.

13 Goode, "Humming Along."

14 Certeau, *The Practice of Everyday Life*.

15 Fox, "National Holiday Commemorations."

16 Tsang and Woods, *The Cultural Politics of Nationalism and Nation-Building*.

17 Anderson, *Imagined Communities*.

18 Fox and Miller-Idriss, "Everyday Nationhood," 549.

19 Edensor, *National Identity, Popular Culture and Everyday Life*, 95–98.

20 Karner, *Ethnicity and Everyday Life*, 27–29.

21 Mazumdar and Mazumdar, "The Articulation of Religion in Domestic Space."

22 Wilton, "Bound from Head to Toe."

23 Carrico, *The Great Han*.

24 Svensson, "Clothing in the Arctic," 72; Quizon, "Costume, Kóstyom, and Dress."

25 Harrell, "Reading Threads."

26 Field observations, Beijing, September 2015.

27 Schein, *Minority Rules*, 6–7.

28 Brady, "'We Are All Part of the Same Family'"; McCarthy, *Communist Multiculturalism*.

29 Gladney, *Dislocating China*, 23; Gladney, "Representing Nationality in China," 92, 95.

30 Gladney, "Representing Nationality in China," 98–103.
31 Liang, "Turning Gwer Sa La Festival into Intangible Cultural Heritage."
32 Interview, XN118041816.
33 Field observations, Xining, April–June 2016.
34 Interview, XN141051616.
35 Interview, XN148053016.
36 Interviews, JN28102215, JN32103115, JN36111015, XN115041516.
37 Interview, JN43112415.
38 Interview, JN51120315.
39 Interview, BJ01082815.
40 Interview, XN144052316.
41 Interview, JN50120315.
42 Interview, JN52120415.
43 For a complete discussion of the various Sufi orders prominent in China, particularly in Qinghai, Gansu, and Ningxia, see Lipman, "Hyphenated Chinese"; Dillon, *China's Muslim Hui Community.*
44 Interviews, YN69012116, YN74012416, XN112041316, XN113041316, XN115041516, XN128043016, XN147052916.
45 Interview, BJ14092415.
46 Interview, XN150061516.
47 See the introduction for an explanation of the relationship between the Yihewani in China and the global Ikhwan.
48 Interviews, LZ03070914, LZ04070914.
49 See Bruinessen, "Global and Local in Indonesian Islam"; Beránek and Ťupek, *The Temptation of Graves in Salafi Islam*; Schmoller, "The Talking Dead."
50 Interview, XN141051616.
51 Ha, "The Silent Hat"; Grose, "Veiled Identities."
52 For a more thorough discussion of the types of women's headcoverings worn in China, see illustrations in Grose, "Veiled Identities"; Leibold and Grose, "Islamic Veiling in Xinjiang."
53 Field observations, Beijing, September 2015.
54 Leibold and Grose, "Islamic Veiling in Xinjiang," 88–97.
55 Interviews, JN37111115, JN57121015, YN108033016, YN80020416, YN84021316, XN117041616, XN121042116.
56 Interview, JN61121615.
57 interview, XN121042116.
58 Interview, YN84021316.
59 Interview, JN34110415.
60 Amer, *What Is Veiling?*, 12–14, 23.
61 Qur'an 24:30–31, 33:53, 59.
62 Amer, *What Is Veiling?*, 28–37.

63 Interview, XN144052316. The respondent phrased this as being a *hege de musilin*.
64 Interview, XN145052516.
65 Interviews, XN120042016, XN134050716.
66 Interview, XN134050716.
67 Interview, YN72012216.
68 Field observations, Beijing, July 2016.
69 Interview, XN118041816.
70 Interview, YN152011816.
71 Interview, JN34110415.
72 Interview, JN23101515.
73 Interview, JN28102215. Though Xi'an and Shaanxi are not typically included in the northwest, the presumed superiority of piety exercised by Hui in these areas grouped them as belonging with Xibei Hui in the mind of the respondent.
74 Interviews, BJ01082815, BJ08091215, JN22101315, JN32103115, JN34110415, JN47112615, JN48112615, JN62122015, YN76012616, YN83021216, XN117041616, XN120042016, XN128043016, XN130050416.
75 Field observations, Beijing, July 2016.
76 Interview, YN77012816.
77 Interview, YN105032316.
78 Turnbull, "In Pursuit of Islamic 'Authenticity.'"
79 Hillman, "The Rise of the Community in Rural China."
80 Interview, JN51120315.
81 Interviews, JN23101515, JN51120315, JN52120415.
82 Interview, JN46112515.
83 Interviews, YN92022216, YN104032216, YN105032316.
84 Interview, YN152011816.
85 Interview, JN61121615.

CONCLUSION

1 Field observations, Yinchuan, March 2016.
2 Miller, *China's Urban Billion*.
3 Interview, XN121042116.
4 Gladney, "Relational Alterity," 445–46.
5 In *Nationalist Politics and Everyday Ethnicity in a Transylvanian Town*, Brubaker et al., address this issue extensively in the appendices.
6 Fox and Jones, "Migration, Everyday Life and the Ethnicity Bias," 387.
7 Glick Schiller, Çağlar, and Guldbrandsen, "Beyond the Ethnic-Lens."
8 Bastia, "Migration as Protest?"
9 Adida, "Too Close for Comfort?"
10 Brubaker, "The 'Diaspora' Diaspora," 6–7.

11 McLoughlin, "Locating Muslim Diasporas."
12 Adida, "Too Close for Comfort?"; Brubaker, "Migration, Membership, and the Modern Nation-State."
13 Redclift, "Displacement, Integration and Identity in the Postcolonial World," 118.
14 Alexander, Chatterji, and Jalais, *The Bengal Diaspora*, 3–4.
15 Brubaker, "Migration, Membership, and the Modern Nation-State," 64.
16 Redclift, "Displacement, Integration and Identity in the Postcolonial World," 125.
17 Dobson, "Unpacking Children in Migration Research."
18 Demintseva, "'Migrant Schools' and the 'Children of Migrants.'"
19 Skrbiš, Baldassar, and Poynting, "Introduction," 263.
20 Hammond, *This Place Will Become Home*, 1–29.
21 Dobson, "Unpacking Children in Migration Research," 358.
22 Light et al., "Internal Ethnicity in the Ethnic Economy."
23 Chandra, "Ethnic Parties and Democratic Stability," 241; Fox and Jones, "Migration, Everyday Life and the Ethnicity Bias," 391.
24 For a more comprehensive assessment of Beijing's migrant population, see especially Zhang, *Strangers in the City*.
25 For extensive firsthand accounts, see Meyer, *The Last Days of Old Beijing*; Dutton, Lo, and Wu, *Beijing Time*.
26 Benjamin Haas, "China: 'Ruthless' Campaign to Evict Beijing's Migrant Workers Condemned," *Guardian*, November 27, 2017; Simon Denyer and Luna Lin, "Mass Evictions in Freezing Beijing Winter Sparks Public Outrage but Little Official Remorse," *Washington Post*, November 27, 2017; Steven Lee Myers, "A Cleanup of 'Holes in the Wall' in China's Capital," *New York Times*, July 17, 2017; Helen Roxburgh, "China's Radical Plan to Limit the Populations of Beijing and Shanghai," *Guardian*, March 19, 2018.
27 Interviews, BJ02082915, BJ30102415, BJ64123015, BJ65010716.
28 Interview, BJ02082915.
29 Interview, BJ30102415.
30 Field observations, Beijing, August 2015.
31 Interview, BJ64123015.
32 Field observations, Beijing, August 2015.
33 Interview, BJ30102415.
34 Interviews, BJ01082815, BJ06090515, BJ10091615.
35 Interview, BJ06090515.
36 Field observations, Beijing, August 2015.
37 Field observations, Beijing, July 2016.
38 Interview, BJ11091615.
39 Interview, BJ12091615.
40 Interview, BJ10091615.

41 Interview, BJ65010716.
42 Interview, BJ14092415.
43 Interview BJ02082915.
44 Interview, BJ30102415.
45 Interview, JN43112415.
46 Interview, JN32103115.
47 Interview, JN50120315.
48 Interview, JN26101915.
49 Interview, JN52120415.
50 Interview, JN61121615.
51 Interview, JN43112415.
52 Interview, XN141051616.
53 Interview, XN112041316.
54 Interview, XN120042016.
55 Interview, XN148053016.
56 Interview, XN150061516.
57 Interview, XN138051316.
58 For a more complete overview of Linxia's historical development and the dynamics of economic and religious life, particularly in the predominantly Muslim *bafang* area, see Erie, *China and Islam*, 86–129.
59 Interview, YN76012616.
60 Interview, YN108033016.
61 Interview, YN73012316.
62 Interview, YN103032216.
63 Interview, YN87021816.
64 Interview, YN105032316.
65 Interview, YN105032316.
66 Interview, YN69012116.
67 Interview, YN92022216.
68 Interview, YN74012416.
69 Interview, YN104032216.
70 Interview, YN92022216.
71 Interview, XN135050916.
72 Interviews, XN112041316, XN115041516, XN121042116, XN129050116, XN143052116, XN145052516.
73 Interview, XN115041516.
74 Interview, XN121042116.
75 Interview, XN129050116.
76 Interview, XN112041316.
77 Interview, XN114041416.
78 Interview, XN115041516.
79 Interview, XN117041616.
80 Interview, YN83021216.

81 Interview, YN72012216.

82 Interviews, XN121042116, XN128043016, XN134050716, XN144052316, XN145052516.

83 Interview, XN145052516.

84 Interview, YN103032216.

85 Interview, XN112041316.

86 Interview, XN143052116.

87 Field observations, Jinan, November 2015.

88 Interview, JN23101515.

89 Interview, JN52120415.

90 Brown, "Ethicity, Nationalism, and Democracy in South-East Asia."

91 Linz, *Totalitarian and Authoritarian Regimes*, 49–61, 159–71.

92 Glasius et al., *Research, Ethics and Risk in the Authoritarian Field*, 38–39.

93 Slater, *Ordering Power.*

94 Soest and Grauvogel, "Identity, Procedures and Performance."

95 Tarrow, *Power in Movement*, 158–80.

96 Earl, "Tanks, Tear Gas, and Taxes."

97 Tarrow, *Power in Movement.*

98 Chen, "China at the Tipping Point?"

99 Tobin, "Worrying about Ethnicity."

100 McCarthy, *Communist Multiculturalism*, 1–19.

101 Mortensen, "Prosperity, Identity, Intra-Tibetan Violence, and Harmony in Southeast Tibet."

102 Leibold, "Interethnic Coflict in the PRC."

103 Leibold, "Interethnic Conflict in the PRC," 240.

104 Gladney, *Dislocating China*, 27.

EPILOGUE

1 Smith Finley, "Securitization, Insecurity and Conflict in Contemporary Xinjiang."

2 Zenz and Leibold, "Chen Quanguo."

3 Roberts, "The Biopolitics of China's 'War on Terror' and the Exclusion of the Uyghurs," 245–52; Byler, "Ghost World."

4 Smith Finley, "Securitization, Insecurity and Conflict in Contemporary Xinjiang," 12–13; Rachel Harris, "Bulldozing Mosques: The Latest Tactic in China's War against Uighur Culture," *Guardian*, April 7, 2019; Eva Xiao and Pak Yiu, "Even in Death, Uighurs Feel Long Reach of Chinese State," AFP News, October 9, 2019.

5 Zenz, "'Thoroughly Reforming Them towards a Healthy Heart Attitude.'"

6 Smith Finley, "Securitization, Insecurity and Conflict in Contemporary Xinjiang."

7 "Uighurs 'Detained for Beards and Veils.'"

8 Stroup, "The De-Islamification of Public Space and Sinicization of Ethnic Politics in Xi's China."

9 Benjamin Haas, "China Bans Religious Names for Muslim Babies in Xinjiang," *Guardian*, April 24, 2017; "Are China's Hui Muslims Next to Face Crackdown?," *South China Morning Post*, May 18, 2017.

10 Nectar Gan, "How China Is Trying to Impose Islam with Chinese Characteristics in the Hui Muslim Heartland," *South China Morning Post*, May 14, 2018.

11 Liu Xin, "Ningxia Changes Halal Label amid Pan-Islam Backlash," *Global Times*, March 26, 2018.

12 Sigal Samuel, "China Is Treating Islam Like a Mental Illness," *Atlantic*, August 28, 2018; "Standoff over China Mosque Demolition"; Nectar Gan, "Chinese Hui Muslim Protest Forces Authorities to Halt Plan to Demolish Weizhou Grand Mosque," *South China Morning Post*, August 9, 2018.

13 Gansu Sheng Huanjing Baihu Ting, "Linxiazhou huanbaoju quanmian guanche luoshi quanzhou Yisilanjiao gongzuo huiyi jingshen."

14 Ji Yuqiao, "Ningxia Learns from Xinjiang How to Fight Terrorism," *Global Times*, November 27, 2018.

15 William Yang, "Chinese Police Officers Have Raided Mosques in a New Crackdown on Religion," *BuzzFeed News*, December 30, 2018.

16 Steven Lee Myers, "A Crackdown on Islam Is Spreading across China," *New York Times*, September 21, 2019; Feng, "'Afraid We Will Become the Next Xinjiang.'"

17 Personal communication, February 2020.

18 Huizhong Wu, "Sign of the Times: China's Capital Orders Arabic, Muslim Symbols Taken Down," *Reuters*, August 1, 2019, https://www.reuters.com/article/us-china-religion-islam-idUSKCN1UQ0JF.

19 Austin Ramzy and Chris Buckley, "'Absolutely No Mercy': Leaked Files Expose How China Organized Mass Detentions of Muslims," *New York Times*, November 16, 2019.

20 Grose, "'Once Their Mental State Is Healthy, They Will Be Able to Live Happily in Society.'"

21 Bunin, "Xinjiang's Hui Muslims Were Swept into Camps alongside Uighurs."

22 Viola Zhou, "'When Are You Going Back to Arabia?' How Chinese Muslims Became the Target of Online Hate," *South China Morning Post*, March 12, 2017.

23 Rose Luqiu and Fan Yang, "Anti-Muslim Sentiment Is on the Rise in China," *Washington Post*, May 12, 2017.

24 Kinling Lo, "Food App's 'Halal' Option Puts China's Social Media in a Stew," *South China Morning Post*, July 24, 2017.

25 Ma, "A New Perspective in Guiding Ethnic Relations in the Twenty-First Century," 214.

26 Sun, "Debating Ethnic Governance in China," 124.

27 Hu and Hu, "Di'erdai minzu zhengce," 1.

28 Hu and Hu, "Di'erdai minzu zhengce," 1–2. A note on translation: in the text (written in Chinese) the authors explain why they dislike using the word *minzu* and instead prefer to use the word *zuqun*, followed parenthetically by *minzu*. To reflect this distinction, which the authors consider meaningful, I have translated *zuqun* as "ethnic groups" and left their parenthetical emphasis as it appears in the text.

29 Leibold, "The Spectre of Insecurity"; Tobin, "Worrying about Ethnicity," 65–93.

30 Tobin, "Minor Events and Grand Dreams," 759–65.

31 Ishaan Tharoor, "The Alarming Rhetoric of China's War on Terror," *Washington Post*, May 30, 2014.

32 Xi, "Secure a Decisive Victory."

33 Xi, "Secure a Decisive Victory."

34 Leibold, "The Spectre of Insecurity," 1–2.

35 Zhao and Leibold, "Ethnic Governance under Xi Jinping," 8.

36 Zhao and Leibold, "Ethnic Governance under Xi Jinping," 9–12.

37 Zhao and Leibold, "Ethnic Governance under Xi Jinping," 8.

38 Leibold, "The Spectre of Insecurity."

39 Sun, "Debating Ethnic Governance in China," 125.

40 Aga and Harrell, "Theory and Practice of Bilingual Education in China."

41 Sun Liping, "'Buwending Huanxiang' Yu Weiwen Guaiquan," *Renming Wang*, July 7, 2010, http://politics.people.com.cn/GB/1026/12079703.html.

42 Leibold, "The Spectre of Insecurity," 9.

43 Lim, "China's Ethnic Policies in the Xinjiang Region."

44 Gladney, *Dislocating China*, 27.

45 Goode, Stroup, and Gaufman, "Everyday Nationalism in Unsettled Times."

46 Author's observations, January–February 2020. Due to heavy domestic censorship of social media platforms, these posts disappeared quickly. In lieu of hyperlinks, I provide the screenshots given in figure E.1.

47 Zhou, "'When Are You Going Back to Arabia?'"

Bibliography

Abrahamson, Mark. *Global Cities*. New York: Oxford University Press, 2004.

Adida, Claire L. "Too Close for Comfort? Immigrant Exclusion in Africa." *Comparative Political Studies* 44, no. 10 (October 2011): 1370–96.

Aga, Rehamo, and Stevan Harrell. "Theory and Practice of Bilingual Education in China: Lessons from Liangshan Yi Autonomous Prefecture." *International Journal of Bilingual Education and Bilingualism*, March 7, 2018, 1–16.

Aldrich, Howard E., and Roger Waldinger. "Ethnicity and Entrepreneurship." *Annual Review of Sociology* 16, no. 1 (1990): 111–35.

Alexander, Claire E, Joya Chatterji, and Annu Jalais. *The Bengal Diaspora: Rethinking Muslim Migration*. London: Routledge, 2016.

Allès, Élisabeth, Leïla Chérif-Chebbi, and Constance-Hélène Halfon. "Chinese Islam: Unity and Fragmentation." *Religion, State and Society* 31, no. 1 (March 1, 2003): 7–35.

Allport, Gordon W. *The Nature of Prejudice*. 25th anniversary ed. New York: Basic Books, 1979.

Al-Sudairi, Mohammed Turki A. "Adhering to the Ways of Our Western Brothers: Tracing Saudi Influences on the Development of Hui Salafism in China." *Sociology of Islam* 4, nos. 1–2 (April 15, 2016): 27–58.

Altner, Diana. "Do All the Muslims of Tibet Belong to the Hui Nationality?" In *Islam and Tibet: Interactions along the Musk Routes*, edited by Anna Akasoy, Charles Burnett, and Ronit Yoeli-Tlalim, 339–52. Farnham, UK: Ashgate, 2011.

Amer, Sahar. *What Is Veiling?* Islamic Civilization and Muslim Networks. Chapel Hill: University of North Carolina Press, 2014.

Andaya, Leonard Y. *Leaves of the Same Tree: Trade and Ethnicity in the Straits of Melaka*. Honolulu: University of Hawai'i Press, 2008.

Anderson, Benedict R. *Imagined Communities: Reflections on the Origin and Spread of Nationalism*. Revised ed. London: Verso, 2006.

Anthias, Floya. "Women and Nationalism in Cyprus." In *Woman-Nation-State*, edited by Nira Yuval-Davis and Floya Anthias, 150–68. New York: Palgrave Macmillan, 1989.

Anthias, Floya, and Nira Yuval-Davis. "Introduction." In *Woman-Nation-State*, edited by Nira Yuval-Davis and Floya Anthias, 1–16. New York: Palgrave Macmillan, 1989.

Atwill, David G. *The Chinese Sultanate: Islam, Ethnicity, and the Panthay Rebellion in Southwest China, 1856–1873*. Stanford, CA: Stanford University Press, 2005.

Atwood, Christopher P. "Bilingual Education in Inner Mongolia: An Explainer." *Made in China Journal* (blog), August 30, 2020.

Bai, Lian. "Identity Reproducers beyond the Grassroots: The Middle Class in the Manchu Revival since the 1980s." *Asian Ethnicity* 6, no. 3 (October 1, 2005): 183–201.

Barmé, Geremie, Jeremy Goldkorn, and Linda Jaivin, eds. *Shared Destiny*. China Story Yearbook 2014. Canberra: Australian National University Press, 2015.

Barth, Fredrik. "Introduction." In *Ethnic Groups and Boundaries: The Social Organization of Cultural Difference*, edited by Fredrik Barth, 9–38. Oslo: Universitetsforlaget, 1969.

Bastia, Tanja. "Migration as Protest? Negotiating Gender, Class, and Ethnicity in Urban Bolivia." *Environment and Planning A* 43, no. 7 (July 1, 2011): 1514–29.

Beech, Hannah. "If China Is Anti-Islam, Why Are These Chinese Muslims Enjoying a Faith Revival?" *Time*, August 12, 2014.

Beijing Municipal Bureau of Statistics (Beijing Shi Tongji ju) and Guo jia tong ji ju. *Beijing Tongji Nianjian*. Beijing: Zhongguo Tongji Chubanshe, 2007–17.

Ben-Dor Benite, Zvi. *The Dao of Muhammad: A Cultural History of Muslims in Late Imperial China*. Harvard East Asian Monographs 248. Cambridge, MA: Harvard University Asia Center, Harvard University Press, 2005.

Beránek, Ondřej, and Pavel Ťupek. *The Temptation of Graves in Salafi Islam*. Edinburgh: Edinburgh University Press, 2018.

Bernard, H. Russell. *Research Methods in Anthropology: Qualitative and Quantitative Approaches*. 4th ed. Lanham, MD: AltaMira Press, 2006.

Biernacki, Patrick, and Dan Waldorf. "Snowball Sampling: Problems and Techniques of Chain Referral Sampling." *Sociological Methods and Research* 10, no. 2 (November 1981): 141–63.

Bilik, Naran. "Language Education, Intellectuals and Symbolic Representation: Being an Urban Mongolian in a New Configuration of Social Evolution." *Nationalism and Ethnic Politics* 4, nos. 1–2 (March 1, 1998): 47–67.

Billig, Michael. *Banal Nationalism*. London: Sage, 1995.

Boland-Crewe, Tara, and David Lea. *The Territories of the People's Republic of China*. London: Europa, 2002.

Bonikowski, Bart. "Nationalism in Settled Times." *Annual Review of Sociology* 42, no. 1 (July 30, 2016): 427–49.

Bonner, Donna M. "Garifuna Children's Language Shame: Ethnic Stereotypes, National Affiliation, and Transnational Immigration as Factors in Language Choice in Southern Belize." *Language in Society* 30, no. 1 (2001): 81–96.

Borchigud, Wurlig. "The Impact of Urban Ethnic Education on Modern Mongolian Ethnicity, 1940–1966." In *Cultural Encounters on China's Ethnic Frontiers*, edited by Stevan Harrell, 278–300. Seattle: University of Washington Press, 1996.

Bracic, Ana. *Breaking the Exclusion Cycle: How to Promote Cooperation between Majority and Minority Ethnic Groups*. Oxford Scholarship Online. New York: Oxford University Press, 2020.

Brady, Anne-Marie. "Ethnicity and the State in Contemporary China." *Journal of Current Chinese Affairs* 4 (2012): 3–9.

———. "'We Are All Part of the Same Family': China's Ethnic Propaganda." *Journal of Current Chinese Affairs* 41, no. 4 (2013): 159–81.

Brose, Michael C. "Permitted and Pure: Packaged Halal Snack Food from Southwest China." *International Journal of Food Design* 2, no. 2 (October 1, 2017): 167–82.

Brose, Michael C., and Su Min. "Marketing as Pedagogy: Halal e-Commerce in Yunnan." In *Ethnographies of Islam in China*, edited by Rachel Harris, Guangtian Ha, and Maria Jaschok, 131–52. Honolulu: University of Hawai'i Press, 2020.

Brown, David. "Ethicity, Nationalism, and Democracy in South-East Asia." In *Ethnicity*, edited by John Hutchinson and Anthony D. Smith, 305–11. Oxford: Oxford University Press, 1996.

Brubaker, Rogers. *Citizenship and Nationhood in France and Germany*. Cambridge, MA: Harvard University Press, 1998.

———. "The 'Diaspora' Diaspora." *Ethnic and Racial Studies* 28, no. 1 (January 1, 2005): 1–19.

———. *Ethnicity without Groups*. Cambridge, MA: Harvard University Press, 2004.

———. "Migration, Membership, and the Modern Nation-State: Internal and External Dimensions of the Politics of Belonging." *Journal of Interdisciplinary History* 41, no. 1 (2010): 61–78.

———. *Nationalism Reframed: Nationhood and the National Question in the New Europe*. Cambridge: Cambridge University Press, 1996.

Brubaker, Rogers, Margit Feischmidt, Jon Fox, and Liana Grancea. *Nationalist Politics and Everyday Ethnicity in a Transylvanian Town*. Princeton, NJ: Princeton University Press, 2006.

Bruinessen, Martin van. "Global and Local in Indonesian Islam." *Southeast Asian Studies* 37, no. 2 (January 1, 1999): 158–75.

Bulag, Uradyn E. "Mongolian Ethnicity and Linguistic Anxiety in China." *American Anthropologist*, new series, 105, no. 4 (December 1, 2003): 753–63.

———. "Seeing Like a Minority: Political Tourism and the Struggle for Recognition in China." *Journal of Current Chinese Affairs* 41, no. 4 (2013): 133–58.

Bunin, Gene A. "Xinjiang's Hui Muslims Were Swept into Camps alongside Uighurs." *Foreign Policy* (blog), February 10, 2020.

Burgjin, Jirgal, and Naran Bilik. "Contemporary Mongolian Population Distribution, Migration, Cultural Change, and Identity." In *China's Minorities on the Move: Selected Case Studies*, edited by Robyn Iredale, Naran Bilik, and Fei Guo, 53–68. New York: Routledge, 2003.

Byler, Darren. "Ghost World." *Logic: A Magazine about Technology* 7 (2019): 89–108.

Callahan, Mary P. "Making Myanmars: Language, Territory, and Belonging in Post-Socialist Burma." In *Boundaries and Belonging: States and Societies in the Struggle to Shape Identities and Local Practices*, edited by Joel S. Migdal, 99–120. New York: Cambridge University Press, 2004.

Callahan, William A. *China Dreams: 20 Visions of the Future*. Oxford: Oxford University Press, 2013.

Carrico, Kevin. *The Great Han: Race, Nationalism, and Tradition in China Today*. Oakland: University of California Press, 2017.

Certeau, Michel de. *The Practice of Everyday Life*. 2nd ed. Berkeley: University of California Press, 2013.

Cesaro, M. Cristina. "Consuming Identities: Food and Resistance among the Uyghur in Contemporary Xinjiang." *Inner Asia* 2, no. 2 (2000): 225–38.

Chandra, Kanchan. "Ethnic Parties and Democratic Stability." *Perspectives on Politics* 3, no. 2 (2005): 235–52.

Chang, Chung-Fu. "Self-Identity versus State Identification of 'Tibetan-Speaking Muslims' in the Kaligang Area of Qinghai—An Ethnographic Analysis." In *Muslims in Amdo Tibetan Society*, edited by Marie-Paule Hille, Bianca Horlemann, and Paul K. Nietupski, 67–86. London: Lexington Books, 2015.

Chen, Aimin, and Jie Gao. "Urbanization in China and the Coordinated Development Model—The Case of Chengdu." *Social Science Journal* 48, no. 3 (September 2011): 500–513.

Chen Jie. "Zhong-A Hezuo luntan li yi lai de zhongguo dui A meiti jiaoliu." *Alabo shijie yanjiu* 5 (September 2014): 81–93.

Chen, John. "Islamic Modernism in China: Chinese Muslim Elites, Guomindang Nation-Building, and the Limits of the Global Umma, 1900–1960." PhD diss., Columbia University, 2018.

Chen, Sanping. *Multicultural China in the Early Middle Ages*. Encounters with Asia. Philadelphia: University of Pennsylvania Press, 2012.

Chen, Xi. "China at the Tipping Point? The Rising Cost of Stability." *Journal of Democracy* 24, no. 1 (January 15, 2013): 57–64.

Cheung, Siu Keung, Joseph Tse-Hei Lee, and Lida V Nedilsky, eds. *Marginalization in China*. New York: Palgrave Macmillan, 2009.

"China Clampdown in Inner Mongolia." *BBC News*, May 30, 2011. www.bbc.com/news/world-asia-pacific-13592514.

Chow, Kai-wing. "Imagining Boundaries of Blood: Zhang Binglin and the Invention of the Han 'Race' in Modern China." In *The Construction of Racial Identities in China and Japan*, edited by Frank Dikötter, 34–52. Honolulu: University of Hawai'i Press, 1997.

Cieciura, Wlodzimierz. "The Crescent and the Red Star: Hui Muslims and Chinese Communism in a Historical Perspective." *Far East / Dálný Východ* 4, no. 1 (January 2014): 6–21.

———. "Ethnicity or Religion? Republican-Era Chinese Debates on Islam and Muslims." In *Islamic Thought in China*, edited by Jonathan Lipman, 107–46. Sino-Muslim Intellectual Evolution from the 17th to the 21st Century. Edinburgh: Edinburgh University Press, 2016.

Citrin, Jack, and David O. Sears. "Balancing National and Ethnic Identities." In *Measuring Identity: A Guide for Social Scientists*, edited by Rawi Abdelal, Yoshiko M. Herrera, Alastair Iain Johnston, and Rose McDermott, 145–74. New York: Cambridge University Press, 2009.

Cliff, Thomas. "Lucrative Chaos: Interethnic Conflict as a Function of the Economic 'Normalization' of Southern Xinjiang." In *Ethnic Conflict and Protest in Tibet and Xinjiang: Unrest in China's West*, edited by Ben Hillman and Gray Tuttle, 122–50. New York: Columbia University Press, 2016.

Comaroff, John L., and Jean Comaroff. *Ethnicity, Inc.* Chicago: University of Chicago Press, 2009.

Cooke, Susette. "Surviving State and Society in Northwest China: The Hui Experience in Qinghai Province under the PRC." *Journal of Muslim Minority Affairs* 28, no. 3 (December 2008): 401–20.

Côté, Isabelle. "The Enemies Within: Targeting Han Chinese and Hui Minorities in Xinjiang." *Asian Ethnicity* 16, no. 2 (April 3, 2015): 136–51.

———. "Horizontal Inequalities and Sons of the Soil Conflict in China." *Civil Wars* 17, no. 3 (July 3, 2015): 357–78.

———. "Internal Migration and the Politics of Place: A Comparative Analysis of China and Indonesia." *Asian Ethnicity* 15, no. 1 (January 2, 2014): 111–29.

Davis, Elizabeth Van Wie. "Uyghur Muslim Ethnic Separatism in Xinjiang, China." *Asian Affairs: An American Review* 35, no. 1 (April 1, 2008): 15–30.

De Cillia, Rudolf, Martin Reisigl, and Ruth Wodak. "The Discursive Construction of National Identities." *Discourse & Society* 10, no. 2 (April 1, 1999): 149–73.

Demintseva, Ekaterina. "'Migrant Schools' and the 'Children of Migrants': Constructing Boundaries around and inside School Space." *Race Ethnicity and Education* 23, no. 4 (July 3, 2020): 598–612.

Denny, Frederick Mathewson. *An Introduction to Islam*. 3rd ed. Upper Saddle River, NJ: Pearson Prentice Hall, 2006.

Dillon, Jim T. *The Practice of Questioning.* International Series on Communication Skills. London: Routledge, 1990.

Dillon, Michael. *China's Muslim Hui Community: Migration, Settlement and Sects.* Richmond, Surrey, UK: Curzon, 1999.

Dobson, Madeleine E. "Unpacking Children in Migration Research." *Children's Geographies* 7, no. 3 (August 1, 2009): 355–60.

Donaldson, John A. *Small Works: Poverty and Economic Development in Southwestern China.* Ithaca, NY: Cornell University Press, 2011.

Dreyer, June Teufel. "China's Vulnerability to Minority Separatism." *Asian Affairs: An American Review* 32 (July 2005): 69–86.

Durkheim, Émile. *The Elementary Forms of the Religious Life: A Study in Religious Sociology.* London: George Allen and Unwin, 1915.

Dutton, Michael, Hsiu-ju Stacy Lo, and Dong Dong Wu. *Beijing Time.* Cambridge, MA: Harvard University Press, 2010.

Earl, Jennifer. "Tanks, Tear Gas, and Taxes: Toward a Theory of Movement Repression." *Sociological Theory* 21, no. 1 (2003): 44–68.

Edensor, Tim. *National Identity, Popular Culture and Everyday Life.* Oxford: Berg, 2002.

Enloe, Cynthia. *Bananas, Beaches, Bases: Making Feminist Sense of International Politics.* London: Pandora, 1989.

Enwall, Joakim. "Inter-Ethnic Relations in Mongolia and Inner Mongolia." *Asian Ethnicity* 11, no. 2 (June 1, 2010): 239–57.

Erie, Matthew S. *China and Islam: The Prophet, the Party, and Law.* Cambridge Studies in Law and Society. Cambridge: Cambridge University Press, 2016.

———. "Muslim Mandarins in Chinese Courts: Dispute Resolution, Islamic Law, and the Secular State in Northwest China." *Law & Social Inquiry* 40, no. 4 (September 1, 2015): 1001–30.

Erie, Matthew S., and Allen Carlson. "Introduction to 'Islam in China/China in Islam.'" *Cross-Currents: East Asian History and Culture Review* 12 (2014): 1–13.

Eroglu Sager, Z. Hale. "A Place under the Sun: Chinese Muslim (Hui) Identity and the Constitutional Movement in Republican China." *Modern China,* May 18, 2020, 1–34.

Fairbank, John King, and Merle Goldman. *China: A New History.* 2nd revised and enlarged ed. Cambridge, MA: Belknap Press, 2006.

Fan Ke. "'Zai difanghua' yu xiangzheng ziben: yige Minnan Huizu shequ jinnian lai de ruogan jianzhu baoxian." *Open Times,* no. 2 (2005): 42–61.

Feng, Chongyi. "The Dilemma of Stability Preservation in China." *Journal of Current Chinese Affairs* 42, no. 2 (June 19, 2013): 3–19.

Feng, Emily. "'Afraid We Will Become the Next Xinjiang': China's Hui Muslims Face Crackdown." *Morning Edition.* National Public Radio, September 26, 2019.

Fox, Jon E. "The Edges of the Nation: A Research Agenda for Uncovering the Taken-for-Granted Foundations of Everyday Nationhood." *Nations and Nationalism* 23, no. 1 (January 1, 2017): 26–47.

———. "National Holiday Commemorations: The View from Below." In *The Cultural Politics of Nationalism and Nation-Building: Ritual and Performance in the Forging of Nations*, edited by Rachel Tsang and Eric Taylor Woods, 38–53. New York: Routledge, 2013.

Fox, Jon E., and Demelza Jones. "Migration, Everyday Life and the Ethnicity Bias." *Ethnicities* 13, no. 4 (August 1, 2013): 385–400.

Fox, Jon E., and Cynthia Miller-Idriss. "Everyday Nationhood." *Ethnicities* 8, no. 4 (December 1, 2008): 536–63.

———. "The 'Here and Now' of Everyday Nationhood." *Ethnicities* 8, no. 4 (December 1, 2008): 573–76.

Gansu Sheng Huanjing Baihu Ting. "Linxiazhou Huanbaoju quanmian guanche luoshi quanzhou Yisilanjiao gongzuo huiyi jingshen." Lanzhou: Gansu sheng huanjing baihu ting, August 30, 2018. www.gsep.gansu.gov.cn/info/1003/50883.htm.

Gao, James Z. "The Call of the Oases: The 'Peaceful Liberation' of Xinjiang, 1949–53." In *Dilemmas of Victory: The Early Years of the People's Republic of China*, edited by Jeremy Brown and Paul G Pickowicz, 184–204. Cambridge, MA: Harvard University Press, 2020.

Garnaut, Anthony. "Pen of the Jahriyya: A Commentary on 'The History of the Soul' by Zhang Chengzhi." *Inner Asia* 8, no. 1 (2006): 29–50.

Gaubatz, Piper Rae. *Beyond the Great Wall: Urban Form and Transformation on the Chinese Frontiers*. Stanford, CA: Stanford University Press, 1996.

George, Alexander L., and Andrew Bennett. *Case Studies and Theory Development in the Social Sciences*. BCSIA Studies in International Security. Cambridge, MA: MIT Press, 2005.

Gillette, Maris Boyd. *Between Mecca and Beijing: Modernization and Consumption among Urban Chinese Muslims*. Stanford, CA: Stanford University Press, 2002.

———. "Children's Food and Islamic Dietary Restrictions in Xi'an." In *The Cultural Politics of Food and Eating: A Reader*, edited by James L. Watson and Melissa L. Caldwell, 106–21. Malden, MA: Blackwell, 2005.

Gil-White, Francisco J. "How Thick Is Blood? The Plot Thickens . . . : If Ethnic Actors Are Primordialists, What Remains of the Circumstantialist/Primordialist Controversy?" *Ethnic and Racial Studies* 22, no. 5 (1999): 789–820.

Gladney, Dru C. *Dislocating China: Reflections on Muslims, Minorities, and Other Subaltern Subjects*. Chicago: University of Chicago Press, 2004.

———. "Islam in China: Beijing's Hui and Uighur Challenge." *Global Dialogue* 9, nos. 1–2 (Winter 2007): 89–95.

———. *Muslim Chinese: Ethnic Nationalism in the People's Republic*. Harvard East Asian Monographs 149. Cambridge, MA: Council on East Asian Studies, Harvard University, Harvard University Press, 1991.

———. "Relational Alterity: Constructing Dungan (Hui), Uygur, and Kazakh Identities across China, Central Asia, and Turkey." *History and Anthropology* 9, no. 4 (June 1, 1996): 445–77.

———. "Representing Nationality in China: Refiguring Majority/Minority Identities." *Journal of Asian Studies* 53, no. 1 (February 1, 1994): 92–123.

Glasius, Marlies, Meta de Lange, Jos Bartman, Emanuela Dalmasso, Aofei Lv, Adele Del Sordi, Marcus Michaelsen, and Kris Ruijgrok. *Research, Ethics and Risk in the Authoritarian Field*. New York: Palgrave Macmillan, 2018.

Glasserman, Aaron. "Making Muslims Hui: Ethnic Bias in the New Curriculum of the China Islamic Association." In *Hui Muslims in China*, edited by Rong Gui, Hacer Zekiye Gönül, and Xiaoyan Zhang, 47–62. Leuven: Leuven University Press, 2016.

Glick Schiller, Nina, Ayşe Çağlar, and Thaddeus C. Guldbrandsen. "Beyond the Ethnic-Lens: Locality, Globality, and Born Again Incorporation." *American Ethnologist* 33, no. 4 (2006): 612–33.

Goldstein, Melvyn C., Ben Jiao (Benjor), Cynthia M. Beall, and Phuntsog Tsering. "Fertility and Family Planning in Rural Tibet." *China Journal* 47 (January 1, 2002): 19–39.

Goode, J. Paul. "Humming Along: Public and Private Patriotism in Putin's Russia." In *Everyday Nationhood: Theorising Culture, Identity and Belonging after Banal Nationalism*, edited by Michael Skey and Marco Antonsich, 121–47. New York: Palgrave Macmillan, 2017.

———. "Love for the Motherland (or Why Cheese Is More Patriotic than Crimea)." *Russian Politics* 1, no. 4 (December 30, 2016): 418–49.

———. "Nationalism in Quiet Times: Ideational Power and Post-Soviet Hybrid Regimes." *Problems of Post-Communism* 59, no. 3 (May 1, 2012): 6–16.

Goode, J. Paul, and David R. Stroup. "Everyday Nationalism: Constructivism for the Masses." *Social Science Quarterly* 96, no. 3 (September 1, 2015): 717–39.

Goode, J. Paul, David R. Stroup, and Elizaveta Gaufman. "Everyday Nationalism in Unsettled Times: In Search of Normality during Pandemic." *Nationalities Papers*, May 22, 2020, 1–25.

Grose, Timothy. "If You Don't Know How, Just Learn: Chinese Housing and the Transformation of Uyghur Domestic Space." *Ethnic and Racial Studies* (July 6, 2020): 1–22. Online.

———. *Negotiating Inseparability in China: The Xinjiang Class and the Dynamics of Uyghur Identity*. Hong Kong: Hong Kong University Press, 2020.

———. "'Once Their Mental State Is Healthy, They Will Be Able to Live Happily in Society': How China's Government Conflates Uighur Identity with Mental Illness." *ChinaFile* (blog), August 2, 2019. www.chinafile.com/reporting-opinion/viewpoint/once-their-mental-state-healthy-they-will-be-able-live-happily-society.

———. "Uyghur University Students and Ramadan." In *Minority Education in China*, edited by James Leibold and Yangbin Chen, 221–38. Hong Kong: Hong Kong University Press, 2013.

———. "Veiled Identities: Islam, Hui Ethnicity, and Dress Codes in Northwest China." *Journal of Islamic and Muslim Studies* 5, no. 1 (2020): 35–60.

Guo Jinbao, Jinan Municipal Bureau of Statistics (Jinan shi tongjiju), and Guo jia tong ji ju. *Jinan Tongji Nianjian 2008*. Vol. 26. Jinan Tongji Nianjian 26. Beijing: Zhongguo Tongji Chubanshe, 2008.

———. *Jinan Tongji Nianjian 2010*. Vol. 28. Jinan Tongji Nianjian 28. Beijing: Zhongguo Tongji Chubanshe, 2010.

———. *Jinan Tongji Nianjian 2011*. Vol. 29. Jinan Tongji Nianjian 29. Beijing: Zhongguo Tongji Chubanshe, 2011.

Guo Jinbao, Jinan Municipal Bureau of Statistics (Jinan shi tongjiju), and National Bureau of Statistics Jinan Interview Team (Guojia Tongjiju Jinan Diaocha dui). *Jinan Tongji Nianjian 2009*. Vol. 27. Jinan Tongji Nianjian 27. Beijing: Zhongguo Tongji Chubanshe, 2009.

Ha, Guangtian. "Hui Muslims and Han Converts: Islam and the Paradox of Recognition." In *Handbook on Religion in China*, edited by Stephen Feuchtwang, 313–37. Cheltenham, UK: Edward Elgar, 2020.

———. "Religion of the Father: Islam, Gender, and Politics of Ethnicity in Late Socialism." PhD diss., Columbia University, 2014.

———. "The Silent Hat: Islam, Female Labor, and the Political Economy of the Headscarf Debate." *Signs: Journal of Women in Culture and Society* 42, no. 3 (February 14, 2017): 743–69.

———. "Specters of Qingzhen: Marking Islam in China." *Sociology of Islam* 8, nos. 3–4 (December 10, 2020): 423–47.

Haleem, M. A. S. Abdel, trans. *The Qur'an*. Reissue ed. Oxford: Oxford University Press, 2008.

Hammond, Laura C. *This Place Will Become Home: Refugee Repatriation to Ethiopia*. Ithaca, NY: Cornell University Press, 2018.

Han, Dong. "Policing and Racialization of Rural Migrant Workers in Chinese Cities." *Ethnic and Racial Studies* 33, no. 4 (April 2010): 593–610.

Handcock, Mark S., and Krista J. Gile. "Comment: On the Concept of Snowball Sampling." *Sociological Methodology* 41, no. 1 (August 2011): 367–71.

Hansen, Mette Halskov. *Lessons in Being Chinese: Minority Education and Ethnic Identity in Southwest China*. Seattle: University of Washington Press, 1999.

Harrell, Stevan. "Introduction: Civilizing Projects and the Reaction to Them." In *Cultural Encounters on China's Ethnic Frontiers*, edited by Stevan Harrell, 3–36. Seattle: University of Washington Press, 1996.

———. "Reading Threads: Clothing, Ethnicity, and Place in Southwest China." In *Writing with Thread: Traditional Textiles of Southwest Chinese Minorities*, edited by Tom Klobe, 99–112. Honolulu: University of Hawai'i Art Gallery, 2009.

———. *Ways of Being Ethnic in Southwest China*. Studies on Ethnic Groups in China. Seattle: University of Washington Press, 2001.

Harris, Rachel. *Soundscapes of Uyghur Islam*. Framing the Global. Bloomington: Indiana University Press, 2020.

Haw, Stephen G. *Beijing: A Concise History*. Routledge Studies in the Modern History of Asia 42. London: Routledge/Taylor & Francis Group, 2008.

———. "The Semu Ren in the Yuan Empire." *Ming Qing Yanjiu* 18, no. 1 (2013): 39–63.

He, Shenjing, and Fulong Wu. "Neighborhood Changes and Residential Differentiation in Shanghai." In *China's Emerging Cities: The Making of New Urbanism*, edited by Fulong Wu, 185–209. New York: Routledge, 2008.

Heberer, Thomas. *China and Its National Minorities : Autonomy or Assimilation?* Armonk, NY: M. E. Sharpe, 1989.

Heckathorn, Douglas D. "Comment: Snowball versus Respondent-Driven Sampling." *Sociological Methodology* 41, no. 1 (August 2011): 355–66.

Hessler, Peter. *Oracle Bones: A Journey through Time in China*. Reprint ed. New York: Harper Perennial, 2007.

Hille, Marie-Paule, Bianca Horlemann, and Paul K. Nietupski, eds. *Muslims in Amdo Tibetan Society: Multidisciplinary Approaches*. Studies in Modern Tibetan Literature. Lanham, MD: Lexington Books, 2015.

Hillman, Ben. "Introduction: Understanding the Current Wave of Conflict and Protest in Tibet and Xinjiang." In *Ethnic Conflict and Protest in Tibet and Xinjiang: Unrest in China's West*, edited by Ben Hillman and Gray Tuttle, 1–18. New York: Columbia University Press, 2016.

———. "The Rise of the Community in Rural China: Village Politics, Cultural Identity and Religious Revival in a Hui Hamlet." *China Journal*, no. 51 (2004): 53–73.

Hillman, Ben, and Gray Tuttle, eds. *Ethnic Conflict and Protest in Tibet and Xinjiang: Unrest in China's West*. New York: Columbia University Press, 2016.

Hirschman, Charles. "The Meaning and Measurement of Ethnicity in Malaysia: An Analysis of Census Classifications." *Journal of Asian Studies* 46, no. 3 (1987): 555–82.

Ho, Wai-Yip. "Mobilizing the Muslim Minority for China's Development: Hui Muslims, Ethnic Relations and Sino-Arab Connections." *Journal of Comparative Asian Development* 12, no. 1 (April 2013): 84–112.

Hong, Meenchee, Sizhong Sun, A. B. M. Rabiul Beg, and Zhangyue Zhou. "Determinants of Halal Purchasing Behaviour: Evidences from China." *Journal of Islamic Marketing* 10, no. 2 (January 1, 2019): 410–25.

Hoshino, Masahiro. "Preferential Policies for China's Ethnic Minorities at a Crossroads." *Journal of Contemporary East Asia Studies* 8, no. 1 (January 2, 2019): 1–13.

Hu Angang, and Lianhe Hu. "Di'erdai minzu zhengce: zoujin minzu jiaorong yiti he fanrong yiti." *Zhongguo Guoji Renwen Shehui Kexue Xinxi Wang* 24 (December 29, 2011): 1–6.

Hua Tao and Zhai Guiye. "Minguo shiqi de Huizu jieshuo yu Zhongguo Gongchangdang 'Huihui minzu wenti' de lilun yiyi." *Minzu yanjiu*, no. 1 (2012): 12–24, 108.

Hwang, Yih-Jye, and Florian Schneider. "Performance, Meaning, and Ideology in the Making of Legitimacy: The Celebrations of the People's Republic of China's Sixty-Year Anniversary." *China Review*, 2011, 27–55.

Information Office of the State Council of the People's Republic of China. "China's Ethnic Policy and Common Prosperity and Development of All Ethnic Groups." White Paper. Beijing, September 9, 2009.

Iredale, Robyn, and Fei Guo. "Overview of Minority Migration." In *China's Minorities on the Move: Selected Case Studies*, edited by Robyn Iredale, Naran Bilik, and Fei Guo, 3–32. New York: Routledge, 2003.

Israeli, Raphael. *Islam in China: Religion, Ethnicity, Culture, and Politics.* Lanham, MD: Lexington Books, 2002.

Jargalsaikhan, Mendee. "Mongolia's Response to China's New Educational Policy in Inner Mongolia." *ASAN Forum* (blog), October 23, 2020. http://www.theasanforum.org/mongolias-response-to-chinas-new-educational-policy-in-inner-mongolia/.

Jaschok, Maria, and Jingjun Shui. *The History of Women's Mosques in Chinese Islam.* Surrey, UK: Curzon Press, 2000.

Jin Zhongjie. "Alaboyu jiaoxue zai Ningxia de lishi yange ji qi minjian tedian." *Xi Bei Di Er Minzu Xueyuan Xuebao (Zhexue Shehui Kexue Xue Ban)* 75, no. 3 (2007): 47–52.

Jinan Municipal Bureau of Statistics (Jinan shi tongjiju) and Guo jia tong ji ju. *Jinan Tongji Nianjian.* Beijing: Zhongguo Tongji Chubanshe, 2007–17.

Jinan Municipal People's Government. "Population of Jinan." Jinan Shi Renmin Zhengfu Men Hu Wang Zhan (Official Website of the Jinan Municipal People's Government), August 22, 2015. http://english.jinan.gov.cn/col/col2235/index.html.

Jinba, Tenzin. *In the Land of the Eastern Queendom: The Politics of Gender and Ethnicity on the Sino-Tibetan Border.* Seattle: University of Washington Press, 2013.

Johnson, Bonnie, and Nalini Chhetri. "Exclusionary Policies and Practices in Chinese Minority Education: The Case of Tibetan Education." *Current Issues in Comparative Education* 2, no. 2 (2002): 142–53.

Jones, Rhys, and Peter Merriman. "Hot, Banal and Everyday Nationalism: Bilingual Road Signs in Wales." *Political Geography* 28, no. 3 (March 2009): 164–73.

Kaltman, Blaine. *Under the Heel of the Dragon: Islam, Racism, Crime, and the Uighur in China*. Athens: Ohio University Press, 2007.

Karner, Christian. *Ethnicity and Everyday Life*. The New Sociology. London: Routledge, 2007.

Kim, Hodong. *Holy War in China: The Muslim Rebellion and State in Chinese Central Asia, 1864–1877*. Stanford, CA: Stanford University Press, 2004.

Kipnis, Andrew. "Neoliberalism Reified: Suzhi Discourse and Tropes of Neoliberalism in the People's Republic of China." *Journal of the Royal Anthropological Institute* 13, no. 2 (2007): 383–400.

Klein, Jakob A. "Everyday Approaches to Food Safety in Kunming." *China Quarterly* 214 (June 2013): 376–93.

Kolås, Åshild. "Degradation Discourse and Green Governmentality in the Xilinguole Grasslands of Inner Mongolia." *Development and Change* 45, no. 2 (March 1, 2014): 308–28.

Koziura, Karolina. "Everyday Ethnicity in Chernivtsi, Western Ukraine." *Anthropology of East Europe Review* 32, no. 1 (May 5, 2014): 1–21.

Kuşçular, Remzi. *Cleanliness in Islam: A Comprehensive Guide to Tahara*. Somerset, NJ: The Light, 2007.

Kvale, Steinar. *InterViews: An Introduction to Qualitative Research Interviewing*. Thousand Oaks, CA: Sage, 1996.

Laferriere, Martha. "Ethnicity in Phonological Variation and Change." *Language* 55, no. 3 (1979): 603–17.

Laliberté, André, and Marc Lanteigne. "The Issue of Challenges to the Legitimacy of CCP Rule." In *The Chinese Party-State in the 21st Century: Adaptation and the Reinvention of Legitimacy*, edited by André Laliberté and Marc Lanteigne, 1–21. New York: Routledge, 2008.

Landau, Ruth. "Religiosity, Nationalism and Human Reproduction: The Case of Israel." *International Journal of Sociology and Social Policy* 23, no. 12 (December 2003): 64–80.

Lee, Ching Kwan. *Against the Law: Labor Protests in China's Rustbelt and Sunbelt*. Berkeley: University of California Press, 2007.

Lee, Yee Lak Elliot. "Muslims as 'Hui' in Late Imperial and Republican China: A Historical Reconsideration of Social Differentiation and Identity Construction." *Historical Social Research* 44, no. 3 (2019): 226–63.

Leibold, James. "Competing Narratives of Racial Unity in Republican China from the Yellow Emperor to Peking Man." *Modern China* 32, no. 2 (April 1, 2006): 181–220.

———. "Ethnic Policy in China: Is Reform Inevitable?" *Policy Studies*, no. 68 (2013): 1–68.

———. "Interethnic Conflict in the PRC: Xinjiang and Tibet as Exceptions?" In *Ethnic Conflict and Protest in Tibet and Xinjiang: Unrest in China's West*, edited by Ben Hillman and Gray Tuttle, 223–42. New York: Columbia University Press, 2016.

———. *Reconfiguring Chinese Nationalism: How the Qing Frontier and Its Indigenes Became Chinese*. New York: Palgrave Macmillan, 2007.

———. "The Spectre of Insecurity: The CCP's Mass Internment Strategy in Xinjiang." *China Leadership Monitor*, no. 59 (March 1, 2019): 1–16.

———. "Toward a Second Generation of Ethnic Policies?" *China Brief* 12, no. 13 (July 2012). https://jamestown.org/program/toward-a-second-generation-of-ethnic-policies/.

Leibold, James, and Timothy Grose. "Islamic Veiling in Xinjiang: The Political and Societal Struggle to Define Uyghur Female Adornment." *China Journal* 76, no. 1 (July 2016): 78–102.

Lenin, Vladimir Ilyich. *National Liberation, Socialism and Imperialism: Selected Writings by V. I. Lenin*. New York: International Publishers, 1968.

———. *The Rights of Nations to Self-Determination: Selected Writings*. New York: International Publishers, 1951.

Leslie, Donald Daniel. *Islamic Literature in Chinese Late Ming and Early Ch'ing: Book, Authors, and Associates*. Canberra: Canberra College of Advanced Education, 1981.

Li, Jieli, and Lei Ji. "Still 'Familiar' but No Longer 'Strangers': Hui Muslims in Contemporary China." In *Ethnic China: Identity, Assimilation, and Resistance*, edited by Xiaobing Li and Patrick Fuliang Shan, 153–70. Lanham, MD: Lexington Books, 2015.

Li Juan, Ma Shaobiao, and Ma Shaohu. "Cong Huizu yuyan jiedu qi minzu rentong." *Gansu Lianhe Daxue Xuebao (Shehui Kexue Ban)* 25, no. 2 (2009): 39–41.

Li Liansheng, "Zhuiyi Jiaozi Hutong." *Beijing Jishi*, no. 9 (2007): 76–78.

Li, Yang. "Minorities, Tourism and Ethnic Theme Parks: Employees' Perspectives from Yunnan, China." *Journal of Cultural Geography* 28, no. 2 (June 1, 2011): 311–38.

Liang Jingyu. *Niu Jie: yige chengshi Huizu shequ de bianqian*. Beijing: Zhong Yang Min Zu Da Xue Chu Ban She, 2006.

Liang Yongjia. "Turning Gwer Sa La Festival into Intangible Cultural Heritage: State Superscription of Popular Religion in Southwest China." *China: An International Journal* 11, no. 2 (September 5, 2013): 58–75.

Light, Ivan, Georges Sabagh, Mehdi Bozorgmehr, and Claudia Der-Martirosian. "Internal Ethnicity in the Ethnic Economy." *Ethnic and Racial Studies* 16, no. 4 (October 1, 1993): 581–97.

Lim, Rosalyn. "China's Ethnic Policies in the Xinjiang Region." *Washington Journal of Modern China* 10, no. 2 (2012): 64–89.

Lin, Hsiao-Ting. *Modern China's Ethnic Frontiers: A Journey to the West.* London: Routledge, 2010.

Linz, Juan J. *Totalitarian and Authoritarian Regimes.* Boulder, CO: Lynne Rienner, 2000.

Lipman, Jonathan N. "The Border World of Gansu, 1895–1835." PhD diss., Stanford University, 1981.

———. "Ethnicity and Politics in Republican China: The Ma Family Warlords of Gansu." *Modern China* 10, no. 3 (1984): 285–316.

———. *Familiar Strangers: A History of Muslims in Northwest China.* Seattle: University of Washington Press, 1998.

———. "Hyphenated Chinese: Sino-Muslim Identity in Modern China." In *Remapping China: Fissures in Historical Terrain*, edited by Gail Hershatter, Emily Honig, Jonathan N. Lipman, and Randall Stross, 97–112. Palo Alto, CA: Stanford University Press, 1996.

Litzinger, Ralph A. *Other Chinas: The Yao and the Politics of National Belonging.* Durham, NC: Duke University Press, 2000.

Liu, Rongduo, Zuzanna Pieniak, and Wim Verbeke. "Food-Related Hazards in China: Consumers' Perceptions of Risk and Trust in Information Sources." *Food Control* 46 (December 1, 2014): 291–98.

Liu, Shuxiang. "Yan'an shiqi de Huizu yu Yisilanjiao gongzuo." *Zhongguo Musilin* 3 (2011): 26–29.

Loubes, Jean-Paul. "Urban Changes in Xinjiang: 'Sinisation' of the Urban Space." *Modumag: A Tale of Urban China* (blog), March 16, 2015. www.modumag.com/focus/urban-changes-in-xinjiang-sinisation-of-the-urban-space-2.

Loyalka, Michelle Dammon. *Eating Bitterness: Stories from the Front Lines of China's Great Urban Migration.* Berkeley: University of California Press, 2012.

Ma, Haiyun. "Fanhui or Huifan? Hanhui or Huimin? Salar Ethnic Identification and Qing Administrative Transformation in Eighteenth-Century Gansu." *Late Imperial China* 29, no. 2 (December 21, 2008): 1–36.

———. "New Teachings and New Territories: Religion, Regulations, and Regions in Qing Gansu, 1700–1800." PhD diss., Georgetown University, 2007.

Ma Hongyan. "Huizu Yuyan Jiqi Fanying de Minzu Rentong Xinli." *Qinghai Minzu Xueyuan Xuebao* 28, no. 4 (2001): 108–10.

Ma, Rong. "A New Perspective in Guiding Ethnic Relations in the Twenty-First Century: 'De-Politicization' of Ethnicity in China." *Asian Ethnicity* 8, no. 3 (October 2007): 199–217.

Ma Shinian. "A Primary Investigation of the History of the Hui People and the Historical Data of Islam Recorded in the Notes Written by Zhou Ma."

In *Islam*, edited by Yijiu Jin, Wai Yip Ho, and Michael Dillon, 87–115. Leiden: Brill, 2017.

Ma Tong. *Zhongguo Xibei Yisilan Jiao Jiben Tezheng.* Xiu ding ben, Di 1 ban. Yinchuan: Ningxia Renmin Chubanshe, 2000.

———. "Zhongguo Yisilanjiao be jiben tezheng." *Ningxia shehui kexue*, no. 6 (1988): 103.

MacFarquhar, Roderick, and Michael Schoenhals. *Mao's Last Revolution.* Cambridge, MA: Belknap Press of Harvard University Press, 2006.

MacInnis, Donald E. *Religion in China Today: Policy and Practice.* Maryknoll, NY: Orbis Books, 1989.

Mackerras, Colin. "Tibetans, Uyghurs and Multinational 'China': Han-Minority Relations and State Legitimation." In *Chinese Politics: State, Society and the Market*, edited by Peter Hays Gries and Stanley Rosen, 222–42. New York: Routledge, 2010.

Madsen, Richard. "The Upsurge of Religion in China." *Journal of Democracy* 21, no. 4 (October 20, 2010): 58–71.

Martin, Terry. *The Affirmative Action Empire: Nations and Nationalism in the Soviet Union, 1923–1939.* Ithaca, NY: Cornell University Press, 2001.

Marx, Anthony W. *Making Race and Nation: A Comparison of South Africa, the United States, and Brazil.* Cambridge: Cambridge University Press, 1998.

Mathieu, Christine. "Lost Kingdoms and Forgotten Tribes: Myths, Mysteries and Mother-Right in the History of the Naxi Nationality and the Mosuo People of Southwest China." PhD diss., Murdoch University, 1996.

Mazumdar, Sanjoy, Shampa Mazumdar, Faye Docuyanan, and Colette Marie Mclaughlin. "Creating a Sense of Place: The Vietnamese-Americans and Little Saigon." *Journal of Environmental Psychology* 20, no. 4 (December 2000): 319–33.

Mazumdar, Shampa, and Sanjoy Mazumdar. "The Articulation of Religion in Domestic Space: Rituals in the Immigrant Muslim Home." In *Contesting Rituals: Islam and Practice of Identity-Making*, edited by Pamela J. Stewart and Andrew Strathern, 125–46. Durham, NC: Carolina Academic Press, 2005.

McCarthy, Susan K. *Communist Multiculturalism: Ethnic Revival in Southwest China.* Studies on Ethnic Groups in China. Seattle: University of Washington Press, 2009.

McClintock, Anne. "Family Feuds: Gender, Nationalism and the Family." *Feminist Review*, no. 44 (1993): 61–80.

McGarry, John. "'Demographic Engineering': The State-Directed Movement of Ethnic Groups as a Technique of Conflict Regulation." *Ethnic and Racial Studies* 21, no. 4 (January 1, 1998): 613–38.

McLoughlin, Seán. "Locating Muslim Diasporas: Multi-Locality, Multi-Disciplinarity and Performativity." *Ethnic and Racial Studies* 40, no. 3 (February 19, 2017): 421–27.

Meer, Nasar. "Muslim Diasporas and Their Framing(s): Muslim Migration Rethought." *Ethnic and Racial Studies* 40, no. 3 (February 19, 2017): 396–400.

Mertha, Andrew C. "From 'Rustless Screws' to 'Nail Houses': The Evolution of Property Rights in China." *Orbis* 53, no. 2 (2009): 233–49.

Meyer, Michael J. *The Last Days of Old Beijing: Life in the Vanishing Backstreets of a City Transformed.* New York: Walker, 2008.

Migdal, Joel S. "The State in Society." In *State Power and Social Forces: Domination and Transformation in the Third World*, edited by Joel S. Migdal, Atul Kohli, and Vivienne Shue, 7–34. New York: Cambridge University Press, 1994.

Miller, Tom. *China's Urban Billion: The Story behind the Biggest Migration in Human History.* Asian Arguments. London: Zed Books, Palgrave Macmillan, 2012.

Millward, James A. "Introduction: Does the 2009 Urumchi Violence Mark a Turning Point?" *Central Asian Survey* 28, no. 4 (December 2009): 347–60.

Minahan, James B. *Ethnic Groups of North, East, and Central Asia: An Encyclopedia.* Santa Barbara, CA: ABC-Clio, 2014.

Mortensen, Eric D. "Prosperity, Identity, Intra-Tibetan Violence, and Harmony in Southeast Tibet: The Case of Gyalthang." In *Ethnic Conflict and Protest in Tibet and Xinjiang: Unrest in China's West*, edited by Ben Hillman and Gray Tuttle, 201–21. New York: Columbia University Press, 2016.

Mullaney, Thomas S. *Coming to Terms with the Nation: Ethnic Classification in Modern China.* Berkeley: University of California Press, 2011.

———. "Critical Han Studies: Introduction and Prolegomenon." In *Critical Han Studies: The History, Representation and Identity of China's Majority*, edited by Thomas S. Mullaney, James Leibold, Stéphane Gros, and Eric Armand Vanden Bussche, 1–22. Berkeley: University of California Press, 2012.

Naughton, Barry. "Deng Xiaoping: The Economist." *China Quarterly* 135 (1993): 491–514.

Oakes, Tim. *Tourism and Modernity in China.* New York: Routledge, 1998.

Ojijed, Wuyuncang. "Language Competition in an Ethnic Autonomous Region: A Case of Ethnic Mongol Students in Inner Mongolia." *Chinese Education & Society* 43, no. 1 (January 1, 2010): 58–69.

Osnos, Evan. "Can China Deliver the China Dream(s)?." *New Yorker*, March 23, 2013.

Özkırımlı, Umut. *Theories of Nationalism: A Critical Introduction.* 2nd ed. Basingstoke: Palgrave Macmillan, 2010.

Pan, Jennifer. *Welfare for Autocrats: How Social Assistance in China Cares for Its Rulers.* New York: Oxford University Press, 2020.

Park, Chai Bin, and Jing-Qing Han. "A Minority Group and China's One-Child Policy: The Case of the Koreans." *Studies in Family Planning* 21, no. 3 (1990): 161–70.

People's Republic of China, National Bureau of Statistics. "Sixth National Population Census of the People's Republic of China, 2010." Beijing, 2013.
Perdue, Peter C. *China Marches West: The Qing Conquest of Central Eurasia*. Cambridge, MA: Belknap Press of Harvard University Press, 2005.
Perry, Elizabeth J. "Chinese Conceptions of 'Rights': From Mencius to Mao—and Now." *Perspectives on Politics* 6, no. 1 (March 2008): 37–50.
———. "Studying Chinese Politics: Farewell to Revolution?" *China Journal*, no. 57 (2007): 1–22.
Petersen, Kristian. *Interpreting Islam in China: Pilgrimage, Scripture, and Language in the Han Kitab*. New York: Oxford University Press, 2018.
Pillsbury, Barbara L. K. "Muslim History in China: A 1300-year Chronology." *Institute of Muslim Minority Affairs Journal* 3, no. 2 (December 1981): 10–29.
Postiglione, Gerard A. "Introduction: State Schooling and Ethnicity in China." In *China's National Minority Education: Culture, Schooling, and Development*, edited by Gerard A. Postiglione, 3–21. New York: Routledge, 1999.
Pullan, Wendy, and Britt Baillie. "Introduction." In *Locating Urban Conflicts: Ethnicity, Nationalism and the Everyday*, edited by Wendy Pullan and Britt Baillie, 1–16. London: Palgrave Macmillan, 2013.
Qian Xuming. "'One Belt One Road' Initiative and China and the Middle East Media Exchanges." *Journalism and Mass Communication* 8, no. 5 (May 28, 2018): 239–45.
Qinghai Provincial Bureau of Statistics (Qinghai sheng Tongji ju) and Guo jia tong ji ju. *Qinghai Tongji Nianjian*. Qinghai Tongji Nianjian 23. Beijing: Zhongguo Tongji Chubanshe, 2007–17.
Quizon, Cherubim A. "Costume, Kóstyom, and Dress: Formulations of Bagóbo Ethnic Identity in Southern Mindanao." *Ethnology* 46, no. 4 (2007): 271–88.
Raento, Pauliina. "Political Mobilisation and Place-Specificity: Radical Nationalist Street Campaigning in the Spanish Basque Country." *Space and Polity* 1, no. 2 (1997): 191–204.
Redclift, Victoria. "Displacement, Integration and Identity in the Postcolonial World." *Identities* 23, no. 2 (March 3, 2016): 117–35.
Rimal, Arbindra, Stanley M. Fletcher, K. H. McWatters, Sukant K. Misra, and S. Deodhar. "Perception of Food Safety and Changes in Food Consumption Habits: A Consumer Analysis." *International Journal of Consumer Studies* 25, no. 1 (2001): 43–52.
Roberts, Sean R. "The Biopolitics of China's 'War on Terror' and the Exclusion of the Uyghurs." *Critical Asian Studies* 50, no. 2 (April 3, 2018): 232–58.
———. *The War on the Uyghurs: China's Internal Campaign against a Muslim Minority*. Princeton, NJ: Princeton University Press, 2020.
Roeder, Philip G. "Soviet Federalism and Ethnic Mobilization." *World Politics* 43, no. 2 (January 1991): 196–232.
Rubin, Herbert J., and Irene S. Rubin. *Qualitative Interviewing: The Art of Hearing Data*. 3rd ed. Thousand Oaks, CA: Sage, 2011.

Sai, Yukari. "Policy, Practice and Perceptions of Qingzhen (Halal) in China." *Online Journal of Research in Islamic Studies* 1, no. 2 (2014): 1–12.
Samuel, Sigal. "China Is Treating Islam Like a Mental Illness." *Atlantic*, August 28, 2018.
Schein, Louisa. "Gender and Internal Orientalism in China." *Modern China* 23, no. 1 (1997): 69–98.
———. *Minority Rules: The Miao and the Feminine in China's Cultural Politics*. Durham, NC: Duke University Press, 2000.
Schell, Orville, and John Delury. *Wealth and Power: China's Long March to the Twenty-First Century*. New York: Random House, 2013.
Schluessel, Eric T. *Land of Strangers: The Civilizing Project in Qing Central Asia*. New York: Columbia University Press, 2020.
Schmoller, Jesko. "The Talking Dead: Everyday Muslim Practice in Russia." *Nationalities Papers* 48, no. 6 (2020): 1036–51.
Scott, James C. *The Art of Not Being Governed: An Anarchist History of Upland Southeast Asia*. Yale Agrarian Studies Series. New Haven, CT: Yale University Press, 2009.
———. *Seeing Like a State: How Certain Schemes to Improve the Human Condition Have Failed*. New Haven, CT: Yale University Press, 1998.
Shen, Kuo. *Meng xi bitan*. Shanghai: Shanghai Shudian Chubanshe, 2003.
Shih, Chih-yu. *Negotiating Ethnicity in China: Citizenship as a Response to the State*. New York: Routledge, 2003.
Shin, Hyun Bang. "Residential Redevelopment and Social Impacts in Beijing." In *China's Emerging Cities: The Making of New Urbanism*, edited by Fulong Wu, 163–81. New York: Routledge, 2008.
Shue, Vivienne. "Legitimacy Crisis in China?" In *Chinese Politics: State, Society and the Market*, edited by Peter Hays Gries and Stanley Rosen, 41–68. New York: Routledge, 2010.
Skey, Michael, and Marco Antonsich, eds. *Everyday Nationhood: Theorising Culture, Identity and Belonging after Banal Nationalism*. London: Palgrave Macmillan, 2017.
Skrbiš, Zlatko, Loretta Baldassar, and Scott Poynting. "Introduction: Negotiating Belonging: Migration and Generations." *Journal of Intercultural Studies* 28, no. 3 (August 1, 2007): 261–69.
Slater, Dan. *Ordering Power: Contentious Politics and Authoritarian Leviathans in Southeast Asia*, Cambridge: Cambridge University Press, 2010.
Smith, Joanne N. "'Making Culture Matter': Symbolic, Spatial and Social Boundaries between Uyghurs and Han Chinese." *Asian Ethnicity* 3, no. 2 (September 1, 2002): 153–74.
Smith, Warren W. *Tibet's Last Stand? The Tibetan Uprising of 2008 and China's Response*. Lanham, MD: Rowman & Littlefield, 2010.

Smith Finley, Joanne. "Now We Don't Talk Anymore." *ChinaFile* (blog), December 28, 2018. www.chinafile.com/reporting-opinion/viewpoint/now-we-dont-talk-anymore.

———. "Securitization, Insecurity and Conflict in Contemporary Xinjiang: Has PRC Counter-Terrorism Evolved into State Terror?" *Central Asian Survey* 38, no. 1 (January 2, 2019): 1–26.

Soest, Christian von, and Julia Grauvogel. "Identity, Procedures and Performance: How Authoritarian Regimes Legitimize Their Rule." *Contemporary Politics* 23, no. 3 (July 3, 2017): 287–305.

Song Qiyuan, Song Xiaole, Li Juan, and Ma Shaobiao. "Cong Huizu Yuyan Kanqi Minzu Rentong." *Longdong Xueyuan Xuebao* 20, no. 4 (2009): 11–13.

"Standoff over China Mosque Demolition." *BBC News*, August 10, 2018. www.bbc.com/news/world-asia-china-45140551.

Stroup, David R. "The De-Islamification of Public Space and Sinicization of Ethnic Politics in Xi's China." Middle East-Asia Project: All About China. Middle East Institute, September 24, 2019. www.mei.edu/publications/de-islamification-public-space-and-sinicization-ethnic-politics-xis-china.

Sturgeon, Janet C. "The Cultural Politics of Ethnic Identity in Xishuangbanna, China: Tea and Rubber as 'Cash Crops' and 'Commodities.'" *Journal of Current Chinese Affairs* 41, no. 4 (2013): 109–31.

Su, Alice. "Harmony and Martyrdom among China's Hui Muslims." *New Yorker*, June 6, 2016.

———. "Meet China's State-Approved Muslims." *Foreign Policy* (blog), November 2, 2016. https://foreignpolicy.com/2016/11/02/meet-chinas-state-approved-muslims-hui-linxia-beijing-compromise.

Sun, Yan. "Debating Ethnic Governance in China." *Journal of Contemporary China* 28, no. 115 (January 2, 2019): 118–32.

Suzuki, Takashi. "China's United Front Work in the Xi Jinping Era: Institutional Developments and Activities." *Journal of Contemporary East Asia Studies* 8, no. 1 (January 2, 2019): 83–98.

Svensson, Tom G. "Clothing in the Arctic: A Means of Protection, a Statement of Identity." *Arctic* 45, no. 1 (1992): 62–73.

Tarrow, Sidney G. *Power in Movement: Social Movements and Contentious Politics*. Revised and updated 3rd ed. Cambridge Studies in Comparative Politics. Cambridge: Cambridge University Press, 2011.

Tian, Ying Ying, and Cecilia Wong. "Large Urban Redevelopment Projects and Sociospatial Stratification in Shanghai." In *China's Emerging Cities: The Making of New Urbanism*, edited by Fulong Wu, 210–30. New York: Routledge, 2008.

Tilly, Charles. *Durable Inequality*. Berkeley: University of California Press, 1998.

Tobin, David. "Minor Events and Grand Dreams: Ethnic Outsiders in China's Postcolonial World Order." *Positions: Asia Critique* 27, no. 4 (November 1, 2019): 739–71.

———. *Securing China's Northwest Frontier: Identity and Insecurity in Xinjiang.* Cambridge: Cambridge University Press, 2020.

———. "Worrying about Ethnicity: A New Generation of China Dreams?" In *China's Many Dreams: Comparative Perspectives on China's Search for National Rejuvenation*, edited by David Kerr, 65–93. New York: Palgrave Macmillan, 2015.

Toqtogha (Tuotuo), ed. *History of the Liao (Liao Shi).* Vol. 30. Dadu, 1344; reprinted Taipei: Dingwen shuju, 1980.

Tsang, Rachel, and Eric Taylor Woods. *The Cultural Politics of Nationalism and Nation-Building: Ritual and Performance in the Forging of Nations.* London: Routledge, 2013.

Tsung, Linda. *Language Power and Hierarchy: Multilingual Education in China.* London: Bloomsbury, 2014.

Turnbull, Lesley. "In Pursuit of Islamic 'Authenticity': Localizing Muslim Identity on China's Peripheries." *Cross-Currents: East Asian History and Culture Review* 3, no. 2 (2015): 35–67.

"Uighurs 'Detained for Beards and Veils': Leak." *BBC News*, February 17, 2020. www.bbc.com/news/world-asia-china-51520622.

Varshney, Ashutosh. *Ethnic Conflict and Civic Life: Hindus and Muslims in India.* New Haven, CT: Yale University Press, 2002.

Vigil, Neddy A., and Garland D. Bills. "Spanish Language Variation and Ethnic Identity in New Mexico." In *Language, Borders, and Identity*, edited by Dominic Watt and Carmen Llamas, 55–69. Edinburgh: Edinburgh University Press, 2014.

Wang, Shouren, and Wenshu Zhao. "China's Peaceful Rise: A Cultural Alternative." *Boundary* 2 33, no. 2 (June 2006): 117–27.

Wang, Wenfei, Shangyi Zhou, and C. Cindy Fan. "Growth and Decline of Muslim Hui Enclaves in Beijing." *Eurasian Geography and Economics* 43, no. 2 (2002): 104–22.

Wang Zhenxiang and Jinan Municipal Bureau of Statistics (Jinan shi tongjiju). *Jinan Tongji Nianjian 2007.* Vol. 25. Beijing: Zhongguo Tongji Chubanshe, 2007.

Weber, Eugen Joseph. *Peasants into Frenchmen: The Modernization of Rural France, 1870–1914.* London: Chatto & Windus, 1979.

Wedeen, Lisa. *Ambiguities of Domination: Politics, Rhetoric, and Symbols in Contemporary Syria.* Chicago: University of Chicago Press, 1999.

Wei, Li. "The 'Why' and 'How' Questions in the Analysis of Conversational Code-Switching." In *Code-Switching in Conversation: Languge, Interaction, and Identity*, edited by Peter Auer, 156–80. London: Routledge, 1998.

White, Sydney D. "State Discourses, Minority Policies, and the Politics of Identity in the Lijiang Naxi People's Autonomous County." *Nationalism and Ethnic Politics* 4, nos. 1–2 (March 1, 1998): 9–27.

Wilczak, Jessica. "'Clean, Safe and Orderly': Migrants, Race and City Image in Global Guangzhou." *Asian and Pacific Migration Journal* 27, no. 1 (March 1, 2018): 55–79.

Wilson, Jonathan A. J., and Jonathan Liu. "Shaping the Halal into a Brand?" *Journal of Islamic Marketing* 1, no. 2 (June 25, 2010): 107–23.

Wilton, Shauna. "Bound from Head to Toe: The Sari as an Expression of Gendered National Identity." *Studies in Ethnicity and Nationalism* 12, no. 1 (April 1, 2012): 190–205.

Wimmer, Andreas. *Ethnic Boundary Making : Institutions, Power, Networks.* New York: Oxford University Press, 2013.

Wu, Fulong. *China's Emerging Cities: The Making of New Urbanism.* London: Routledge, 2008.

Xi, Cui. "Media Events Are Still Alive: The Opening Ceremony of the Beijing Olympics as a Media Ritual." *International Journal of Communication* 7 (June 14, 2013): 1220–35.

Xi Jinping. *Kexue yu aiguo: yan fu sixiang xintan.* Beijing: Qinghua Daxue Chubanshe, 2001.

———. "Secure a Decisive Victory in Building a Moderately Prosperous Society in All Respects and Strive for the Great Success of Socialism with Chinese Characteristics for a New Era." Address to the 19th National Party Congress of the Communist Party of China, Beijing, October 18, 2017.

Ya Hanzhang and Li Weihan. *Huihui minzu wenti.* Yan'an: Yan'an Jiefang She, 1941.

Yang, Huaizhong, and Zhen'gui Yu, eds. *Yisilan yu Zhongguo wenhua.* Yinchuan: Ningxia Renmin Chubanshe, 1995.

Yi Muzhi. *Jinan Yisilan jiao lishi.* Beijing: Zhongguo Dang'an Chuban she, 2006.

Yuan, Lu, and Sam Mitchell. "Land of the Walking Marriage." *Natural History* 109, no. 9 (November 2000): 58.

Yuval-Davis, Nira. *Gender and Nation.* Politics and Culture. London: Sage, 1997.

———. "National Reproduction and 'the Demographic Race' in Israel." In *Woman-Nation-State*, edited by Nira Yuval-Davis, Floya Anthias, and Jo Campling, 92–109. London: Palgrave Macmillan, 1989.

Zang, Xiaowei. "Ethnic Differences in Neighbourly Relations in Urban China." *Asian Ethnicity* 7, no. 2 (June 2006): 195–207.

———. "Hui Muslim–Han Chinese Differences in Perceptions on Endogamy in Urban China." *Asian Ethnicity* 6, no. 1 (February 1, 2005): 51–68.

Zenz, Adrian. "'Thoroughly Reforming Them towards a Healthy Heart Attitude': China's Political Re-Education Campaign in Xinjiang." *Central Asian Survey* 38, no. 1 (January 2, 2019): 102–28.

Zenz, Adrian, and James Leibold. "Chen Quanguo: The Strongman behind Beijing's Securitization Strategy in Tibet and Xinjiang." *China Brief* 17, no. 12 (September 21, 2017). https://jamestown.org/program/chen-quanguo-the-strongman-behind-beijings-securitization-strategy-in-tibet-and-xinjiang.

Zhang, Chenchen. "Governing Neoliberal Authoritarian Citizenship: Theorizing *Hukou* and the Changing Mobility Regime in China." *Citizenship Studies* 22, no. 8 (November 17, 2018): 855–81.

———. "Governing (through) Trustworthiness: Technologies of Power and Subjectification in China's Social Credit System." *Critical Asian Studies* 52, no. 4 (October 1, 2020): 565–88.

Zhang, Li. "Migrant Enclaves and Impacts of Redevelopment Policy in Chinese Cities." In *Restructuring the Chinese City: Changing Society, Economy, and Space*, edited by Laurence J. C. Ma and Fulong Wu, 243–59. New York: Routledge, 2005.

———. *Strangers in the City: Reconfigurations of Space, Power, and Social Networks within China's Floating Population*. Palo Alto, CA: Stanford University Press, 2001.

Zhao, Taotao, and James Leibold. "Ethnic Governance under Xi Jinping: The Centrality of the United Front Work Department and Its Implications." *Journal of Contemporary China* 29, no. 124 (2020): 487–502.

Zhaxi, Duojie. "Housing Subsidy Projects in Amdo: Modernity, Governmentality, and Income Disparity in Tibetan Areas of China." *Critical Asian Studies* 51, no. 1 (January 2, 2019): 31–50.

Zhou, Chuanbin, and Xuefeng Ma. *Development and Decline of Beijing's Hui Muslim Community*. Chiang Mai: Silkworm Books, 2009.

Index

A

B

I

STUDIES ON ETHNIC GROUPS IN CHINA
Stevan Harrell, Editor

Cultural Encounters on China's Ethnic Frontiers, edited by Stevan Harrell

Guest People: Hakka Identity in China and Abroad, edited by Nicole Constable

Familiar Strangers: A History of Muslims in Northwest China, by Jonathan N. Lipman

Lessons in Being Chinese: Minority Education and Ethnic Identity in Southwest China, by Mette Halskov Hansen

Manchus and Han: Ethnic Relations and Political Power in Late Qing and Early Republican China, 1861–1928, by Edward J. M. Rhoads

Ways of Being Ethnic in Southwest China, by Stevan Harrell

Governing China's Multiethnic Frontiers, edited by Morris Rossabi

On the Margins of Tibet: Cultural Survival on the Sino-Tibetan Frontier, by Åshild Kolås and Monika P. Thowsen

The Art of Ethnography: A Chinese "Miao Album," translation by David M. Deal and Laura Hostetler

Doing Business in Rural China: Liangshan's New Ethnic Entrepreneurs, by Thomas Heberer

Communist Multiculturalism: Ethnic Revival in Southwest China, by Susan K. McCarthy

Religious Revival in the Tibetan Borderlands: The Premi of Southwest China, by Koen Wellens

Lijiang Stories: Shamans, Taxi Drivers, and Runaway Brides in Reform-Era China, by Emily Chao

In the Land of the Eastern Queendom: The Politics of Gender and Ethnicity on the Sino-Tibetan Border, by Tenzin Jinba

Empire and Identity in Guizhou: Local Resistance to Qing Expansion, by Jodi L. Weinstein

China's New Socialist Countryside: Modernity Arrives in the Nu River Valley, by Russell Harwood

Mapping Shangrila: Contested Landscapes in the Sino-Tibetan Borderlands, edited by Emily T. Yeh and Chris Coggins

A Landscape of Travel: The Work of Tourism in Rural Ethnic China, by Jenny Chio

The Han: China's Diverse Majority, by Agnieszka Joniak-Lüthi

Xinjiang and the Modern Chinese State, by Justin M. Jacobs

In the Circle of White Stones: Moving through Seasons with Nomads of Eastern Tibet, by Gillian Tan

Medicine and Memory in Tibet: Amchi *Physicians in an Age of Reform,* by Theresia Hofer

The Nuosu Book of Origins*: A Creation Epic from Southwest China,* translated by Mark Bender and Aku Wuwu from a transcription by Jjivot Zopqu

Exile from the Grasslands: Tibetan Herders and Chinese Development Projects, by Jarmila Ptáčková

Pure and True: The Everyday Politics of Ethnicity for China's Hui Muslims, by David R. Stroup

CPSIA information can be obtained
at www.ICGtesting.com
Printed in the USA
BVHW030855130222
627674BV00009B/4